This book renders a unique service to everyone concerned with improving intercultural relations—layman and specialist alike. Here in compact form the growing body of knowledge concerning race and ethnic relations, yielded by more than twenty years of scientific research, is integrated and distilled into a single volume—offering to a wide audience the ammunition necessary to combat prejudice.

Summarizing the contributions of psychologists and psychiatrists, sociologists and anthropologists, educators and experts in the field of industrial relations, the book relates the major findings in three main branches of intercultural research: the extent and origin of racial differences, the nature and causes of prejudice and discrimination, and methods and programs undertaken to reduce these causes. The significance of the findings, and the need for putting them to practical use are brought into new focus with actual illustrations of the broad problem of prejudice and its costs to society.

"P
tion
new,
read
large
know
shou
in th
and
appr

"It
eithe
are t
we a
failu
able
we st

ed a valuable func-
aterial—much of it
nd presenting it in
drawn on his own
de and penetrating
ten a book which
ts, to practitioners
to intelligent men
bout the scientific
oblems.

rd to neglect, on
st be solved if we
cy at home, and if
t apologies for our
y derive consider-
recent years, but

"The contributions of psychology and the other social sciences have already begun to have a practical impact, as Professor Saenger demonstrates. His own work, and the pages which follow, represent a valuable addition to the goodly store of psychological material which can aid us all to think more clearly, and to act more effectively, in this important area."

THE SOCIAL PSYCHOLOGY
OF PREJUDICE

THE SOCIAL PSYCHOLOGY

OF PREJUDICE

Achieving Intercultural Understanding
and Cooperation in a Democracy

By GERHART SAENGER

Assistant Professor of Psychology
New York University

HARPER & BROTHERS PUBLISHERS

NEW YORK

THE SOCIAL PSYCHOLOGY OF PREJUDICE

16929

To

OLLY AND HERMAN

CONTENTS

vii

PART III

WHAT CAN BE DONE ABOUT PREJUDICE AND DISCRIMINATION?

PART IV

IN CONCLUSION

FOREWORD

By OTTO KLINEBERG

Professor of Psychology, Columbia University

It is not uncommon to hear the view expressed that one of the major difficulties in the world today arises from the fact that the physical sciences have progressed too fast, and the sciences of man, including psychology, too slowly. The physicists have let loose forces which, though they may be used for constructive purposes, are potentially capable of doing incalculable harm. If the psychologists knew enough about man—so the argument runs—they could tell man how to control these forces; or rather, how to control his relations with his fellow men so that such forces will not be used for destructive purposes; it is because the sciences of man cannot do this that we are now faced with the possibility of catastrophe.

There is another way of looking at the situation, however, which may be considerably more accurate. There are at least some facts in the possession of psychologists and other social scientists which are really capable of transforming human relations, and of improving the state of the world, if only such facts were more widely known, more fully accepted, and more constantly applied in actual practice. In this category are the facts concerning race—the lack of validity in the notion of superior and inferior ethnic groups, the irrationality of prejudice, and the harm which it causes to the whole fabric of our society.

This does not mean that we know all we need to know about these important problems. Much remains to be done, particularly regarding the practical techniques which can be brought into operation in specific situations. We know too little, also, about the methods which should be employed in order that the information possessed by social scientists may enter into the lives of people in such a manner as to affect their attitudes and behavior. On these and other related questions, research is still in progress, and it may be a long time before all the answers become available. It remains true that the material already collected is impressive not only for its quantity but also for its relevance to the fundamental problem of man's relations to his fellow men.

Professor Gerhart Saenger has performed a valuable function in organizing and integrating this material—much of it new, some of it relatively inaccessible—and presenting it in readable and interesting form. He has drawn on his own large research experience, as well as his wide and penetrating knowledge of the literature. He has written a book which should be useful to educators and to students, to practitioners in the field of intergroup relations, and to intelligent men and women who want to know more about the scientific approach to one of our most important problems.

It is a problem which we cannot afford to neglect, on either moral or practical grounds. It must be solved if we are to be truly satisfied with our democracy at home, and if we are to face the rest of the world without apologies for our failure to practice what we preach. We may derive considerable satisfaction from the progress made in recent years, but we still have a long way to go.

The contributions of psychology and the other social sciences have already begun to have a practical impact, as Professor Saenger demonstrates. His own work, and the pages which follow, represent a valuable addition to the goodly store of psychological material which can aid us all to think more clearly, and to act more effectively, in this important area.

PREFACE

This book was written for persons interested in improving the relations between the different racial and ethnic groups that live in our country. It may be used as a textbook for courses in "race relations," "intergroup" or "intercultural relations," or as a supplementary text for courses in "social psychology," "American minority groups," "race differences," and related subjects. *The Social Psychology of Prejudice,* however, has not been written primarily as a textbook. It is addressed to the student as a future leader in his community, and with the hope that it will be of value to all those in a position to influence intergroup relations in their dealings with their fellow Americans. The book is intended to be of service to teachers and psychologists, social workers and psychiatrists, public officials and civic leaders, representatives of management and labor, in short all those who in the pursuit of their work have to deal with the prevention and cure of prejudice and discrimination, as they affect the individual or the group.

During the last two decades in particular there has been a steadily growing literature in the field of race and ethnic relations. Attention was given first to the study of the extent and origin of racial differences. There was the simultaneous study of the cultural background of America's various immigrant groups and of their adjustment to their new country. Somewhat later research began to concentrate on the study of the nature and extent of prejudice and discrimination, to be followed by intensive and extensive research into their causes. Different investigators began to search into the economic and political, social and psychological causes of prejudice, as well as the ways and means in which prejudiced beliefs are passed from generation to generation. The last few years finally saw a growing scientific interest in the analysis of the methods most useful in combating prejudice and discrimination. Some concerned themselves mainly with the study of the potential impact of education on bringing about more democratic attitudes, others occupied themselves more with the study of the techniques useful in abolishing discrimination and intergroup tension.

In the present volume I attempt to bring together and to integrate these different approaches for the specialist as well as the educated layman. The first part of the book attempts to familiarize the reader with the scope of the problem, as well as the cost we pay for the continued existence of undemocratic practices. Attempts to improve relations between different racial and ethnic groups require a thorough knowledge of the nature of the interacting groups as well as of the various factors which contribute to prejudice and discrimination.

The second part of the book is hence devoted to an analysis of the differences between the various groups. The question is raised whether these differences can be explained on biological grounds or must be attributed to differences in culture and the differential treatment experienced by majority and minority groups in a prejudiced society. In analyzing the origins of prejudice and discrimination equal attention was given to its various and interrelated causes, in accordance with the author's belief that a number of different, almost equally important factors are responsible for the emergence of prejudice and discrimination. To understand prejudice and discrimination we must have recourse to the contributions of psychologists as well as psychiatrists, sociologists and anthropologists, educators and experts in the field of industrial relations.

The integration of so many different approaches is admittedly a difficult undertaking. Yet, as the last and largest part of this book attempts to demonstrate, the successful reduction of prejudice and discrimination requires insight into the prejudiced individual as well as into processes of group interaction. This truth becomes evident in the first chapters of the last part, which deal primarily with the educational attack on prejudice, as well as the subsequent chapters dealing with the reduction of discriminatory practices. Whenever possible examples of successful programs have been given and attempts made to explain the success of the undertaking in terms of our knowledge of the causes of prejudice and discrimination.

Prompted by the desire to keep this volume short and easily readable, I necessarily had to be selective in the choice of references given and the studies reported. These choices are necessarily subject to the personal bias of the writer and in no sense provide an adequate coverage of the literature.

I wish to express my deeply felt appreciation to Prof. Otto Klineberg of Columbia University, who critically read the whole manuscript. I am greatly indebted also to Prof. Isidor Chein of New York

University for his many valuable suggestions. Individual chapters were discussed with Professor Gladys Meyer of Barnard and Dr. John Harding, Prof. Dan Dodson, as well as Garda Bowman and John Sullivan of the New York State Commission against Discrimination, for whose comments I am grateful. I am also indebted to Prof. Stuart W. Cook for his constant encouragement in the writing of this book. The following organizations have provided valuable material: The National Association for the Advancement of the Colored People, The Urban League, The National Conference of Christians and Jews, The Anti-Defamation League of B'nai Brith, The American Jewish Committee, The Commission on Community Interrelations of the American Jewish Congress, and the Center for Human Relations Studies of New York University.

Able secretarial help was provided by Eleanor Pearlson, Reby Evans, Hope Giordano, Nancy Goldstein, and Isabel Whitehill.

GERHART SAENGER

New York University
New York

PART I. THE PROBLEM OF PREJUDICE AND DISCRIMINATION

The achievement of good relations between different racial and ethnic groups continues to be a major problem of our time.

In the present struggle between democracy and authoritarianism the continued existence of undemocratic practices at home endangers our relations with other nations. Perhaps even more important are the consequences of prejudice and discrimination for the welfare of our own country. Prejudice undermines our national unity. The "racial problem" often distracts us from seeking a realistic solution for other pressing social and economic problems. Discrimination and segregation constitute economic waste and lead to the impoverishment of the discriminating group and its victims.

We pay for our prejudices in terms of human happiness. Intolerance leads to fear and uneasiness among members of the privileged majority as well as its victims. Neurotic hatred of others fails to make the maladjusted person essentially more secure and socially adapted. Prejudice not only severely limits the opportunities of minority people, it makes it harder for them to develop an integrated and well-adjusted personality.

It is the object of this volume to lead to a fuller understanding of the ways and means to combat prejudice and discrimination based on insight into the causes of these twin evils. But we cannot appreciate the need for the solution of our problem completely until we have gained a clearer understanding of the nature and extent of prejudice and its costs to society and the individual.

CHAPTER 1

THE NATURE AND EXTENT OF

PREJUDICE AND DISCRIMINATION

"Sidney Levy is a nice person. Personally, I would not mind if he would join the club. But you know how it is. He is definitely Jewish, and, as a matter of principle we don't take Jews as members. . . . Sure, he seems nice, but you never know with them. Sooner or later their true nature will show through. Moreover, once we take him, he may invite his Jewish friends and before long the whole club will be overrun by these kikes."

NATURE OF PREJUDICE AND DISCRIMINATION

Such statements exemplify many of the typical characteristics of the prejudicial attitude. There is the tendency to evaluate the person not as an individual but as a member of his group, as well as the belief in the inferiority of all its members. This belief in turn is rooted in the assumption of the essential likeness of all its members, the overlooking of individual differences. The conviction that whatever differences exist are innate often constitutes an important part of such faulty generalizations.

Originally the term prejudice is derived from "pre-judgment." We judge a specific person or idea on the basis of preconceived notions, without bothering to verify our beliefs or to examine the merits of our judgment. If I am prejudiced against Italian cooking, I may refuse to taste any new Italian dish offered to me. I know it will not taste good, and am sure that I shall not like it. If friends serve an Italian dish under the pretense that it is French, I may greatly enjoy it, particularly if I am prejudiced in favor of French cooking. The same dish might not have tasted good at all had I known its true origin. Our tastes, our *perceptions*, are influenced by our prejudices.

Prejudices always involve feelings and a system of more or less outspoken stereotyped beliefs. If we are prejudiced against Jews, we

3

feel antagonistic toward them and may *believe* that they are aggressive and ill-mannered.

Feelings and beliefs determine at least partially what we see. The person we meet at a party appears to be gay and outgoing. After we learn that his name is Giordano Bruno he begins to look to us— provided we dislike Italians and consider them emotional—as being uncontrolled and overemotional.

The relationship between the emotional component of an attitude and the beliefs associated with it (known as the "cognitive" component of the attitude) will be more difficult to ascertain. We may dislike a group simply because we have been taught to do so, but do not have any specific ideas concerning the type of people they are. On the other hand it is not impossible to hold a number of negative stereotypes about another group without feeling especially hostile toward them. One may consider the French as "unreliable," "fickle," "aggressive," yet like them. Whenever our overt beliefs concerning the nature of other groups do not furnish the real reason for our likes or dislikes, the reduction of false beliefs may not be expected to be very helpful in changing our feelings toward others.

Prejudices, like all attitudes, may *motivate us* to act in a friendly or hostile way toward the objects of our prejudice, depending upon the nature and intensity of our feelings. But in common with all attitudes, prejudice does not necessarily lead to action. After an examination students may refrain from expressing their hostile attitudes toward the teacher if they are afraid that such expression of hostility may affect their mark. Nor can it be assumed that all actions are reflections of underlying attitudes. The young bride may go to a concert not because she loves music but because she loves her husband. She may not even tell him how she really feels about classical music.

The determination of the circumstances under which underlying attitudes correspond to expressed opinions or overt behavior as well as an examination of the conditions which lead to discrepancies between them will be of major importance. Much will depend here upon the influence of the environment. A relatively unprejudiced banker who for business reasons joins a swanky yacht club, may not only condone its anti-Semitic practices, but join in deriding Jews since, as a new member, he feels the need to conform in order to be accepted. The member of a liberal union may express a tolerant attitude toward his Negro fellow workers at a union meeting and beat up a Negro in a race riot where the anonymity of the mob protects him, and the mass outbreak of hatred activates his own aggressive feelings.[1]

More often than not prejudicial attitudes conform with prejudicial opinions and behavior. But the possibility of inconsistencies makes it important to study attitudes of prejudice to some extent independently from and prior to the study of discriminatory behavior. These attitudes may decline without a corresponding decrease of discriminatory action. On the other hand, no overt increase in hostile actions against minorities may be found, although there may be an increase in hostile feelings which only wait for a favorable opportunity to erupt into violent action.

Though discrimination may be caused by prejudice, unlike the latter it is not a state of mind but consists of clearly observable behavior of the individual or society. It has been defined as any type of action "which denies to individuals or groups of people equality of treatment which they may wish."[2] Discrimination may involve differential treatment, for example, when the same crime is followed by different punishment for Negroes and whites, or when women are given lower wages than men for the same type of work. Discrimination may consist in the exclusion of members of a given group from specific jobs, from higher education, or from the vote.

Segregation, as distinguished from voluntary separation, must be considered discrimination when it occurs against the desire of the segregated group, or at least without the consent of both parties. Whether enforced by law or by social custom it implies the assumption of the inferiority of the segregated group on the part of the dominant group. In social interaction discrimination may express itself all the way from mere expressions of disrespect, as in the use of different forms of address, to open expressions of hostility toward members of different groups.

The report of the United Nations subcommittee concerned with the evils of discrimination demands that . . .

. . . some means must be found to suppress or eliminate inequalities of treatment which may have harmful results, aiming at the prevention of any act or conduct which implies that an unfavorable distinction is made between individuals solely because they belong to certain categories or groups of society. The aim is to prevent any act which might imply inequality of treatment on grounds of race, colour, sex, language, religion, political or other opinion, national or social origin, property, birth, or status.[3]

How widespread is prejudice and discrimination? The extent of prejudicial attitudes found in any specific group is difficult to gauge. Prejudice has many facets, and may vary from mild antagonism to violent hatred. Our reply will be different if we only measure wrong beliefs concerning another group, than if we measure antagonistic feelings concerning the same group. Some people may be prejudiced only against one ethnic group, others might be prejudiced against any group differing in looks or behavior from their own.

Gordon Allport, the well-known psychologist, believes on the basis of a survey of public opinion poll data that

> . . . one-fifth of our people are implacable Anglophobes; five or ten percent are violently anti-Semitic, while perhaps forty-five percent more are mildly bigoted in the same direction. At least forty percent express prejudice against the Negro. The numbers that are anti-Catholic, anti-Protestant vary, but in all cases the proportion is fairly high.[4]

These figures, high as they are, probably represent an understatement. Expressions of anti-minority feelings are frowned upon in democratic countries. Many may hesitate to express their prejudices in public, may even be unaware that they have any.

BELIEFS AND STEREOTYPES

Prejudice has many dimensions. We need to study the *beliefs* held toward different ethnic groups; the quality and intensity of popular *feelings* directed toward them (for example, fear or disgust), and, finally, the *desire to take* hostile *action* against them.[5]

One hundred Princeton University students were asked to pick from a prepared list of personality traits those they considered most typical for different ethnic groups.[6] Repeated in the same institution eighteen years later, the study indicated that although there had been a substantial decrease in the tendency toward generalization, by and large, the same stereotypes of the "lazy, happy-go-lucky Negro," the "shrewd, mercenary, ambitious Jew," the "impulsive and artistic Italian" prevailed. Moreover, these generalizations have since been found to hold not only for Princetonians, but to be shared by students as well as other individuals in different parts of this country and abroad.[7,8]

The widespread acceptance of major stereotypes[9] is perhaps mainly indicative of the tendency to think in general terms of a specific ethnic group. Such generalizations, unless they have definite derogatory meanings, do not in themselves necessarily imply hostile feelings toward other ethnic groups, although they may tend to block the possibility of a fresh, unbiased approach to the individual member of a group toward whom we harbor specific stereotypes.

FEELINGS AND MOTIVATIONS

It is a different matter if we find in a recent nationwide public opinion poll that 36 per cent of the population express the belief that the Jews "are getting more power than is good for the country,"[10] and 12 per cent harbor the same opinion about the Catholics.

An even larger proportion feels more or less hostile toward Negroes. Asked whether they would mind having a Negro nurse if they were sick in a hospital, 45 per cent of a sample of 7000 high school students from 17 Midwestern and Eastern states declared that they would not like it, another 16 per cent were undecided. More than half of the group would not approve of a law compelling owners of recreational centers to admit Negroes and other minority group members.[11] In 1948 as much as 42 per cent of the adult population of the country preferred not to work with Negroes.[12]

Different intensities of prejudicial feelings can be distinguished by the same method. While about one half of the population reveals at least slight anti-Semitism, only 14 per cent of the United States population preferred not to work side by side with Jews on the same job. The intense hostility toward Jews revealed in a few interviews of a sample of typical Chicago veterans is probably even rarer.

> Yeah, the Hebes . . . I think Hitler did a good thing. They're born that way, they can make a dollar where a white person starves. Where they come in, the niggers follow and knock the property down. They're awfully clannish for another thing. Take the Irish, they don't trust each other. The Jews patronize each other. . . . I think they should put them all in Africa.[13]

While the sample is small (150 cases), its careful selection permits us to consider it as typical enough to show the characteristic distribution of different intensities of prejudice in a group. Only one out of every twelve veterans appeared to be free of anti-Negro prejudice, one fourth held stereotyped beliefs concerning Negroes, while the remainder showed outspoken or intense hostility (16 per cent) toward members of the colored race. In comparison four out of every ten veterans appeared to be free of anti-Semitism, three tended to stereotyped beliefs, and another three showed pronounced hostility.[14]

The scientific study of the motivational component in prejudicial attitudes was introduced by Bogardus, who in 1926 asked a sample of upper-class Americans from all sections of the country how closely they were willing to associate with different ethnic groups. At that time about 35 per cent of those replying were willing to have Italians live on the same street with them, but 55 per cent were willing to have them employed "in my occupation." Only 10 per cent wanted the Irish excluded from their occupation, as compared to 61 per cent unwilling to work with Negroes.

Table 1. Reactions of 1725 Americans toward Association with Eight Different Ethnic Groups

	Ethnic Groups %							
Would admit to:	Eng-lish	Amer-ican	Irish	Ger-man	Ital-ian	Jews (German)	Jews (Russian)	Negroes
Kinship by marriage	94%	90%	70%	54%	15%	8%	6%	2%
My club	96	92	83	54	26	22	18	9
My street	97	92	86	79	35	26	16	12
My occupation	95	92	90	83	55	40	30	39
As citizens of my country	96	91	91	87	71	54	45	57

Adapted from Bogardus, E. S., "The Measurement of Social Distance," in Newcomb, T. M., and Hartley, E. L.: *Readings in Social Psychology* (Holt, New York, 1947, pp. 504 ff.). A repetition of this study in 1946 again showed the consistency of ethnic preferences. When all groups were arranged in terms of preferential rank order, by and large the same groups occupied the same places.[15]

The findings of the Bogardus study do not necessarily give us a clue as to the actual or potential behavior of the population. The ratings appear to be indicative rather of approval of the existing rank order of preference for specific racial and ethnic groups.[16] On the basis of contemporary research, it appears safe perhaps only to state that the group which expresses willingness to campaign actively against Jews or other minority groups, which spontaneously makes anti-Semitic and anti-Negro remarks, is unlikely to number at present more than 10 per cent of the total population of the United States.[17] Moreover, their expressed desire toward more vigorous action against the victims of prejudice does not necessarily mean that they actually participate in hostile action either as initiators or as followers.

Considering the difficulties of ascertaining the prevalence of hostile predispositions toward minority groups, which can be inferred only indirectly, it appears more helpful to describe the possible types of interaction and then proceed to an estimate of the extent of the various types of discrimination found in this country.

INTENSITY OF PREJUDICE

Overt relations between different ethnic and racial groups—as well as prejudice itself—can be classified on a continuum from extremes of friendliness to extremes of hostility, from the cordial relations between French, German and Italian citizens of Switzerland to the mass extinction of the Jews by Hitler. The various levels of prejudice and prejudicial action have been defined by the United Nations Commission on Human Rights:

1. Prejudice which is merely an opinion which is not given outward expression either in word or by positive conduct of hostility or contempt toward members of a particular group, but which consists rather in a negative attitude of avoiding contact with members of that group as much as possible without expressing such dislike.

2. Prejudice which consists of internal opinion but which is expressed outwardly in some relations with the member of a disliked group, such as showing a definitely cold attitude toward them. In this case, there is a mild expression of antipathy, dislike, or devaluation in social relations, in which no legal problem is involved and in which no discriminatory act occurs.

3. Prejudice which does not go so far as to deny legal rights to the members of a disliked group, but which leads to some form of social discrimination, as for example, intentionally and manifestly avoiding any social contact with members of the disliked group.

4. Prejudice which leads to discriminatory acts, denying rights to individuals belonging to a group discriminated against.

5. Prejudice which leads not only to discriminatory behavior but goes further and gives rise to propaganda for further discrimination. This propaganda may be confined to certain private circles (for example, trying to convince friends,) or it may develop into public manifestations such as speeches or written incitements to acts of discrimination.

6. Prejudice which leads to acts of violence against the members of a group, committed either by an individual or by a group of individuals, or committed or tolerated by public authorities.[18]

The United Nations report is in need of some supplementation. The absence of prejudice in the relations between different ethnic groups living in close proximity is usually related to cooperation. The members of the different groups work together, play together, live together, and tend to help each other. Even though differences between them may be acknowledged, the other group is not disliked or held inferior. The differences between the groups may even be appreciated.

In true intergroup cooperation there is no conflict either within the individual or between him and his environment. There are no mental reservations, cooperation is voluntarily and gladly given. When overtly good relations coincide with underlying prejudice, we may speak of "tolerance." On the surface tolerance in its manifestations may not differ at all from true cooperation. Psychologically, however, tolerance is a distinct state of mind. It means to be fair, to tolerate another person. Etymologically, the word "tolerate" means to "suffer," and we tend to suffer or tolerate persons we do not like or toward whom we have mixed feelings, such as unwanted relatives honoring us with a visit. One often feels superior to the person one tolerates. The true meaning of the word is perhaps best expressed in the words of a high school girl. "Tolerance," she said, "is when you put up with certain people but you don't like to have them around anyhow."[19]

Contrary to cooperation, tolerance usually implies conflict. Such conflict may exist between the individual's prejudices and his democratic belief in equality and fairness; or it may represent the outcome of a conflict between his prejudices and his need to give in to the demands of an unprejudiced environment. In the latter case, a lessening of the curbs imposed by the environment, a decline in societal sanctions against prejudice, may change tolerance to overt discrimination.

Tolerance is not likely to create ideal intergroup relations if for no other reason than that the tolerated person feels humiliated, resents such an attitude. Even with the best intentions, the tolerant person usually gives his true feelings and beliefs away, acts condescending, magnanimous, expects praise for his behavior. The minority's reaction toward tolerance here resembles the reaction of the receiver of charity from the proverbial Lady Bountiful. With all its faults, however, tolerance is decidedly better than overt discrimination.

POLITICAL AND LEGAL DISCRIMINATION

Discrimination can be practiced officially by government authorities with the backing of law, or unofficially by private individuals or associations such as business organizations or educational institutions.

Official discrimination often encourages the rise, and supports the perpetuation, of private discrimination and prejudice. Where it includes segregation it encourages the emergence of false beliefs concerning minority members which would be more difficult if close contact between the groups prevailed.

In spite of widespread anti-Semitic propaganda in Germany the boycott of Jews after Hitler's rise to power was a partial failure until legislation succeeded in segregating Jews and gentiles completely. Previously those who had known Jews socially as well as through business connections continued to associate with them. Once segregation had been accomplished, the lies of Nazi propaganda concerning the nature of Jews were no longer contradicted through intimate day-to-day contact between gentiles and Jews.[20]

In the United States legal discrimination in our Southern States does not by itself engender much prejudice and private discrimination; it is more a consequence of prior antagonistic feelings. It tends to perpetuate the prejudices already existing by interfering with the full intellectual and emotional development of the colored people. The legally enforced segregation in housing and social life prevents satisfactory contact and insight into the essential likeness of Negro and white family life, and encourages the persistence of derogatory stereotypes.

Official as well as private discrimination can be subdivided further in terms of the area where discrimination is exhibited. We may group these under the heads of political and legal discrimination, and segregation in public facilities and in education.

Political discrimination consists in the denial of the vote or equal representation to any group of citizens. Laws which tied the right to vote to property either by denying the franchise to persons without property or by giving more votes to the well-to-do citizens were directed against Negroes and poor whites.

The poll-tax laws, most of them enacted in the period between 1890 and 1910, were passed for two main reasons: first, to eliminate the Negro from politics after Reconstruction; second to crush the radical agrarian movement which swept the West and parts of the South in the 1890's and the 1900's. The Populist movement threatened for a time to unite the poor white and black masses against the ruling class in the South. In Georgia and Alabama, where the Populist movement was very strong, the poll tax laws were the most severe. The application of this tax, which keeps about half of the whites and nearly all the Negroes from voting, marked the beginning of the Southern oligarchy that continues to hold sway in the seven poll-tax states.[21]

In addition to the poll tax, which in 1951 was still on the statutes of five states, Negroes were and still are substantially prevented from participation in the democratic process by the institution of the white primary. Various state laws prevented the participation of Negroes in the primaries, but were recently declared unconstitutional by the Supreme Court.

Another method of preventing Negroes from voting consists in the discriminatory application of "educational" requirements in which the prospective voter has to satisfy the registrar (always a white man) of his ability to read and write. "While a white man is rarely 'insulted' by being given the test," many Negro teachers and even college professors were disqualified because they mispronounced a single word.[22]

Attempts to prevent Negroes from voting are not restricted to legal and pseudo-legal practices. "Violence, terror, and intimidation have been, and still are, effectively used to disfranchise Negroes in the South."[23] Hence, in spite of great recent improvements, in 1947 only 610,000 or 12 per cent of the 5,069,085 Negroes of voting age were qualified to vote.[24]

Political discrimination is closely related to legal discrimination. The same political system which guarantees in the South the survival in power of an oligarchy favoring the maintenance of the status quo also determines the election of law-enforcement officers. In practice this leads to an unequal administration of justice ranging from differential punishment for the same crimes to lack of fair trials by impartial judges, from inequalities in judicial guarantees to differences in protection of life and property by the law.

The rape of a white woman by a Negro is usually followed by the imposition of a death sentence, whereas the rape of a Negro woman by a white man leads to mild if any punishment at all. Inequalities in the administration of justice also exist with regard to crimes against property. In many cases Negroes have been convicted to long prison terms (five to ten years), if not life, for petty thievery.

The means of obtaining a confession as well as the manner in which trials are conducted differ greatly for members of majority and minority groups:

In various localities, scattered throughout the country, unprofessional or undisciplined police while avoiding brutality, fail to recognize and to safeguard the civil rights of citizenry. Insensitive to the necessary limits of police authority, untrained officers frequently overstep the boundaries of their proper duties. At times this appears in unwarranted arrest, unduly prolonged detention before arraignment, and abuse of the search and seizure power. . . . The frequency with which such cases arise is proof that improper police conduct is still widespread, for it must be assumed that there are many instances of the abuse of police power which do not reach the courts. Most of the victims of such abuse are ignorant, friendless persons, unaware of their rights, and without the means of challenging those who have violated those rights. . . . Unpopular, weak, or defenseless groups are most apt to suffer.[25]

Discrimination in trial procedure is found frequently. In many cases evidence in favor of the accused Negro is not admitted.

In a trial for rape of four Negroes in Florida all four were condemned to death in spite of the fact that testimony was never printed, medical evidence on which the charge was based, not published. When conviction was set aside by the superior court and re-trial ordered, the sheriff shot and killed one of the four defendants, mortally wounding one other (one had been shot two years earlier for the same reason) in an attempt to "flee" in spite of the fact that the Negroes were not armed. They were shot at the side of the car previously stopped for repair kneeling at the side of the car, and continued being shot at while lying wounded on the ground. Again, medical evidence contradicting the sheriff's story was excluded, and the same biased jury cleared the officer.[26]

In the majority of cases Negroes are tried by white juries. Such discriminatory court practices are by no means restricted to Negroes. In a study of fifty Texan counties having a "Latin American" population ranging from 15 to 40 per cent no persons of Mexican descent have ever been called for jury service.[27] In contrast to the stern justice meted out to the Negro the vast majority of Southerners who participated in lynchings and other acts of violence against Negroes have never been caught or, if arrested, were freed by a jury of their peers who did not find them guilty.

SEGREGATION

Official restrictions in freedom of movement and choice of residence, as practiced in South Africa, are almost absent in this country. But segregation is required by law in the South for all transportation, places of public assembly, and public services such as hospitals, welfare agencies, and, most important, educational institutions.

To comply with the constitutional requirement of equal treatment the South advanced the theory of "separate but equal" facilities for Negroes and Whites, which in practice has inevitably led to extreme inequalities in every area.

Grade for grade, the education offered in Negro schools is vastly inferior to that offered to white children. Rural school houses in the deep South are usually without comfort, equipment, proper lighting, and sanitation; and usually fail to provide transportation to and from school.[28] Negro teachers are badly trained and receive only a fraction of the salaries paid to white teachers. Much more money—particularly in the deep South—is expended for the education of white children. Partly as a result of such discriminatory practices, 62.8 per cent of the Negro population but only 17.1 per cent of the white population failed to complete grammar school.[29]

Table 2. Current Expenses for Negro and White Pupils in Average Daily Attendance, and Salaries for Negro and White Teachers, in Selected States and Average for all States Practicing Segregation Reporting, 1947-1948

States	Expenses Per Pupil		Instructional Salaries	
	White	Negro	White	Negro
Mississippi	$114.74	$ 23.86	$1,703	$ 638
Georgia	126.87	58.73	1,924	1,281
Florida	177.47	112.70	2,777	2,214
Maryland	200.51	165.06	3,369	3,137
All states reporting*	136.73	74.67	2,271	1,742

* Of sixteen states practicing segregation, nine reported expenditures per pupil, and fourteen teacher's salaries. Adapted from *Biennial Survey of Education in the United States.* U. S. Office of Education, Washington, D. C., 1947-48.

Official and unofficial discrimination in the field of medical care jeopardized the health of the colored races. A white inhabitant of the United States had fourteen times as good a chance for proper hospital care as had the colored citizens.[30] The national proportion of physicians to population is about 1 doctor to each 750 persons, the accepted minimal standard 1 to 1500; the proportion of Negro physicians to Negro population is 1 to 3377.[31] When in 1943 two and a half times as many Negro mothers than white mothers died in childbirth; lack of adequate medical care is at least partly to blame.[32] Together with inadequate schooling, neglect of proper medical care lowers the employment chances of members of minority groups.

Private discrimination is even more widespread. It is directed not only against Negroes and Orientals but also Jews and Catholics, immigrants, particularly those from Southern and Eastern Europe, as well as women. If we consider as the main targets of discrimination the members of the colored races (about fifteen million), Jews (about five million) and Catholics (about twenty-five million), we find that altogether at least forty-five million Americans are subject to discrimination at one time or another.

EDUCATION

Private discrimination has been studied most thoroughly in education and employment, housing, and public accommodation. In higher education it is the rule rather than the exception. According to a recent nation-wide study, 44 per cent of all applications to colleges by Jews and 33 per cent by Catholics were rejected as compared to 23 per cent of all applications by Protestants.[33]

The exclusion of Jewish and to a lesser extent of Catholic students is based on the so-called quota system tacitly endorsed by most American colleges. It is usually defended by stating that American colleges have to conform to the prejudices of students and communities (notwithstanding the fact that with regard to other issues colleges often claim leadership), that colleges would be swamped with minority members if they abolished the quotas, and, not infrequently, that too many minority members in a given institution would increase the prejudices of the majority student body.

Because the quota system limits the ability of minority group members to get into a college of their own choosing, it severely restricts their opportunities to enter a professional career. A study published in 1948 indicates during the period of 1935-1939 one third of Protestant applications, 40 per cent of non-Italian Catholic applications and over 90 per cent of Jewish applications to medical schools were rejected.[34] Undesirable personality characteristics are often used as an excuse for the refusal to admit minority students on an equal basis. The Dean of a medical school explained that "emotional stability" and personality were more important than a high average.

But at the same time he admitted that the rejected students had been refused without an interview to determine their "emotional stability" or personality.[35]

The situation for Negroes is worse. Of the estimated 75,000 Negroes in college in 1947, only 11,000 attended non-segregated schools. In 1946 592 Negroes were enrolled in medical schools, 507 of them in the two Negro medical schools.[36] The South maintains only two law schools and no school of engineering for its colored students. While almost one fourth of its population is non-white, twelve times as much money is spent on higher education for whites than for Negroes.[37]

DISCRIMINATION IN EMPLOYMENT

Discrimination in employment takes a variety of forms which need to be distinguished.
1. Total exclusion of members of a specific group;
2. Access to lower grade (e.g. menial) jobs only;
3. Limitations in numbers of group members hired (many firms, in order to escape the onus of discrimination, hire a token number of minority members);
4. Unequal labor conditions for minority members;
5. Inequalities in wages and salaries;
6. Prohibitive or unequal standards for promotion.

The total effects of discrimination in the employment of minority group members can partially be ascertained by studying the occupational distribution of different groups. In spite of considerable improvement during the last decade, in 1950 at least 51.3 per cent of all non-white workers fell into the unskilled categories ("laborers," "farm laborers," "private household," and "service workers") as compared to only 18.6 per cent of the white working force.[38]

Over-all discrimination against Jews is somewhat less widespread, and is most severe in banking, finance, insurance, and heavy industry.[39] It often does not take the form of total exclusion, but may consist in obstacles in the way of promotion.

Discrimination is not always the fault of the employer. Some unions exclude Negroes from membership either directly in their bylaws or by tacit consent. Where they control hiring practices, or where membership in the union is a condition of employment, members of the colored race can be automatically excluded from employment in the industry.[40]

Differential pay for the same type of job is given not only to minority members but often to women. A method of studying the existence of unequal pay for identical jobs held by Negroes and whites has been worked out in the "Northtown Survey" conducted by the

Commission on Community Interrelations of the American Jewish Congress. Equating for training and length of experience on the job, they found that the earnings of the "typical" white worker in this "typical" Northern town was $1.49 as compared to $1.08 for the "representative" Negro worker. Particularly during the last century, and to a lesser degree today, immigrant labor has been paid less than native-born labor. The possibility of obtaining labor at a low cost was indeed one of the main factors leading to the importation of immigrant labor from Europe.

Partially as a result of the widespread existence of discrimination in America minority members usually enjoy a much lower standard of living than majority members, who have the better jobs at a higher pay, and usually are the first to be hired and the last to be fired during a decline in the business cycle.[41] In 1949 the median income of nonwhite families was $1,533 as compared to $3,138 for white families.[42]

HOUSING AND RECREATION

Even if discrimination in housing were nonexistent, Negroes would occupy the less desirable houses because they could not afford higher rents. Their situation is further aggravated by the fact that they have to pay more for the same accommodations than white because they are restricted to small, densely populated sections of our cities. Not only in the South but throughout the nation Negro housing is more often characterized by defective plumbing and toilet facilities, and an inadequate state of repair, than the dwellings of whites.

Table 3. Percentages of Substandard Dwellings in Each Rental Group in Sixteen Northern and Western Cities and Twenty-six Southern Metropolitan Areas, for Houses occupied by Negroes and Whites

| Rental Group | Occupancy | | Ratio |
(Dollars)	White	Negro	Negro:White
Below 5	90.2	97.6	1.1
5– 9	87.7	94.7	1.1
10–14	69.4	79.4	1.1
15–19	42.1	55.3	1.3
20–24	25.0	43.8	1.8
25–29	14.4	31.0	2.2
30–39	7.7	20.9	2.7
40–49	4.0	13.5	3.4
50–59	3.2	10.9	3.4
60–74	2.8	9.1	3.3
75–99	2.7	10.1	3.9
100	2.8	13.4	4.8
Number of units	6,385,845	850,063	

Robinson, C. K., "Relationship between Conditions of Dwellings and Rentals By Race," *Journal of Land and Public Utility Economics*, 3:296-312, August, 1946. XXII.

REFERENCES

1. Jahoda, M., in "Consistency and Inconsistency in Intergroup Relations." *Journal of Social Issues,* 5:4, 1949.
2. United Nations, *Report on the Main Types and Causes of Discrimination.* Lake Success, N. Y., 1949, p. 2.
3. *Ibid.,* p. 3.
4. Allport, G. W., "The Bigot in Our Midst." *Commonweal,* 40:582-586, 1944.
5. Kramer, B. M., "Dimensions of Prejudice." *Journal of Psychology,* 27:389-451, 1949.
6. Katz, D., and Braly, K. W., "Racial Stereotypes of 100 College Students." *Journal of Abnormal and Social Psychology,* 28:280-290, 1933.
7. Gilbert, G. M., "Stereotype Persistence and Change among College Students." *Journal of Abnormal and Social Psychology,* 46:245-254, 1951.
8. Eyesenck, H. J., and Crown, S., "National Stereotypes: An Experimental and Methodological Study." *International Journal of Opinion and Attitude Research,* 1:26-39, 1948.
9. Klineberg, O., *"Tensions Affecting International Understanding."* Social Science Research Council, Bulletin 62, pp. 103-112, 1950.
10. *Fortune Survey,* October 1947.
11. Remmers, H. H., and Gage, N. L., "Patterns of Attitudes toward Minorities among High School Youth in the United States Middlewest." *International Journal of Opinion and Attitude Research,* 1:106-109, 1947.
12. Roper poll, 1948.
13. Bettelheim, B., and Janowitz, M., *Dynamics of Prejudice.* Harper & Brothers, New York, 1950, p. 17.
14. *Ibid,* pp. 16 and 26.
15. Bogardus, E. S., "Changes in Racial Distances." *International Journal of Opinion and Attitude Research,* 1:55-62, 1947.
16. Krech, D., and Crutchfield, R. S., *Theory and Problems of Social Psychology.* McGraw-Hill, New York, 1948, pp. 222 ff.
17. Forster, A., *A Measure of Freedom.* Doubleday, New York, 1950, p. 101.
18. United Nations, *op. cit.,* p. 14.
19. Montagu, F. M. A., *Man's Most Dangerous Myth, The Fallacy of Race.* Columbia University Press, New York, 1942, p. 94.
20. Saenger, G., *Today's Refugees, Tomorrow's Citizens.* Harper & Brothers, New York, 1941, p. 21.
21. Davie, M. R., *Negroes in American Society.* McGraw-Hill, New York, 1949, p. 267.
22. Myrdal, G., *An American Dilemma: The Negro Problem and Modern Democracy.* Harper & Brothers, New York, 1944, p. 484.
23. *Ibid,* p. 485.

24. Jackson, L. P., "Race and Suffrage in the South since 1940." *New South*, 3:1-26, 1948.
25. *To Secure These Rights*. The Report of the President's Committee on Civil Rights, October, 1947.
26. N.A.A.C.P. Report, Groveland, Florida, 1951.
27. *To Secure These Rights, ibid.*
28. Davie, *op. cit.*, p. 150.
29. *Sixteenth Census of the United States, 1940*, Population II, Characteristics of the Population, Part I, United States Summary. Government Printing Office, Washington, D. C., p. 41.
30. Myrdal, *op. cit.*, p. 172.
31. *Medical Care and the Plight of the Negro.* N.A.A.C.P, New York, 1947, pp. 1-28.
32. Davis, M. M., "What Color Is Health." *Survey Graphic*, January, 1947, pp. 85 ff.
33. Roper, E. *Factors Affecting the Admission of High School Seniors to College.* American Council on Education, Washington, D. C., 1949.
34. *Multiple Applications for Admission to American Medical Schools.* American Jewish Congress, New York, 1948, p. 11.
35. Dodson, D., "Anti-Semitism in New York Medical Schools." *American Mercury*, pp. 53-63, July 1947.
36. Ivy, A. C., and Ross, I, *Religion and Race, Barriers to College,* Public Affairs Pamphlet No. 153, New York, 1949, pp. 18 and 20.
37. Report of the President's Commission on Higher Education, Government Printing Office, Washington, D. C., Vol. 7, pp. 5 and 11.
38. U.S. Department of Commerce, 1950 Census, Preliminary Report, Series PC-7, No. 2, Table 6. Government Printing Office, Washington, D. C.
39. Saenger, G., and Gordon, N., "The Influence of Discrimination on Minority Group Members in its Relation to Attempts to Combat Discrimination." *Journal of Social Psychology*, 31:100, 1950.
40. Northrup, H., *Organized Labor and the Negro.* Harper & Brothers, New York, 1944.
41. Weaver, R., *Negro Labor, A National Problem.* Harcourt Brace, New York, 1946, Ch. 1.
42. Deutsch, M., Helper, R., and Selltiz, C., *Studies of Interracial Housing.* New York University, Preliminary Report, 1952.
43. Myrdal, *op. cit.*, p. 375.
44. Saenger, G., and Shulman, H., "Some Factors Determining Intercultural Behavior and Attitudes of Members of Different Ethnic Groups in Mixed Neighborhoods." *Journal of Psychology*, 25:373, 1948.
45. Lee, A. M., and Humphrey, N. D., *Race Riot.* Dryden Press, New York, 1943.

CHAPTER 2

THE COST OF PREJUDICE

THE COST TO SOCIETY

Prejudice not only harms its victims; the whole nation pays the price for intolerance and discrimination.

Russian propaganda sees to it that a race riot in Gary, Indiana, will be known to millions of colored people throughout the world. During the last war the Japanese presented themselves as the liberators of the yellow and brown races from white domination. The existence of large scale discrimination in this country is often cited as evidence that we do not practice the democracy we preach.

Not only our foreign relations but also our domestic politics are handicapped by racial and ethnic cleavages. One need not go as far as some authors who claim that the "Southern demagogy is one way in which the South pays for its prejudices."[1] But there appears little doubt that in the South many elections center around the issue of white supremacy. Preoccupation with the race question often prevents attention to the very real economic and social problems of the area. Perhaps regardless of the merits of the individual candidate and his program, he is liable to be defeated if his opponent is known to be a more ardent advocate of white supremacy. By and large Southern politicians fighting for the preservation of the status quo in race relations have not been in the ranks of the more progressive legislators.

In the one-party South senators are elected by a small minority of the voters. But ethnic and religious differences also play an important role in the North. The background of the candidate influences many voters. A deliberate appeal to prejudice has marred many municipal and state elections. In the United States as in Europe fascist movements employed racial intolerance as a propaganda appeal and a program for action in a conscious effort to change democratic institutions.[2]

During war and peace the consequences of prejudice influence our national welfare. One of Hitler's principal weapons during the last

21

world war was the use of the fifth column. Existing political, social, and economic tensions between majority and minority groups in different countries were skilfully exploited to undermine the enemies of the third Reich.[3] While the attempts by Nazi agents to disrupt national unity in America met with limited success only, the existing cleavages impaired our efficiency. Discrimination in industry still leads to an inadequate utilization of the nation's manpower resources. In the early stages of the last war, major defense industries which were starved for workers refused to hire Negroes.[4]

The treatment of Negroes and other minorities as second class citizens rarely fails to undermine their morale. Segregated army units do not fight as well for democracy as Negroes fighting together with their white fellow country men.[5] The loss to the nation of many potential scientists who could not develop their talents because they were Negro, Italian, Greek, is another consequence of discrimination. It is worth remembering that the whole program for the storing and distribution of blood plasma was originated by Dr. Charles Drew, a Negro.

There are no accurate ways to measure the financial cost of discrimination. Particularly in smaller communities, the maintenance of separate schools, libraries, and recreational centers in the South is an expensive business. In the interest of maintaining segregation, the region which already pays more per capita for education than other parts of the country in relation to income, has repeatedly opposed federal aid to schools because the funds were not earmarked for Jim Crow. When in 1951 60.7 per cent of all South Carolina draftees failed the army intelligence tests the high cost of maintaining separate schools perhaps bore part of the blame.

Discrimination limits the buying power of the minorities and, therefore, indirectly the standard of living of the population as a whole. Groups suffering from discrimination not only consume less but also pay fewer taxes. Forced to live in slums they require a disproportionately high outlay of public moneys for crime protection, health, and social services. In Atlanta, Georgia, "slum areas, predominantly segregated, paid only 5.5 per cent of the city's real property tax revenue and cost the city 53 per cent of its police, fire, health and other service costs. . . . Again in Springfield, Illinois, it costs $3,200,000 a square mile to maintain slums which only contribute $586,000 in tax collections."[6]

Negroes in segregated areas are even worse off than white slum dwellers. If they are able to advance financially they cannot move out of the area. With an already lower income they have to pay proportionately more for the same accommodations than whites. The resulting extremes of overcrowding together with the absence in most communities of adequate social and sanitary services, medical care and schools for their colored quarters, tend to make segregated slums breeding grounds for delinquency and crime.

If Negroes have a higher crime rate than whites, we cannot explain the difference only in terms of discrimination in the administration of justice, by the fact that Negroes are arrested more often and punished more severely for the same behavior than whites.[7] The extremely poor living conditions of a disproportionately large number of Negroes must also be considered. More often than in other groups both father and mother have to work. Particularly in Negro slums there is a lack of supervised recreational facilities. Hence, the children are left to themselves, with no place to go, exposed to the dangers of the street.

The stigma of inferiority placed on the minority member in a prejudiced society, with the consequent thwarting of normal aspirations, may also predispose minority members toward crime more often than other groups in the population. "The Italian boy who might have been another Joe DiMaggio may turn out to be a gangster . . . the Negro who might have been a C.P.A. may end up in the numbers racket."[8] Add to this the psychological tensions resulting from the inability of the victims of discrimination and intimidation to act out their aggression against the suppressors whom they fear, and their accumulated fear and resentment, and it becomes evident why discrimination and prejudice may contribute to crime.[9]

Tuberculosis and venereal diseases are found most often in the slums inhabited by the underprivileged, but they are bound to spread to the rest of the community. The tensions which exist in the border areas of segregated quarters and which are often expressed in gang warfare along racial and ethnic lines affect both groups. Both the majority and the minority pay the price in money and in a deterioration of human relations.

EFFECT ON MAJORITY PERSONALITY

Judging from the example of Germany, violence and hatred tend to brutalize those who practice it. Segregation severs the lines of communication between white and black and permits unfounded rumors to flourish. Where the ignorant and prejudiced person lives in an atmosphere of fear and hate of those whom he exploits a coarsening of the emotions, a more general callousness to human suffering, may well result and affect the total range of human relations. More tender feelings are bound to suffer where hostility prevails. While no objective research has been undertaken on the effects of social prejudice on those who harbor it, it is the consensus of experts in the field that discrimination and segregation has an effect on those who indulge in it.[10]

The effect on the segregating group is that it develops a crass super-ficiality that does not allow for responsiveness for other people's needs and wants, that it overcompensates by developing an attitude of self-righteousness which blinds it to its own problems, that it makes the group warlike and subject to fascist types of domination.[11]

Such an attitude of self-justification, typical of many prejudiced individuals, is related to the need to defend oneself in the face of a prevailing democratic ideology. The existence of large-scale discrim-ination directed particularly against the Negro is embarrassing, makes for moral uneasiness in the face of our belief in freedom and equality of opportunity. Even though the conflict is likely to be repressed in most people most of the time, it is likely to lead to more or less unconscious guilt feelings producing mental strain.[12]

To counter such guilt feelings an elaborate system of rationalization concerning the necessity of keeping the Negro in his place has to be developed. Its core is the assumption that the Negro is innately in-ferior. It is assumed that he could not benefit from better educational facilities, not occupy difficult jobs. But the more thoughtful white must somehow know that there are individual differences in the Negro group as well as the white group, recall wartime experiences with skilled Negro labor.

There is the subsidiary belief that the Negro is happy with the place assigned him by white society. But why then the fear that he may revolt and the feeling steps must be taken to keep him in his place? Why the often heard statement that segregation must be kept at all price, the constant fear that any break in the solid wall of discrimi-natory practices would lead to the demand for full social equality?

These beliefs are necessary to avoid guilt feelings and explain the hostility which is aroused when they are challenged. It is at best hard to maintain the whole host of irrational beliefs "justifying" existing race relations, and it becomes even more difficult when the errors of prejudicial beliefs are pointed out by others. The discriminating person needs to hold on to his excuses for exploiting other groups.

Preoccupation with prejudice requires time and energy which could be better spent in improving one's own position; working out one's own economic, social, and psychological problems. The prej-udiced worker who sees to it that the minority worker gets paid less still does not make more money. The feeling of superiority which bolsters the self-esteem of the insecure and impoverished white does not really make him feel secure. It certainly often prevents him from advancing himself. Only real accomplishments can give real security.

The division of mankind into inferior and superior groups may well lead to an exaggerated feeling of one's own worth among the members of the privileged group. But since this emphasis on one's superior status may easily take the place of working to improve oneself, it impoverishes the growth of personality.

FAITH IN DEMOCRACY

We cannot deny that the simultaneous teaching of democracy and the practice of discrimination contributes to cynicism and lack of faith. The young child soon realizes that the high-sounding ideals learned in school are at odds with what he sees around him. He learns to watch what people do rather than to listen to what they say. While again no scientific data are available it is known that the discrepancies between parental teachings and the way they act in front of the child generally tend to have an unfavorable influence on his development.

The conflict between the ideas of our culture and reality also affects the minority. Like all Americans minority members are indoctrinated in the prevailing ideology that one should try to advance oneself socially and economically, and that success in this endeavor depends largely upon the merits of the individual. Like everyone else they are taught that they have a right to freedom of opportunity, only to see it denied in practice. Their chances to improve their standard of living depend—at least in part—on the extent of discrimination against the particular group to which they belong. It is this discrepancy between expectation and reality which, perhaps more than the actual amount of discrimination, determines the extent of frustration felt.

It would not be surprising if the experience of discrimination should lead to a decline in the minority's belief in the American dream. But contrary to expectations a recent study showed that the faith in the American dream is as strong in the minority as it is among majority group members. Notwithstanding existing inequalities, minority group members fully shared with their fellow Americans the belief in the American dream, that personal qualities such as drive and ambition rather than external factors such as luck, pull, race, or religion determine success.[13]

While such failure to face reality might be considered politically desirable in the interest of our national unity, it constitutes a definite psychological conflict for those who show it. Sometimes, this belief can be upheld by withdrawal. The Jew who only goes to Jewish resorts, applies for jobs only at Jewish firms, will not encounter discrimination.

In spite of all attempts of evasion, exposure to prejudice is bound to influence the development of the young child. Feelings of humiliation, hurt, and frustration, may result from avoidance, derision, ridicule, and sometimes open attack experienced by the minority children at the time when they enter school. If the child lives in the protection of a minority "ghetto" he may not be exposed to prejudice until later in life, perhaps when he enters business or is drafted for the army. But the unexpected exposure to prejudice in later life may have an even more severe effect, particularly where there has been no parental preparation for such experiences.

Wherever minority groups possess a common culture, have a tradition or language of their own, it is easier to reject the stigma of its inferiority claimed by the majority group. Under attack the minority group will tend instead to value its own culture even more.

The American Negro, one of the earliest immigrant groups in this country, has no such culture of his own. Similarly, among reformed Jews in many countries of Western Europe consciousness of an independent culture was dead; they were aware only of having a common religion and perhaps a common fate. But a defensive reaction may set in even where no indigenous culture exists. The development of "racial pride," a feeling of the superiority of one's own group, is a reaction to prejudice and discrimination. It may take the form of "pointing with pride" to the number of famous group members contributing to politics, arts, and science; or of being proud of the group's survival under the most adverse circumstances. But to some extent there is usually less satisfaction in such empty "racial" pride. It is psychologically sounder to build one's self-esteem on positive values worth preserving. Otherwise, inferiority feelings are likely to be only suppressed rather than eliminated.

The existence of a sound self-esteem depends in large measure upon successful identification with one's own group, which is fundamental for the development of a well-adjusted personality. When the child reaches greater awareness of the outside world, his capacity to identify with the parents is influenced by their position in the outside world, the respect they enjoy in their immediate environment. The child of the village drunk will find it harder to respect his father than the son of the banker or doctor. Where his group is considered inferior by the larger society, a positive identification with his ethnic group becomes more difficult for the Negro, Italian, or Jewish child.

PROBLEMS OF IDENTIFICATION

Minority children develop a group consciousness at a relatively early age. In an attempt to ascertain at what age Negro children were able to identify with their own racial group, 253 Negro children ranging from three to seven years of age were presented with two white and two colored dolls and asked to choose between these dolls in answer to the following questions by the experimenter:

1. Give me the doll that you like to play with—like best.
2. Give me the doll that is a nice doll.
3. Give me the doll that looks bad.
4. Give me the doll that is a nice color.
5. Give me the doll that looks like a white child.
6. Give me the doll that looks like a colored child.
7. Give me the doll that looks like a Negro child.
8. Give me the doll that looks like you.

Analysis of the data indicated that the ability to differentiate between the two racial groups arises early in life, with 77 per cent of all three year old children giving the colored doll upon request. All children could distinguish white and colored dolls by the time they had reached their seventh year. With increasing age the colored children became more and more aware of being Negro. But they did not tend to prefer the black dolls which represented their own group. Instead they showed a decided preference for white skin.[14]

This study indicated that a substantial proportion of the Negro children reject their own group at an early age. Such rejection is a consequence of the negative evaluation by the majority group, which is taken over by our Negro children. They accept the standards of the white majority if they label the white doll as "nice," "clean," the black as "ugly." Instead of being proud of their group, they are ashamed of it and deny membership in it.

EFFECT OF EXPOSURE TO PREJUDICE

The fact that there are more light skinned Negroes among upper class Negro society is in itself a consequence of the tendency of the minority to look at itself in terms of majority values. Parents prefer their lighter children, upper class Negroes choose lighter skinned girls as wives. This does not necessarily mean that the upper class light skinned Negro always has a desire to draw closer to white society, to "pass over." Rather, the sensitivity to color is a result of the fact that color has become the basis of social distinction within Negro society. The light colored Negro has a greater chance to rise in Negro society and thus even benefits from segregation. Not only because of his color but also because he is more successful and more cultured, passing over appears more feasible and he is more acceptable to majority group members. Hence the member of the upper strata of Negro society finds himself more in a conflict situation than the members of the lower strata, has less well developed ties to his own group.[15]

The reactions of minority groups to discrimination will depend also on the extent and severity of discriminatory practices. These reactions must guarantee the survival of the individual, must keep him out of danger and as much as possible advance his chances in a competitive society. They must be able to protect his self-esteem and provide an outlet for the pent-up aggressive feelings resulting from the frustrations of minority life.

Where discrimination is relatively light we may find a tendency to overcome the additional obstacles resulting from minority status. Minority members may work harder, be more aggressive, and more likely to protest. Militant reactions require the possibility of success, demand that the punishments of revolting against inequalities be not too severe.

As the amount of discrimination rises, the likelihood of resignation and apathy increases, and, ultimately, a lowering of aspirations may occur. An example of such adaptation to pressure can be seen when the children of unemployed workers experience a lowering of ambitions and a narrowing of the range of phantasy in the realm of daydreams.[16]

Studies of underprivileged white workers have shown us that the person whose skill and station in life makes it unlikely that he will succeed and climb even the lower rungs of the social ladder, adjusts by lowering his ambition, stressing cooperation rather than competition, live for the day rather than for the future.[17] Exclusion from many types of work and from rewards and recognition has in many cases lowered the aspirations of Negro youth. Instead of futile striving many youths possess and pursue a *carpe diem* philosophy. A poll in New York City showed that Negroes had an aspiration level considerably lower than whites, whereas the Jewish group had the highest ambitions in terms of the jobs they desired. A lowering of ambitions among Negroes helped them to ward off extreme frustration. The Jews, on the other hand, suffering from discrimination to a lesser extent, could adjust to an unfavorable situation through increased effort.

ACCOMMODATION TO PREJUDICE

Accommodation to prejudice is largely a matter of necessity for lower class Negro society in the deep south. To the extent that the white population prefers the meek, childish, "good" Negro and severely punishes transgressions from this norm, the assumption of a servile, childish character becomes advantageous. The Negro is rewarded for acting humble, childish, clownish.[18] The jovial, happy-go-lucky Negro stereotype may in some case actually exist. Clowning helps to release tension. While actually most of this type of behavior is a surface phenomenon, a mask the Negro is forced to wear, much of this behavior may have become virtually second nature.

The behavior of self-abasement, bowing to majority demands, tends to produce a loss of self-respect, if not self-hatred. Psychologically, adjustment to such feelings may be accomplished in part by secretly despising the majority group. As Powdermaker has pointed out, gratification can be derived from the feeling of having successfully fooled the white man about one's real feelings, by despising his stupidity in failing to see that one lies.[19]

To preserve their self-esteem, the minority members may also identify with their oppressors, take over their system of values, their modes of behavior. Through such identification the minority members gain strength, enjoy vicarious gratification of their need for power, accomplishment, and success. To a minor extent we find similar tendencies in the white collar worker in our society. Prevented from securing financial success and unable to advance himself in conformity with the demands of the American creed, she may derive satisfaction through identification with her boss, whose success becomes her own.

The effect of extreme oppression on its victims has been described by Bettelheim in his study of concentration camp inmates.

The prisoners suffered from the steady interference with their privacy on the part of the guards and other prisoners. So a great amount of aggression accumulated. In new prisoners it vented itself in the way it might have done in the world outside the camp. But slowly prisoners accepted, as expressions of verbal aggressions, terms which definitely were taken over from the vocabulary of the Gestapo. From copying the verbal aggressions of the Gestapo to copying their form of bodily aggressions was but one step, but it took several years to make it. . . .

Old prisoners tended to identify with the Gestapo not only in respect to aggressive behavior. They tried to arrogate to themselves old pieces of Gestapo uniforms . . . loved to look like one of the guards. . . .

Among the old prisoners one could observe other developments which definitely could not originate in propaganda. It seems that since they returned to a childlike attitude toward the Gestapo, they had a desire that at least some of those whom they accepted as all-powerful father images should be just and kind. They divided their positive and negative feelings—strange as it may be they had positive feelings—toward the Gestapo in such a way that all positive emotions were concentrated on a few officers who were high up in the hierarchy of camp administrators . . .[20]

Acceptance of suppression is most likely when resistance becomes hopeless. Erich Fromm has shown how the Jewish people, after decades of futile resistance against their Roman conquerors, finally accepted their fate and, expecting deliverance after death, became ripe for the emergence and acceptance of the Christ story.[21] Similarly, the belief in being rewarded for the sufferings on earth is particularly strong in Negro revival forms of religion. In this case, aggressive tendencies are repressed, considered sinful. Suffering is seen as the prelude to reward and ultimate triumph over the adversary in the future, in heaven. Such attitudes enable the minority person to restrain his aggression and to keep out of trouble, and at the same time to preserve his self-esteem by feeling better than others, the true children of God, the chosen race.

Resignation to prejudice was found also among contemporary American Jews, though only in a minority. One fourth of all New York Jews questioned considered the fight against discrimination as hopeless.[22] They stated that the attempt to fight prejudice would only make matters worse. It would be better to avoid bringing anti-Semitism to public awareness. They, too, accepted the doctrine of the inferiority of their group, of the minority.

To protect their self-esteem, they held at the same time the belief that while anti-Semitism was due to the behavior of the Jews, not all Jews showed the behavior causing prejudice. If all Jews would behave like they did themselves, anti-Semitism would disappear. Blaming other members of their group for their fate, they show considerable hostility toward them. Not only are the other Jews responsible for their misfortunes, but their very existence prevents the "good Jews" from being accepted by the majority whom, they believe, they resemble.

Sharing the prejudice of the majority, the resigned individual tends to be prejudiced against other minority groups as well. He thus gains not only an additional outlet for his aggressive needs (resulting from discrimination as well as from his inability to escape the situation due to his resignation) but also an additional support for his self-esteem. While he may be aware of not being accepted, not being quite as good as the majority individual, he feels superior to other members of his group as well as other minorities.

From here it is only one step toward releasing the accumulated hostility toward members of one's own group or other minorities. Jews become anti-Semites, Negroes fight Negroes. Such intragroup hostility tends sometimes to be encouraged by a prejudiced majority. We recall the low penalties for Negro violence against Negroes. The price, however, which the minority members pays for such neurotic outlet is the inability to identify with his own group. Rejected by the majority and by the minority such individuals are often quite isolated.

While resignation and withdrawal, accommodation to existing inequities, forms one way of adjustment, the active attempt to change one's position in society constitutes the other alternative. It may take the form of militant action against discriminatory treatment. Where possible, minority groups might attempt to assimilate themselves.

Overt protest against discrimination constitutes the best form of adjustment. Active opposition to oppression tends to enhance the individual's self-esteem. The individual here identifies with his own group, gains support from it. He rejects the negative evaluations of the majority. Additional feelings of strength are gained where the militant minority cooperates with the progressive, unprejudiced elements in the majority group as well as with other minority groups rather than blindly attacking the majority group as a whole. Needless to say, in situations where suppression operates by force, militant action may lead to danger and create counter-aggression. While the possibilities of reprisal might cause anxiety, nevertheless, the assertion of protest and action within the limits set by the situation is likely to produce the best adjusted minority members.

EFFECTS ON ASSIMILATION

The process of assimilation is likely to create conflict. In the isolation of the ghetto, the Jews were exposed to strong tension, but the pressure was felt as being directed against the whole group, not the individual as such. The individual Jew possessed some "region in which he felt at home, in which he could act freely."[23] Stringent restrictions made it impossible for him to leave his group. Hence, one may assume there was little tendency to identify with the majority group, to take over their evaluation of one's own group.

This situation changed radically when emancipation set in, when the barriers between majority and minority groups were gradually lowered. The dispersal of the Jews, who now gained closer contact with majority group members, made the individual exposed to personal pressure. Living within the gentile community he now became the direct target of individual attack.

At the same time, the possibility of emancipation offers the opportunity to escape the disadvantages of minority membership by adopting the ways of the majority. Such adaptation may imply a greater acceptance of the majority's evaluation of the minority group as inferior. It tends to lead to a lowering of strong feelings of belonging to one's old group and at least temporarily to increased insecurity.

The lower-middle class individual attempting to rise to the next higher class of society experiences a similar decline in his feelings of belonging to his group of origin. He tends to emulate the values and standards of the group into which he is trying to move, looks at his old group through the eyes of the group into which he plans to penetrate. Like the Jews, he will find it difficult to be accepted. The conflict resulting from increased emancipation of minority groups can be fairly unsettling:

Jeanne Smith's [name fictitious] general outlook towards life is highly idealistic, but for the purposes of preserving her self-esteem and as a result of the constant pressure of discrimination which she had experienced in her attempts to secure a white collar job, she has adopted an attitude of scepticism. Her basic insecurity and frustration, and the realization that she may not be accepted because she is a Negro, has led to a certain generalized lack of trust in people, and a qualified coldness to all but a few friends, with whom she feels totally accepted. She has a need to disguise her natural warmth towards people behind a veneer of cynicism and aloofness. Once she has achieved a degree of acceptance among a white group, she unconsciously propagandizes on behalf of Negroes, in terms of what she is trying to do in the line of education.

"Oddly enough," she states, "I have never had the desire to be born white." She is infinitely proud of her ethnic group, and feels that the Negroes have accomplished a great deal since their liberation from slavery, against tremendous odds of restriction and discrimination in every field. She believes that Negroes have done well in combating the problems of a highly scapegoated minority group. However, she does feel somewhat hostile towards her own group, feeling that the Negroes plight is partially their own fault. In her eyes, the majority of Negroes have adopted an attitude of resignation towards their problem. She finds them too apathetic in their combat, their attempts to understand.

Jeanne identifies strongly with both Negro and white groups. She has the need to identify with the former for a sense of belonging and for the sense of security that that group identification provides. At the same time, in reaction to the barriers of discrimination, she has identified with the majority group in an attempt to further racial understanding. In mixed groups, where she more often identified more strongly with whites than Negroes, depending on the individuals involved, she experiences guilt feelings due to the other Negroes who she realizes have not succeeded in identifying with the white group to the extent she has.[24]

Jeanne Smith represents many of the problems of the person on the boundary between groups whom the sociologists call the "marginal" man. She participates in the social life of both majority and minority groups. Being partially accepted by the socially "superior" group, which she admires and resents at the same time, still being tied to the minority group, she feels at home in neither group. She harbors hostility also toward the minority group leading to feelings of shame, guilt, and desertion.

The reactions of minority members who mix with the majority group, particularly those attempting to assimilate to it, have a direct effect on intergroup relations. Particularly where they suspect prejudices against their own group they tend to overemphasize their minority origin, or deliberately underplay it. They may be constantly aware of their minority membership, proud of it, or be ashamed of it.

To some extent, all of us are usually aware of ourselves not only as individuals but as members of groups. If I ride on a bus and the bus driver passes by a stop, I am annoyed at him in my capacity as a passenger. We, the passengers, and hence I, the individual riding in the bus, have been insulted. When I buy bread in the grocery store and am made to wait, I may think of myself as a "neglected customer," or, and this is decisive, as a "foreigner" if I believe that the grocer is prejudiced against foreigners.[25] It is symptomatic for the minority member that he thinks of himself more often as a member of an ethnic group than as a member of a group defined in terms of the momentary situation, as a passenger on a bus or a customer in a store.

Whenever the member of the minority has experienced rejection, and at the same time tends to reject his own group, he may become exaggeratedly self-conscious, sensitive, tend toward introspection. He not only feels under observation, he is at the same time looking for the appearance of those "despised" personality traits which he considers as "typical" for his own minority group. He is, as it were, preoccupied with his Jewishness, his being a Negro, a foreigner, and finds it difficult to merge himself into the social situation merely as a participant.[26] In mixed company members of the minority often do not tend to be themselves. They may act reflectively instead of spontaneously, feel ill at ease. In other cases they do not act in an inhibited manner but compensate by being exaggeratedly outgoing and gay. Whatever their reaction, its deviation from normal, matter-of-fact spontaneous behavior, without emphasizing or hiding their group membership, not only tends to have a negative effect on interpersonal relations, but also shows the minority in an unfavorable light.

Such reactions tend to be lessened, if not absent, whenever there is an entirely positive identification of the minority member with his own group. The individual Italian or Jew who is proud of Italian or Jewish accomplishments does not feel on the defensive. Hence he is less likely to be self-conscious or introspective. He does not need to comply with the wishes of others, or overcompensate by stressing his own worth unduly. Nor does he need to be overmodest.

One may perhaps argue that while the sufferings of the persons attempting to assimilate are deplorable, they are also inevitable. In order to be motivated to adopt majority behavior, it might be considered necessary that minority members develop first a negative attitude toward the values and behavior patterns of their own culture. But the danger is that prejudice and discrimination on the one hand, the ensuing negative evaluation of minority characteristics by minority members on the other hand, may create precisely those characteristics in the minority which furnish fuel for further prejudice. The reaction to prejudice itself brings forth aggression and clannishness, introspective tendencies and the development of compensatory "racial pride" as well as the assertion of the group's superiority. It appears likely that whenever an increased demand for conformity leads to a greater stress on assimilation the progress of assimilation is actually slowed down.

The child who is sent to the kitchen and permitted to return only after he has learned proper manners so that he can eat with his parents, is unlikely to learn good manners. In the kitchen he ceases to be exposed to the example of parental behavior which he can imitate. Moreover, he will develop resentment against the punishing parents, which is not conducive to learning. It is the child who is permitted to eat with his parents, who is not constantly told about his inferiorities, the loved child, who will imitate his parents and learn the approved behavior.

If we substitute our minorities for the child, and the ghettos for the kitchen, it becomes apparent why the demand for speedy Americanization together with the punishment for behaving in foreign ways may retard assimilation. It not only creates racial pride, but it fosters the formation of ghettos, where the immigrant, the Jew, the Negro, receive recognition denied to them by the outside world, where they maintain a feeling of belonging and being accepted. One may, of course, question whether complete assimilation, the disappearance of cultural differences, is in itself desirable. Assimilation would not be necessary if we did not tend to exploit those who are different. The need for conformity itself will be found to be anchored in psychological factors such as insecurity and fear. Prejudice looks at difference not as desirable but as a threat. If we should be able to cease to look at other groups as inferior, if we could give up the need to proclaim the superiority of our own group, it would not be necessary to prove the innate equality of the different racial and ethnic groups.

The widespread existence of prejudice and discrimination at a high cost for all parts of the nation requires a thorough analysis of the factors which are responsible for its growth. We need to look for their causes both in the nature of the interacting groups and the process of interaction.

SELECTED READINGS

1. Sartre, J. P., "Portrait of the Inauthentic Jew." *Commentary*, 5: pp. 389-397, 522-531, 1948.
2. Clark, K. D., and M., "Racial Identification and Preference in Negro Children," in *Readings in Social Psychology*, ed., Newcomb, T. M. and Hartley, E. L. Holt, New York, 1947, pp. 169-178.
3. Lewin, K., *Resolving Social Conflicts*. Harper & Brothers, New York, 1948, chs. 9-12.
4. Hughes, E. C., "Race Relations in Industry," in *Industry and Society*, ed., Whyte, W. F., McGraw-Hill, New York, 1946, ch. 6.

REFERENCES

1. Moon, B., *The High Cost of Prejudice*. Julian Messner, Inc., New York, 1947, p. 83.
2. Janowitz, M., "America's Black Legions: Nativist Agitation During the Great Depression," in *America in Crisis*, ed., Aaron, D. Knopf, New York, 1952.
3. Farago, L., ed., *German Psychological Warfare*. Committee for National Morale, New York, 1941.
4. Moon, *op cit.*, p. 20.
5. Saenger, G., "The Effect of the War on Our Minority Groups." *American Sociological Review*, 8:15-22, 1943.
6. Moon, *op. cit.*, p. 37.
7. Davie, M. R., *Negroes in American Society*. McGraw-Hill, New York, 1949, ch. 12.
8. Moon, *op. cit.*, p. 48.
9. McLean, H. V., "Psychodynamic Factors in Racial Relations." *The Annals of the American Academy of Political and Social Science*, 244:161, 1946.
10. Deutscher, M., and Chein, I., "The Psychological Effects of Enforced Segregation, a Survey of Social Science Opinion." *Journal of Psychology*, 26:259-287, 1948.
11. *Ibid.*, p. 280.
12. Myrdal, G., *An American Dilemma*. Harper & Brothers, New York, 1944, p. XLV.
13. Saenger, G., and Gordon, N. S., "The Influence of Discrimination on Minority Members in its Relation to Attempts to Combat Discrimination." *Journal of Social Psychology*, 31:95-120, 1950.
14. Clark, K. D., and Clark, M., "Racial Identification and Preference in Negro Children," in *Readings in Social Psychology*, ed., Newcomb, T. M., and Hartley, E. L. Holt, New York, 1947, pp. 169-178.

15. *Characteristics of the American Negro*. Klineberg, O., ed. Harper & Brothers, New York, 1944.
16. Jahoda-Lazarsfeld, M., and Zeisel, H., *Die Arbeitslosen von Marienthal*, Leipzig, Hirsel, 1932.
17. Davis, A., "The Motivation of the Underprivileged Worker," in *Industry and Society*, ed. Whyte, W. F. McGraw-Hill, New York, 1946.
18. Sutherland, R., *Color, Class and Personality*. American Council on Education, Washington, 1942, p. 56.
19. Powdermaker, H., "The Channeling of Negro Aggression by the Cultural Process," *American Journal of Sociology*, 48:750-758, 1943.
20. Bettelheim, B., "Individual and Mass Behavior in Extreme Situations," in *Readings in Social Psychology*, ed., Newcomb, T. M., and Hartley, E. L. Holt, New York, 1947, pp. 637 ff.
21. Fromm, E., *"Zur Entstenhung des Christusdogmas."* Wien, 1931.
22. Saenger and Gordon, *op. cit.*, pp. 108 ff.
23. Lewin K., *Resolving Social Conflicts*. Harper & Brothers, New York, 1948, p. 155.
24. Cherner, F., and Frankel H., Unpublished case history.
25. Lewin, *op. cit.*, p. 146.
26. Sartre, J. P., *op. cit.*, p. 389 ff.

CHAPTER 3

FACING THE PROBLEM

What can be done to overcome the widespread prejudice and discrimination that proves so costly to everybody? In asking this question it is of course necessary to admit that not everyone is even aware of the existence of the problem. And those who are aware of it may believe that nothing can be done about it, because of "human nature."

Members of minorities suffering from suppression and exploitation will, as a rule, be aware of the problem. Many of them, though by no means all as we have seen, will feel unjustly treated. Others agreeing with the majority group, tend to blame themselves, their own group. Some, of course, we noted, may attempt to protect their self-esteem by repressing any awareness of their special situation and by pretending that they are no different from anyone else.

The members of the majority group, and especially the more prejudiced ones, may not be aware of the evils of prejudice and discrimination at all. They may deny that it exists or that they themselves are afflicted with it. In this "best of all worlds" everyone occupies his proper place. There may be tensions and race riots. But to those who are blind to the realities of prejudice and discrimination these tensions are caused by those who revolt and fail to recognize the natural order of things, in which every group occupies the place it deserves in terms of their own worth. Only misguided liberals and "do-gooders," communists and "uppity" Negroes want change, fail to realize that everyone is better off with the way things are now.

Most prejudiced persons do not ascribe to the extreme position just described. They will readily admit that there are excesses, usually committed by others. They agree that these excesses must be erased in due time. But they hold on to their position that there are superior and inferior people, and believe that the superior people should keep the place in the sun, and perhaps have a greater say in the affairs of the nation. In some cases the prejudiced person may grant the one or other minority a better place in the future, provided they mend their "evil" and "undesirable" ways, become educated in the ways of the majority.

Not everybody is considered capable of such improvement. In general it is assumed that the children of immigrants will become true Americans. At least they always did become Americanized in the past. But doubts exist among the prejudiced that all ethnic or nationality groups can be equally easily assimilated. The perpetuation of discriminatory immigration quotas favoring North Europeans in the McCarran-Walters Bill of 1952 made many people ask whether we still believe that the French and Italians are inferior to the British and Germans.

A substantial proportion of the population believes that not everyone is capable of improvement. They believe that Negroes, and perhaps Jews, cannot be assimilated. They frown upon the attempt to integrate members of the colored race whom they consider biologically inferior.

THE POPULAR DIAGNOSIS AND THE SCIENTIFIC APPROACH

Are the premises of the prejudiced part of the population correct? Are there superior and inferior races? What causes difference? Are these differences responsible for the existent relations between majority and minority peoples? These questions need an answer.

If the popular diagnosis of the origin of prejudicial treatment in racial and ethnic differences proves correct there may be some justification for differential treatment, always provided we omit ideological and humanitarian considerations. On the other hand, if the opinions of prejudiced people concerning the nature of racial and ethnic differences should prove wrong, they need to be corrected. Prejudiced people must be taught the facts concerning racial and ethnic differences, will have to learn that existing ethnic differences could result from cultural differences or differences in treatment rather than heredity.

The facts about race are today known to a fairly large educated public. In summarizing the work of psychologists and anthropologists on racial and ethnic differences we shall have to concern ourselves not only with the results of their investigations, but also with the ways by which the prejudiced individual arrives at wrong conclusions.

We shall have to concern ourselves not only with the correction of false beliefs concerning the innate superiority of one group, but also with an analysis of the real differences which exist today between majority and minority group members due to differences in upbringing and opportunities. The student of racial and ethnic relations needs to be informed about the scope of existing physical, social, and psychological differences regardless of their origin.

Relevant here is the question of the extent to which people who are different can live in peace with each other. Is ethnocentrism, the preference for one's own group, universal or is it more correct to say that some people get along with those who differ from them, while others are afraid of and hostile toward those who differ and hence demand conformity? The nature of the interacting groups requires as much attention as the processes of interaction between them.

With this discussion we have left the realm of the popular diagnosis of the problem of human relations and entered the realm of scientific inquiry and diagnosis. If people insist in harboring false beliefs, are prejudiced against each other and discriminate, in spite of the price they pay, how do we explain these phenomena?

One major avenue of inquiry is concerned with the relation of prejudice and discrimination to economic and social problems. We shall have to ask ourselves to what extent the desire to gain by exploiting others is responsible for the persistence of prejudice and discrimination. To what extent can social prestige be gained through exclusion? Under what circumstances and through what means do prejudiced people try to restrict open competition for material and social advantages?

The question will have to be asked whether or not economic and social causes are solely responsible for the existing situation. Prejudices, we know, exist in individual life as well as in intergroup relations, even where economic and social factors could not possibly matter. If we are shy and timid we may become prejudiced against the stranger who is the life of the party even though he has a background identical to ours. Similarly, if we have doubts (probably unconscious) about our own sexual capacities, it is easy to imagine that members of other groups are remarkably endowed, and to condemn them for these very traits which we ourselves desire; hence, Negroes, for instance, are often accused of being dangerously oversexed. What then is the actual extent to which psychological factors play a role in explaining prejudice?

The widespread existence of racial prejudice in some countries and its almost complete absence in others poses another problem. Are some of the economic and social conditions which cause prejudice at home absent abroad? Are the inhabitants psychologically better adjusted? Have they chosen other means to cope with their problems?

If we find that even young children not yet burdened with economic and social problems show prejudice, we need to know to what extent intolerance is transmitted through parents, the school, and the community at large.

Our knowledge of the manifold causes of prejudice provides us with cues for action. What needs to be done in the individual case may depend on the particular reasons for the emergence of prejudice and discrimination in a given group in a particular situation. There may be no over-all cure for prejudice, no one superior method to combat it.

Superficially, the problem of the reduction of prejudice and discrimination appears simple. If social, economic, and psychological factors cause prejudice, why not attempt to remove the factors which make people look down upon others and exploit them? But this may only rarely be possible. Economic insecurity cannot be completely removed within the framework of our society—even if this were desirable. And even where we may be able to succeed in improving the lot of prejudiced persons we still have to deal with the heritage of intolerance transmitted from generation to generation and firmly anchored in our folkways—as, for example, the traditional southern pattern of segregation.

Education may be the answer here. Yet education will encounter serious resistance. Large proportions of our population have been brought up to look down upon others and to treat them as inferior. The prejudiced individual lives in a society in which his friends and neighbors are also prejudiced and where sometimes the very laws encourage discrimination and segregation, brand others as second-class citizens. Can people be taught the facts about the nature of racial and ethnic differences if the acceptance of the truth brings them into conflict with those on whom they depend? It might prove difficult to make people listen if the acceptance of the facts would cause them to appear uninformed and undemocratic and prevent them from feeling superior.

The question also arises as to who is to teach the prejudiced person the errors of his ways. He is unlikely to associate with people whose opinions differ markedly from his own. Perhaps we should start early in life, with the young child whose prejudices have not had time to develop. But even if the schools should attempt to do the job of education for democracy, how successful can they be in the face of counter-indoctrination by the parents? Moreover, the teachers and school administrations are dependent upon the good will of an often prejudiced community. How far can they go in teaching even scientifically verified facts which contradict the beliefs of large sections of the community? What would happen if they encourage a lowering of the barriers between groups?

If these difficulties exist in the field of formal education of our children, how much more difficult will it be to re-educate the adult, particularly when powerful psychological and economic motives make it advantageous for him to cling to prejudice and discrimination? In the face of the difficulties facing successful education, might it not perhaps be better to concentrate on the removal of discriminatory practices instead upon the prior removal of prejudice?

If we should succeed in bringing together into close contact the prejudiced groups with those about whom they are prejudiced, we might accomplish what education fails to do. People learn more from what they themselves experience than from what they are being told. The Negro or Jew with whom they associate daily is not the same person as the imaginary Negro or Jew who exists only in the prejudiced person's phantasy. But will they be able to see? We have already observed how attitudes color our perception. Contact between majority and minority members has always existed. The problem here will be to ascertain what kind of contacts permit learning and which are detrimental to the establishment of good intergroup relations.

Even if we should find that beneficial contact provides an answer, how do we manage to get people together? The prejudiced person will be inclined to shy away from contact with those whom he dislikes. In the face of opposition how can we bring about improvements in patterns of discrimination? We need to analyze the relative strength of the opposition toward the abolition of discriminatory practices in employment, housing, or education; which may differ in various regions. We shall have to know to what extent the prejudiced person has a realistic awareness of the climate of public opinion favoring or opposing discrimination. Can we make the prejudiced person aware that he, too, suffers, when he discriminates against others?

Changes often tend to be initiated not so much by the population at large, but by its leaders. They carry prestige and power, and people are likely to listen to them. They can take the initiative. But the leaders themselves may be prejudiced, or they may be afraid of the consequences of change. Hence it becomes necessary to examine under what conditions change will lead to a minimum of friction, and when resistance to change may become so severe that it obviates the possibility of progress.

We have to analyze what support can be given through the authority of laws passed to guarantee civil rights, and how these have to be implemented. What kind of laws can be passed, and which are likely to be rejected?

While political and economic factors determine to a considerable extent the course of racial and ethnic relations, much can be done to influence the course of events. In the United States the tradition of intolerance and prejudice has always been opposed by strong equalitarian and democratic beliefs. An informed and determined leadership can do much to combat intolerance and strengthen democracy. Success in this endeavor does not depend on good will alone, but on a thorough understanding, based on a knowledge of the science of human relations, of the causes of prejudice and the ways and means useful in reducing tension.

SELECTED READINGS

1. Smith, L., *Strange Fruit*. Reynal and Hitchcock, New York, 1944.
2. Berlin, Elin, *Lace Curtain*. Doubleday, New York, 1948.
3. Wright, R., *Black Boy*. Harper & Brothers, New York, 1945.
4. Hobson, L., *Gentleman's Agreement*. Simon & Schuster, New York, 1947.
5. White, W. L., *Lost Boundaries*. Harcourt, Brace, New York, 1948.
6. Di Donato, P., *Christ in Concrete*. World, New York, 1944.

PART II. WHAT CAUSES PREJUDICE AND DISCRIMINATION

A. THE INTERACTING GROUPS

Who are the main victims of prejudice and discrimination in contemporary America? Negroes and Orientals, Jews and Catholics, Mexicans and Puerto Ricans, as well as other immigrant groups, constitute America's minorities. What do all these minority groups have in common? With the possible exception of the Catholics, a prejudiced population tends to consider them all as more or less racially different, with distinct physical and related psychological attributes, which brand them as inferior. Usually these attributes are considered innate and typical for most if not all members of the group, such as the "swarthy" complexion of the Italian or the "cunningnesss" of the Jew.

Scientists use the term "race" only when a given group can be described in terms of some inborn physical characteristics, such as skin color, hair, a head shape. There is a legitimate question whether such physical characteristics are genetically linked with specific psychological characteristics such as high or low intelligence, or other differences in personality or emotionality. But they do not consider it permissible to speak of a distinct racial group when two groups differ only in terms of acquired social or psychological characteristics.

We speak of "ethnic groups," as distinct from "racial groups," when a group has a common culture, however vague, and may have had or still has a distinct religion, language, and national origin; perhaps also distinct manners or ways of dressing or modes of self-expression. Most ethnic groups have a strong sense of belongingness. They feel at home with each other and consider others as outsiders. All minority groups are ethnic groups, and some of them are not only culturally different but also belong to a different race. But for purposes of convenience we shall here use the term "ethnic group" only if we speak of a group which does not differ from other groups in regard to physical characteristics, is not a distinct racial group.

43

The determining factor in human relations is neither the actuality of racial boundaries nor the existence of psychological differences between racial and ethnic groups, but the *beliefs* people have concerning the nature of racial groupings. When the people of Salem hanged some of their female citizens as witches it mattered little whether witches existed. What counted was that they believed in witches. Similarly, people's attitudes toward Jews are partially determined by the fact that they consider them as a distinct race with specific physical and psychological characteristics, which are inherited and hence can never be completely changed. In terms of the prejudiced person's attitude and actions, it is relatively irrelevant whether there is a Jewish, Italian, or Mexican race.

While the essential likeness of all minority problems leads us to combine our discussion of the relations between racial and ethnic minorities and the majority, we find some differences when we enter into an analysis of the ways and means of reducing prejudice. Ethnic minorities may be completely assimilated; all differences with the majority group can disappear. But the inherited physical differences between racial groups cannot be erased. In discussing the nature of the interacting groups we shall, therefore, first have to distinguish racial and ethnic groups, next determine to what extent different racial groups differ, and finally discuss existing differences between majority peoples and both racial as well as ethnic minorities insofar as these may influence their interaction.

CHAPTER 4

NATURE AND DEVELOPMENT OF THE

RACES OF MAN

The term "race" designates "a group or population characterized by some concentrations, relative as to frequency and distribution, of hereditary particles (genes) or physical characters, which appear, fluctuate, and often disappear in the course of time by reason of geographic and/or cultural isolation."[1]

RACE, A BIOLOGICAL ENTITY

Racial groupings are defined in terms of hereditary differences. They must not be confused with the division of mankind into national, religious, or linguistic groups.[2] We cannot scientifically speak of an American or Russian, Mexican or Chinese race. Their countries are inhabited by members of different races. The Jews as well as Christians are religious groups. "Latin," "Semitic" or "Aryan" are terms which designate languages, spoken by different racial and national groups.

Earlier scientific attempts to divide mankind into a number of racial groups began with the classification of men in terms of a single physical characteristic such as skin color, head form, height, hair structure. But the choice of each different characteristic leads to a different system of classification. Using head form as the criterion, it became necessary to combine into one racial group the populations of Northern Europe and of Africa. The choice of skin color as criterion leads to the inclusion of such diverse people as the aborigines of Australia and many inhabitants of Africa in the same racial group.

It appears possible, however, to divide mankind into racial and subracial groups on the basis of a complex of traits, including skin color, head form, stature, form of the nose, and type of hair. The choice of these characteristics leads to a division of mankind into four major racial groups, the Negroid, Australoid, Caucasoid, and Mongoloid stock.[3] Some scientists prefer to consider the American Indian

45

as a separate group.[4] Within each stock subgroups are distinguished. The Caucasoid group includes the Nordic, Alpine, Dinaric, Armenoid, and Mediterranean peoples.[5] Among the Negroid group large differences exist between the Bushmen, Negrito, Melanesian, and Negro groups.

Table 4.   A Classification of Racial Groups

Race	Subgroup	Skin Color	Head Form	Stature	Nose	Hair
Caucasoid	Nordic	Blond-Light brown	D, M	170+	L	S,W
	Alpine		B	165	Me	S,W
	Dinaric		B	170	Me	S,W
	Armenoid		BB	170	Me	S,W
	Mediterranean		D, M	160	L	W
Mongoloid	Mongoloid	Yellow-Brown	B	160	Me	S
	Indo-Malay		M, B	170	Me	S
	American		D, B	170	Me	S
	Polynesian		B	170+	Me	W
Australoid	Ainu	Light-Dark brown	B	155	Me	W
	Dravidian		D	155	Me	C
	Australian		D	165	P	C
Negroid	Bushman	Brown-Black	D	140	P	Wo
	Negrito		B	140	P	Wo
	Melanesian		D	160	P	Wo
	Negro		D	170	P	Wo

Adopted from "The Concept of Race," W. M. Krogman, in "The Science of Man in the World Crisis," edited by Linton, R. Columbia University Press, New York, 1945, p. 52.

Explanation of symbols: Headform: D—dolichocephalic (longheaded), M—mesocephalic (mid-headed), B—brachycephalic (roundheaded); Stature measured in centimetres; Nose: L—narrow-nosed, Me—median nose, P—broadnosed; Hair: S—straight, W—wavy, Wo—wooly.

The characteristics selected here for distinguishing the various races and subraces constitute mere surface traits. All men are alike with regard to the really important characteristics, such as structure of the brain, the nervous system, the heart, blood and blood vessels, and with regard to almost all details of their anatomical structure.

With rare exceptions it is not even possible to say that each differentiating trait is characteristic of one race only.[6] There are round-headed as well as longheaded individuals in all major stocks. Occasionally, some characteristics are absent in some regions of the earth. There are no persons with frizzy hair among the Eskimos and no blue eyed Negroes in Central Africa.

But the differences particularly between subracial groups such as the Nordic and Mediterranean stock, which "racists" consider of such importance, are differences in average only. We find instead considerable overlap, which usually makes it impossible to tell whether we are dealing with a short individual of a tall race or a tall individual of a short race, a light member of a dark group or a darker member of a light-skinned group. On the other hand it is not difficult to distinguish a Scotchman from a native inhabitant of Central Asia. Average differences in terms of the differentiating physical characteristics are large. There are a few characteristics found in one group but not in the others such as the eyelid fold found among Mongolians.

GENETIC BASIS OF RACIAL DIFFERENCES

Differences between racial groups reflect a difference in the distribution of the genes, the raw material of heredity, in these various populations. Every physical trait, as well as mental ability, is determined by a number of different genes.

We may be able to understand better the nature of race and racial mixtures if we look for a moment at the nature of heredity. Father and mother contribute to an equal extent to each of their offspring. Their various children will differ from each other because at each mating only one half of the gene pairs found in each sex cell of either parent enters into the union. If we consider a great number of couples where the fathers had genes both for relatively light and relatively dark skin, and the mothers also had these two types of genes, the chances are that one fourth of their children would inherit two light genes, one fourth two dark genes, and two fourths a combination of light and dark skin genes from their parents. Actually more than one gene for the determination of skin color must exist in order to explain the fact that we have relatively large differences in shading even among "pure" whites.

Genes for different traits can combine independently of each other. If both parents have "brown" and "blue" eye genes, and both genes for "blond" and "dark" hair, they can have children with blond hair and blue eyes as well as blond hair and brown eyes, or the children may have dark hair either with blue or brown eyes. This is known to geneticists as the principle of independent assortment, which explains why we can and do find persons with dark skin and frizzy hair as well as wavy hair, individuals with light skin and frizzy hair or light skin and wavy hair.

We are now able to define races in genetic terms:

Races are populations which differ in the relative commonness of some of their genes. If we make a careful study of the populations not only of different countries but even of provinces or districts of the same country, in fact of neighboring villages, we certainly find them somewhat different. In one village there will be relatively more brunettes and in

the other more blonds, in one district the universal blood donors will
be more frequent than in the other.[7]

The geographic distribution of specific genes, however, is by no
means a stable one. If, for example, the inhabitants of the first village
become economically better off and, therefore, have more children,
there would be in their county in time an increased number of
brunettes.

Finally, mixture can cause ever new combinations. Suppose that at
any one time the inhabitants of one country were all blond and blue
eyed, and those of the neighboring country brunettes and brown eyed,
a new variety of men will arise when the inhabitants of these two
countries intermarry, namely blondes with brown eyes and brunettes
with blue eyes. All these events have occurred in the history of mankind. Climatic conditions have favored one group over the other.
Social preferences have influenced the distribution of genes. Different
racial and subracial groups have mixed.

But we still have not answered the most fundamental question of
what caused the original diversity of human types. Mankind has
always shown great curiosity concerning its antecedents. Most religions dealt at length with the divine origin of man. Some people
thought to justify their discriminatory practices by proclaiming that
God has created white man and black man and hence did not desire
them to mix. Until the advent of Darwin's theory of evolution man
was considered as unique, basically different from all animals. We
now know that he is only the culmination of a long upward development from the most primitive animals on to higher and higher forms
of living, through the fishes to amphibians, reptiles, and mammals to
man.

All species of animals from the beginning of the evolutionary ascent
on are the result of accidental mutations or changes of the gene structure which, as we saw, determines the form of the living animal. These
mutations, which are exceedingly rare and occur perhaps once in a
hundred thousand cases, are responsible for the upward development
of the species and lead to the constant development of new varieties.

Occasionally, some individuals or groups of the same type of animal
become separated from each other, and different mutations take place
in the two isolated groups. Moreover, in different environments different types of characteristics may increase the chance of survival.
Since isolation prevents them from mixing, the two groups will thus
become more and more unlike and finally become mutually infertile,
unable to reproduce with each other. When this point has been reached
we speak of a difference in species.

This process of constant divergence, the emergence of ever new species, finally led, about forty or sixty million years ago, to the development of the primate, the ancestor of man. The first beings which can be called man were the Java and Pekin man, living approximately half a million to a million years ago, followed by the Heidelberg man about half a million years ago. These men have been named according to the locations where their skeletons had been found. They differed from modern man in their heavy chinless lower jaws, small skulls, and many other apelike traits. Much nearer to modern man was Neanderthal man, who roamed the earth about a hundred thousand years ago. He differed from modern man chiefly in being thick-set, with receding chin and long arms.

According to most authorities modern man, or *Homo sapiens,* originated at most some fifty thousand years ago in the region where Europe, Asia, and Africa join. From here modern man has spread over the whole world, a process taking thousands of years. It was not until approximately fifteen thousand years ago that the first men set foot on the American continent by crossing the Bering Strait from Siberia.

EVOLUTION OF THE RACES OF MANKIND

It appears as if the development of the major stocks of mankind took place roughly during the first twenty-five thousand years of this migration. *Homo sapiens* must have been a rather heterogenous group, with all or almost all the genes now found in the different races of mankind. Similar occurrences are found among many mammals who exhibit a great variety of size and color within a single species. Yet there is no reason to believe that the various groups migrating to different parts of the world were exactly alike, even though they all came from the same source.

It looks as though the whole human race had got its genes from the same source. One can imagine a huge aquarium tank in which a great variety of differently colored fish are swimming. There comes an order for fish to populate an aquarium in Utah and the shop keeper dips in his net and brings it up full of flashing fishes—many gold, some silver, a few black, some with fantails, some plain and many other kinds in different quantities. From this collection, there is established a population in a Salt Lake City pool, which may eventually be known as the Salt Lake City race. In response to a request from Buenos Aires the net dips again and comes up with another collection, containing many of the same kinds as went to Salt Lake City, but in somewhat different proportions, lacking entirely a few of the rarer kinds but containing one or two different rare ones. Moreover, in Argentina it turns out that the customers, naturally enough, like silver fish, so these are bred in larger numbers than the others and proportions of the original sample are changed further. Everyone can recognize that the fish of the Salt Lake City pool and the inhabitants of the aquarium in Buenos Aires all came from the same source and that many of the same colors and kinds are found in each population, but the kind of mixture is distinctive for each "race" of fish. The original pool of course represents the collection of genes from which our ancestors and we of our particular race received our own particular collection.[8]

In addition to the diversity introduced by migration other changes may have occurred as the result of mutations. Montagu considers it possible that the kinky hair of the Negro may well be of such origin. While this characteristic has no adaptive value as far as known, some of those characteristics which now distinguish the major types of races may have survival value. Broad noses are found particularly among populations living in dry, hot zones as did the Negroes. People who originally lived in the temperate zones are distinguished by thin and narrow noses. A broad nose permits a greater air intake than a thin and narrow nose, an advantage in a tropical climate. A thin and narrow nose gives a greater opportunity to warm the air which proves advantageous in cold regions. Similarly, dark pigment proves to be more resistant to the intense sunlight of the tropics. If an originally fairly white group migrates into a tropical climate, they would over long stretches of time become darker, due to the greater survival chance of those carrying darker genes, as happened to the early "Aryan."

Differences in mutation, the influence of selective survival operating in isolated groups, as well as the original small accidental differences in gene distribution in groups which had become separate, always finally led to the emergence of groups which became mutually infertile, i.e. species. Man is unique in that this degree of separation has never been reached. This can be explained only if we assume that the periods of comparative isolation had not been sufficiently extended and that even during prehistoric times periods of isolation were always followed by periods of intermixture.[9]

RACE MIXTURE AND RACIAL INSTABILITY

During recent times, since the advent of recorded history some six thousand years ago, this process of intermixture has taken place at a greatly accelerated rate. All racial groups existing today are known to have mixed with other racial groups. The ancestors of the American Negro, for example, had white genes even before their arrival on the American continent since Arabic caravans penetrated deep into the heart of Africa.[10] But the greatest intermixture and hence the greatest variety of human forms is found in Europe. We may remind our readers here of the invasion of Spain in the eighth century by the "Moors," as well as the later invasion of Eastern Europe by the Mongols.

Homogeneous populations are not even found in the more isolated parts of Europe such as Sweden. The Swedish anthropologist Retzius found that in his country, which has frequently been described as 100 per cent Nordic, only 11 per cent could be classified as pure or "typical Nordics." On the other side of Europe, we find in Sicily types immediately classifiable as "Greek," "Moorish," and "Norman," as well as those with certain Negroid characteristics.[11] Perhaps the greatest racial mixture, however, exists in the United States, where all the European populations have mixed with each other and to a lesser extent with the American Indian and the American Negro.

The great apparent variety of racial forms is due not only to intermixture, but is partially the result of the relative instability of racial characteristics. The appearance of the individual is determined by the interaction of his hereditary equipment and his environment. Height, for example, is determined not only by genes but also by nutrition. Few modern whites would be able to fit into the medieval armor worn by the knights of the Crusades. The American soldier of World War II was on the average an inch taller than his father from World War I. A change of environment also affects head form within the short time of one generation.[12] The children of Jewish immigrants from Eastern Europe are more longheaded than their relatively round-headed parents. The American-born children of Italians from Sicily, on the other hand, are more round-headed than their relatively long headed parents. The net effect is that the two fairly distinct groups come to resemble each other within one generation after being transplanted to a new environment.[13]

Some so-called racial characteristics have no genetic antecedents whatsoever. The tendency toward fat among Jews, Italians, and Germans, often mentioned by prejudiced individuals, is solely the result of a diet containing a high amount of fat and starch. In view of the extensive racial intermixture as well as the instability of racial type, further aggravated by the fact that many so-called racial characteristics are determined by external rather than hereditary factors, it becomes scientifically incorrect to speak of pure races. Race relations, however, as we noted earlier, are not determined by scientific facts but by people's beliefs, by social convention. Some Americans classify as a Negro everyone known to have a Negro ancestor, no matter how long ago, and treat such person as a Negro even though he may now not possess any Negro genes whatsoever. We arbitrarily call "colored" many individuals whose racial traits are mainly "white." It would be equally logical to call "white" all those individuals who had white ancestors, no matter how few, reserving the term Negro to those not having any white ancestors.

BIOLOGICAL SUPERIORITY OF RACIAL GROUPS

The reason for this arbitrary division is the belief that other races are inferior to our own and that intermixture would contaminate the "superior white." Prejudiced individuals often assume that the colored races are more animal-like, more primitive. There is no denying that the more protruding lower portions of the Negro race make him appear closer to the higher apes, compared to whites and Mongolians.[14] But if we take thickness of the lip as a criterion, we find that the Mongolians are closest to the animals followed by the Caucasians, with the Negroes the most human, since the higher apes have practically no lips. With regard to hairiness of face and body, however, the white race appears much closer to the animals than either of the other two major stocks.[15]

Racial differences, we noted, are restricted only to those physical characteristics used to separate populations into different groups. Moreover, according to the operation of the principle of independent assortment, there is no reason to assume that any other physical characteristic determined by heredity should appear linked to racial differences. Nevertheless, many persons reason that since Negroes differ in skin color, hair, and nose form from whites, they may also differ with regard to other physical traits. With rare exceptions the existing evidence contradicts this belief. This does not preclude the existence of large differences between racial and ethnic groups on a nonhereditary basis. The Negro death rate for tuberculosis and pneumonia is twice as high as that among whites in this country. These diseases are related to undernourishment, poor housing, and sanitation, to which Negroes are more exposed as the result of discrimination.

It has often been stated that Negroes have an obnoxious body odor compared with whites. Experimental comparisons of Negro and white students have been unable to find such difference. Variations in body odor may result from different living conditions. If Negroes are often given only the dirtiest jobs and not paid enough to afford adequate sanitation, differences in body odor are not surprising.

Equally widespread is the belief that Negroes are more highly sexed than whites, and possess larger sex organs. The Kinsey report has contributed largely to the elimination of this misconception. Middle class Negroes and middle class whites tend to be equally restrained; lower class whites and Negroes tend to be equally uninhibited.[16] But there are more Negroes than whites in the lower class, hence we should find proportionately more Negroes lacking in inhibitions.

"HYBRIDIZATION"

Those who believe that Negroes are inferior to whites, often also consider members of "pure races" to be superior to mixtures, the so-called hybrids. What happens if a "pure" Negro and a "pure" white, each one having only the skin color genes peculiar to their race, marry? All their children will be mulattoes of an intermediate shade with genes from both Negro and white parents. The marriage between two mulattoes, however, can produce all types of skin color from the darkest black to white. Moreover, the intermarriage between a white person and a mulatto cannot produce children darker than the darker of the two parents.

A further complication is added if we consider the simultaneous interaction of more than one racial trait. If, for example, two mulattoes marry, most of the children will be of intermediate skin color. Some of these children, however, will have Negroid or medium broad noses, others "European" or narrow and thin noses. Similarly, the "white" offspring of a mulatto and white parent can have children with medium broad as well as long and narrow noses. It often happens that the child of a quadroon (one out of the four grandparents is a "Negro," three are whites) and a white person has no distinguishing Negro characteristics whatsoever, is biologically speaking, entirely white.[17]

Prejudiced persons tend to object to race mixture on the grounds that Negroes are of inferior intelligence. Even prejudiced individuals, however, may concede that there are more intelligent as well as less intelligent whites, as there are Negroes of different degrees of intelligence. A person believing in eugenics—the art of improving the race—should consequently seek to marry a person his equal or superior in intelligence. Such persons may be found among whites, and, though perhaps in smaller numbers, among Negroes (actually there is no scientific evidence for the theory that there are fewer Negroes than whites possessing high intelligence). The average white would obviously improve his chances to have bright children if he married a Negro of above average intelligence.

Persons opposed to racial intermixture also claim that the hybrid offspring would be biologically weaker or show signs of disharmony in body structure. According to Wirth and Goldhamer,[18] evidence concerning the lowered fecundity of hybrids is conflicting. A study of an old racial mixture between Hottentots and Boers showed "7.7 children per family several generations after the original crossing"; surely no evidence of lowered fecundity. The mutineers of the Bounty who married native Polynesian women have left children of great physical vigor and exuberance. We may expect fewer children wherever society disapproves of hybrids, weaker individuals where discrimination depresses the living standard of the hybrid group.

If we compare racial intermixture among humans with our experiences with animals we have reasons to believe that the hybrids may even be stronger than either parent.[19, 20] The phenomenon of hybrid vigor, the greater strength of the crossing of two dissimilar groups, is well known. The chance that two defective recessive genes come together in the offspring is lessened in the crossing of heterogeneous groups.

There is no reason to fear that race mixture may lead to disharmony in the hybrid, and that the offspring of a crossing between Negroes and whites might perchance have the relatively longer legs of the Negro parent and the shorter arms of the white parent. The actual differences between average length of the leg in the two races is only about one fifth of an inch. But even if the differences would be greater we could not expect a disharmonic body. Otherwise we should find also that if a tall white man marries a short white woman, the son would have father's long legs and mother's short arms, and, *mirabile dictu,* father's big head on mother's thin neck.

Where hybrids show undesirable characteristics, social pressure tends to be responsible. If the parents of a child come from two different religions or racial groups in a society where one group looks down on the other and disapproves of intermarriage, where friends and relatives make things difficult for the couple, it would be unreasonable not to expect the child to suffer the consequences of a divided home.

Intermarriage usually happens only where prejudice is low. Yet not all occurrences of racial mixture are achieved by voluntary and peaceful means. While the United States provides perhaps the greatest example of modern intermixture of a peaceful and voluntary nature, it harbors in its boundaries at the same time the descendants of a race which came here against its will as a result of brute force.

What caused the widespread mixture of Negroes and whites within the United States? It has been estimated that not more than 22 per cent of today's Negroes are unmixed.[21] Often Negro women had no choice but to submit to their white masters. Moreover, sexual intercourse with whites proved to be advantageous for the Negro slave women, who had no inducement to be chaste. Her person was the only means of purchasing favors, indulgences, and presents. To become the favorite of the master or of his sons even lent some dignity to her life.[22]

In discussing the morals of Negroes we must also consider the fact that for economic reasons the slave owners actively interfered with the formation of a stable Negro family life. Families were torn apart without the slightest compunction. Nobody, therefore, should blame the Negro girl for her promiscuousness. Similar reactions may be expected among women of all races under similar circumstances. In spite of their "racial pride" German girls prostituted themselves to American soldiers after the fall of Germany for a cigarette or a bar of chocolate.

In the United States "miscegenation received a further impetus from the fact that the children of slave women were the legal property of the woman's owner. The prevailing purchase price of slaves made it generally cheaper to breed slaves than to buy them" writes Klineberg.[23] Since mulatto children commanded a higher price than pure Negro children, such interbreeding was encouraged by the white master. Apparently the rise of the so-called "instinctual aversion" toward sexual intercourse between Negro and white is thus of relatively recent vintage.

By and large, mixture between different racial and ethnic groups takes place more frequently as the result of peaceful means rather than by force. Where prejudice is absent man chooses his mate on the basis of character, common interests, personality needs, individual standards of beauty, rather than in terms of racial characteristics.

Perhaps few groups have mixed with others as often as the Jews. Jews tended to intermarry, whenever—sometimes over stretches of centuries—persecution and prejudice were at a minimum. As a result, in the twentieth century Jewish populations in different countries differ profoundly from each other. Where they have resided for long stretches of time in any one country they often can no longer be readily distinguished from the rest of the population. German census figures taken during the end of the nineteenth century indicate that German Jews show the same distribution of hair color and eye color as the non-Jewish population. In commenting on the argument that at least in America it appears often possible to distinguish Jews from other ethnic groups, Montagu states:

> Just as there is such a thing as an English, a German, a French, an Italian, and even an American cast of features, so there is such a thing as a Jewish cast of face. This cast of face is often taken to be biologically determined, but the fact is that it is culturally determined. . . . Add to the culturally determined cast of face traditionally determined gesticulations of the face and the body, character of speech, together with certain

likewise culturally determined preferences for color combinations, style, and total ensemble of clothes, and we have a powerful association of traits which readily enables us to distinguish certain Jewish persons from non-Jews.[24]

The identifiability of Jews goes back to precisely the same factors that make the European able to identify the American tourist even before the latter begins to speak. Much depends on the relative stage of assimilation of a specific Jewish group in a given country, as well as on their original habitat, as compared to that of the non-Jewish population. Jews coming mainly from Eastern and Southern Europe cannot be easily distinguished on the basis of their physique alone in Eastern and Southern Europe, but are more visible among a predominantly Nordic population. Similarly, Italians settling in French Canada will differ from the native population less than Italians settling in Wisconsin whose population was recruited to a considerable extent from Scandinavian countries.

Whatever the origin of difference, the very diversity of racial and ethnic groups, the fact that visible differences exist facilitates the emergence of prejudice. The average individual, aware of physical differences, tends to assume that these must be accompanied by psychological differences between groups. Since it is popularly believed that all differences between racial and ethnic groups are inherited, it appears only logical to believe also that perhaps differences in behavior and manner are also inherited.

SELECTED READINGS

1. Dunn, L. C., and Dobzhansky, T. H., *Heredity, Race and Society*. Penguin Books, 1946 (popular).
2. *What Is Race?* UNESCO, Paris, 1952 (popular).
3. Leiris, M., *Race and Culture*. UNESCO, Paris, 1951.

REFERENCES

1. *What Is Race?* UNESCO, Paris, 1952, pp. 81-96.
2. Klineberg, O. *Race Differences*. Harper & Brothers, New York, 1935, pp. 25 ff.
3. Montagu, M. F. A., *Man's Most Dangerous Myth: The Fallacy of Race*. Columbia University Press, New York, 1945, p. 4.
4. Boyd, W., *Genetics and the Races of Man*. Little, Brown & Co., Boston, Mass. 1950.
5. Krogman, W. M., "The Concept of Race," in *The Science of Man in the World Crisis,* ed., Linton, R. Columbia University Press, New York, 1945, pp. 38-62.

6. Klineberg, O., *op. cit.,* p. 18.
7. Dunn, L. C., and Dobzhansky, T. H., *Heredity, Race and Society.* Penguin Books, New American Library of World Literature, New York, 1946, p. 108.
8. *Ibid,* pp. 105 ff.
9. Huxley, J. S., *The Uniqueness of Man.* Chatto and Windus, London, 1941, p. 6.
10. Seligman, C. G., *The Races of Africa.* London, Butterworth, 1930, pp. 53 ff.
11. Huxley, *op. cit.,* p. 120.
12. Boyd, *op. cit.,* p. 152.
13. Boas, F., *Abstract of the Report on Changes in Bodily Form of Descendants of Immigrants.* Columbia University Press, New York, 1911.
14. Boas, F. *The Mind of Primitive Man.* Macmillan, New York, 1938, p. 102.
15. Klineberg, *op. cit.,* pp. 33 ff.
16. Kinsey, A. C., Pomeroy, W. B., and Martin, C. E., *Sexual Behavior in the Human Male.* Saunders, Philadelphia, 1948.
17. Day, C. B., *A Study of Some Negro-White Families in the United States.* Harvard African Studies, Vol. X, Cambridge, 1932.
18. Wirth, L., and Goldhamer, H., "The Hybrid and the Problem of Miscegenation," in *Characteristics of the American Negro,* ed. Klineberg, O. Harper & Brothers, New York, 1944.
19. Dickinson, A., "Race Mixture, A Social or a Biological Problem." *Eugenics Review,* 41:81-85, 1949.
20. Angel, J. L., "A Racial Analysis of the Ancient Greeks." *American Journal of Physical Anthropology,* 31:374, 1944.
21. Herskovits, M. J., *The Anthropometry of the American Negro.* Columbia University Press, New York, 1930, p. 18.
22. Calhoun, A. W., *A Social History of the American Family.* Clark, Cleveland, 1917, Vol. II, pp. 291 ff.
23. Wirth and Goldhamer, *op. cit.,* p. 264.
24. Montagu, *op. cit.,* p. 231.

CHAPTER 5

THE INTELLIGENCE OF RACIAL AND

ETHNIC GROUPS

THE MEANING OF DIFFERENCE

Prejudiced people consider their antagonistic feelings toward minorities to be a natural reaction to these minorities' "inferiority" or "undesirable personality." Opinions like "Negroes are dumb and emotional," "Jews are bright and aggressive," are frequently expressed by biased people, discussing the "nature" of different racial and ethnic groups.

Before we can examine the truth of these statements we have to analyze their meaning. They usually tend to indicate the speaker's belief that compared to himself Negroes are less intelligent and more emotional, the Jews more intelligent and more aggressive. But our "experts" on the relative merits of others are themselves of different intelligence or personality. A college professor, for example, may consider his son as "dumb." His less intelligent playmates, however, think of him as "quite bright." Much depends upon the intelligence level of the person or group who judges another individual or group.

It is possible that our professor knows that his son is more intelligent than other boys in his class. Yet his emotional reaction to his child is determined by comparing his son with himself, as well as by his expectations. Such difficulties become even greater if we discuss characteristics like aggression or emotionality. Americans tend to consider the French as emotional, the British as cold and unemotional. But to the French we ourselves may appear as unemotional, and to the British as overemotional. The standards of our own group invariably furnish the point of reference from which we judge others.

To make our judgments even more unreliable we may overrate our intelligence and underrate those of others. A man who calls his wife unintelligent may overestimate his own accomplishments and depreciate her intellectual prowess. An unintelligent white man calling Negroes dumb may be unaware of his own deficiency. To pass judgments on the intelligence and emotionality of parents and children, husbands and wives, Jews and Negroes, Japanese and French, we need objective measures rather than the subjective judgment of the individual.

In calling Negroes "dumb" our white observer may imply that all Negroes are less intelligent than he himself; or he may mean that most Negroes are dumb. If pressed, the more sophisticated individual will explain that he only means there are more intelligent whites than Negroes, or, that the average Negro is not as bright as the average white. He would allow that there are some whites of low intelligence and Negroes of exceptional intelligence such as George Washington Carver and Ralph Bunche.

We have now reduced our original ambiguous statements to the question of comparisons between averages of populations. This reduction, however, is not sufficient. If we say that men are somewhat taller than women, this may mean that all or almost all men are of superior height compared to women. It may also mean that though differences in average exist, we can still find a relatively large number of women who are taller than the average man.

Much depends here on the actual difference in average height, which amounts to four inches approximately, and the "spread" or "variation" from the mean, which is 5 feet 4 inches for women and 5 feet 8 inches for men, in the United States at the present day, within each group. We shall find considerable overlap since large differences in height exist within each sex. There are many men below 5 feet 4 inches and many above 5 feet 8 inches. Similarly there are even more women smaller than 5 feet 4 inches and a somewhat smaller though still fairly large group of women taller than 5 feet 8 inches.

The same type of analysis applies to group differences in intelligence. Large differences between the least and most intelligent group members are found within each group as for example among men and women or whites and Negroes. All modern scientists, even the few who still adhere to the belief in racial differences, agree that such average differences between groups, if they existed at all, would have to be fairly small. (Actually, of course, there is no scientific evidence that any differences exist.) Only if differences in average Negro and average white intelligence were large or if all whites were of the same (high) intelligence and all Negroes were of the same (low) intelligence could we say that all or most whites are superior to all or most Negroes.

This is of practical importance in so far as it means that we could find for almost every group of whites of a given intelligence a group of Negroes (perhaps somewhat smaller) of greater intelligence. Even if Jews were more intelligent than Gentiles there would be many Jews of lower intelligence than the average Gentile. Finally, even if men were more intelligent than women, many women would be brighter than the average man. To go a step further, the less intelligent a particular white man, the larger is the number of Negroes surpassing his intelligence, a disturbing thought for the prejudiced individual of low intelligence, who needs to bolster his self-esteem by claiming that "Negroes are dumb."

Superiority of one group as compared to another could be acquired or inherited. When the prejudiced man states that women are of low intelligence, he believes in the innate superiority of men. The prejudiced white individual thinks that white people are born superior. At various times this belief has been used to justify the denial of equal educational opportunities, or the refusal of access to jobs presumed to require high intelligence, for women or Negroes. Hence we must attempt to separate acquired skill and knowledge from true hereditary differences in comparing different racial and ethnic groups.

Until the advent of modern psychology, it had generally been assumed that innate differences in intelligence were reflected satisfactorily in the achievements of individuals, for example, school grades. Modern psychology has taught us that school marks are by no means determined solely by intelligence. The sick child often falls behind in school, as does the child who is given to worrying, or the child who does not get along with the teacher, or is disinterested. The general living standard, nutrition, and many other environmental factors will have an influence on the child's grades.

In explaining differences in performance and accomplishment occurring between children of the same family or between different groups, both hereditary and environmental factors must be considered. If we find that there are fewer female than male scientists, artists, or politicians, we have to ask ourselves whether these differences are the result exclusively of hereditary factors or whether environment plays a role. The answer is well known. There are fewer female scientists because our graduate schools were only recently opened to them. Society did not encourage women to become artists or politicians.

Modern intelligence tests are intended to study a person's native intelligence, independent of acquired knowledge. They unquestionably come closer to measuring the actual potentialities of the individual than school examinations, which measure only how much the individual has learned.

But closer examination of contemporary intelligence tests makes it clear that these tests do not succeed in measuring "native" intelligence. They fail to eliminate completely environmental factors, such as quality of schooling, motivation to study, emotional factors, to name but a few. Even if environmental factors could be eliminated to a much greater degree than appears to be the case in today's intelligence tests, they still might not reveal the true extent of a person's intellectual capacity. Intelligence, in order to reveal itself fully in solving the problems constituting an intelligence test, may have to be trained and exercised. Hence, intelligence tests can be used to compare the intelligence of two individuals fairly only if they came from the same background, had the same opportunity to develop their hereditary ability.

Yet intelligence tests can be used to compare racial and ethnic groups precisely because we have learned a great deal about the factors determining test performance. An examination of these factors is in fact indispensable for our purposes because it shows us how to account for the apparent differences in intelligence (as opposed to true hereditary differences) between different groups in our society.

To accomplish our objective we need to know something about the nature of intelligence tests, to understand the concept of IQ or "Intelligence Quotient." An intelligence quotient is a score based on the number of correct replies to an intelligence test, an example of which appears below. The items given are taken from the Army Classification Test of World War I.

1. If 5½ tons of bark cost $33, what will 3½ tons cost?
2. A train is harder to stop than an automobile because
   (   ) it is longer (   ) it is heavier (   ) the brakes are not so good.
3. Truth is to gentleman as lie is to——
   rascal   live   give   falsehood   (Underline correct word)
4. x x x x o o o x x o x x x x o o o x x—o o o
   (Complete the series.)

A person who solves as many questions (but not more) than fifty per cent of the population, i.e., the average person, is given an IQ of 100. The exceptional individual who answers correctly more questions than did 97 per cent of the population obtains an IQ of 130. Two thirds of the population have an IQ between 86 and 115.

INTELLIGENCE OF RACIAL AND ETHNIC GROUPS

We are now ready to compare the IQ's of the average native-born, white American with those of other ethnic groups residing in this country. A few years ago Klineberg[1] arranged a table summarizing the results of intelligence tests for all groups for which more than four studies were available.

Table 5.   The Intelligence of Ethnic and Racial Groups

Ethnic group	Number of studies	IQ range	Median IQ
American Control Groups	18	85–108	102
Jews	7	95–106	103
Germans	6	93–105	100.5
English and Scotch	5	93–105	99
Japanese	9	81–114	99
Chinese	11	87–107	98
American Negroes	27	58–105	86
Italians	16	79–96	85
Portuguese	6	83–96	84
Mexicans	9	78–101	83.5
American Indians	11	65–100	80.5

Adapted from *Characteristics of the American Negro*. Ed., Klineberg, O. Harper & Brothers, New York, 1944.

Among the groups studied Jews had the highest average IQ, followed closely by the Germans and English. The median IQ of the two mongolian populations studied was only slightly lower. Negroes, on the other hand, had a much lower IQ than native white Americans.

Even if we could take the results of this comparison at face value it would not give clear-cut evidence for the superiority of the white race. We note that two white groups, Italians and Portuguese, have a lower IQ than Negroes. The Japanese and the American Indian are racially members of the Mongolian stock, but differ widely in their average IQ. Differences between various ethnic groups within the same major race are greater than differences between the major races. Moreover, on the one extreme we find a Japanese group which had an average IQ of 81, whereas another group of Japanese rated as high as 114. Similarly, numerous studies have shown that Northern Negroes have a higher IQ than Negroes living in the South.[2] Apparently neither of these groups can be considered as representative for all Japanese or Negroes.

If Northern and Southern Negroes have different IQ's in spite of evidence that they do not actually differ in intelligence, we have to account for these differences in test performance. Intelligence tests require a sustained effort, concentration, and attention. A person's score on an intelligence test, therefore, depends to a considerable extent on his motivation. There is no reason to exert ourselves unless a good performance is properly rewarded.[3] Usually our desire to prove superior in a competitive world would provide adequate motivation. But some ethnic groups are denied equal opportunities regardless of their native abilities. Hence it is likely that they make less of an effort to do as good as they can on an intelligence test.

There is reason to suspect also that differences in IQ between such groups as the Japanese and the American Indian, Italians and American Jews are to some extent the result of cultural differences. The imprisonment of the Jews in the ghettos and their exclusion from manual occupations has through the centuries led to an enforced emphasis on abstract intelligence which became a part of the Jewish tradition. This emphasis on learning was further reinforced by the existence of discriminatory practices. If two candidates applying for a job perform equally well it is usually the non-Jew who is hired. In order to be accepted the Jew has to excel. The desire to overcome discrimination may furnish the motivation for studying harder, which in turn may account for the high Jewish IQ. On the other hand, the absence of competitive tendencies among several Indian tribes, as well as their different attitude concerning speed, may contribute to the low IQ of the American Indian.[4] The tests operate against members of groups who see no special virtue in working fast or who frown upon competition with each other.

A glance at our intelligence test items shows that the correct solution of most problems requires familiarity with the English language. The low IQ of Italians and Mexicans in this country has been shown to be due at least partly to language difficulties.[5] One half of the difference in IQ between native-born Americans and Italians or Mexicans disappears if performance tests are substituted for linguistic tests. In the same study, the Japanese had an IQ of 89.1 when verbal tests were used, but achieved an IQ of 101.5 in a performance test. Parenthetically, prejudiced individuals at home and abroad often consider the inability of others to speak correct English as a sign of their "stupidity," even if they themselves do not speak other languages.

Most existing intelligence tests tend to favor specific groups as the result of the type of problems used.[6] They favor urban rather than rural populations and perhaps middle class over lower class people.[7] Klineberg demonstrates this point by citing the following sentence completion question: ". . . should prevail in churches and libraries." The right answer "silence" may be familiar to the Northern middle class white but it is most likely unknown to the Southern lower class Negro considering the prevalence of revivalist forms of religion among lower class Southern Negroes.

The score an individual makes on an intelligence test may be determined also by the amount and quality of schooling he has received. Studies of both white and Negro population showed a rise in IQ roughly proportionate to the amount of school training received by the testees.[8] One may, of course, argue that "the more intelligent pupils go to school more regularly and stay there longer," rather than that "they have higher IQ's because of their longer school attendance."

But length and regularity of school attendance is largely determined by social factors. Parents in lower class families[9] do not encourage their children to stay in school since they do not feel that a longer period of schooling would be rewarded in terms of better jobs and wages. They do not emphasize education to nearly the same extent as middle class parents for whom education becomes a matter of status and prestige. Moreover, because of their large families and scanty income, lower class families need the earnings of their children to implement the family budget. They often tend to encourage their children to work as early as they possibly can. Since a disproportionately large proportion of Negroes are members of the lower class, they tend to have lower class attitudes toward education. To aggravate the situation further, a large number of Southern Negroes are sharecroppers, who require the help of all family members in planting and harvesting.[10] The majority of their children, therefore, attend school only for a few months each year. Whereas during the school year of 1943-1944 eleven Southern states (where most Negroes reside) spent $84.79 per capita for the education of white children, they spent only $36.97 per capita for Negro children.[11]

DETRIMENTAL EFFECTS OF INSUFFICIENT SCHOOLING

The test performance of children depends not only on the length of schooling, but also on the quality of the schools they attend. We noted earlier that segregated schools for Negroes are of inferior quality. The importance of adequate schooling becomes apparent if we find that Negro children migrating from the inferior schools of the South to New York City schools experienced an increase in IQ amounting to six points after four years of residence in the North.[12] Members of the lower classes not only find it harder to send their children to good schools, to afford the luxury of a long education, but suffer from other handicaps as well. Their living standard, the houses in which they dwell, and the food they eat, is inferior to those of the middle and upper classes. Their families are larger; hence their parents can spend less time with each child in the family. To make things worse often both parents have to work in order to make ends meet. Their children are left by themselves. These factors, too, appear to have an influence on the relatively low IQ of their offspring.[13]

While the results of these studies certainly tend to discredit the assumption of the superior intelligence of the white race in general, and Nordics in particular, they are significant far beyond their bearing on the problem of racial differences in intelligence. To the extent that different classes of the population, and different racial and ethnic groups are exposed to different amounts of education and schools of different quality, to that extent are they handicapped in a competitive struggle in which the outcome is at least partially determined by the degree to which a person has been able to develop his native intelligence and acquire skill and knowledge.

Differences in schooling do not only deprive the underprivileged groups of equal opportunities. They reinforce the myth of their intellectual inferiority. Prejudiced persons find proof for their beliefs concerning the Negro's low intellectual capacity by pointing to their lower IQ's, their "general ignorance," not realizing that these differences are in themselves to a considerable extent the result of prejudice leading to the denial of equal educational opportunity.

While we discovered that racial and ethnic differences in intelligence in terms of the ability to solve problems were due largely to a more or less favorable environment, the prejudiced member of the majority group observes only the apparent differences in skill, knowledge, and applied intelligence. It is to his "interest" to attribute existing differences to differences in innate intelligence, as well as in other psychological characteristics related to success. Having been brought up to believe that one's station in life depends on one's intelligence, on one's drive, application, he will believe that he is a member of a superior group by virtue of his own merits. To believe otherwise would lead to loss of self-esteem and feelings of insecurity as well as a fear of social decline. The member of the privileged group might be more afraid of the competition of the underprivileged if he realized that as a group they are as gifted as he and his class. Guilt feelings may arise whenever the person holding a privileged position and believing in equal opportunity for all would realize that the low position of the Negro is not the result of his innate inferiority, but stems from the social and educational handicaps under which minorities labor.

SELECTED READINGS

1. *Characteristics of the American Negro,* ed. Klineberg, O. Harper & Brothers, New York, 1944 (technical).
2. Klineberg, O., *Race and Psychology,* UNESCO, Paris, 1951 (semi-popular pamphlet).
3. Davie, M. R., *Negroes in American Society.* (Chap 6, "The Education of the Negro.") McGraw-Hill, New York, 1949.

REFERENCES

1. *Characteristics of the American Negro,* ed., Klineberg, O. Harper & Brothers, New York, 1944, p. 35.
2. Klineberg, O., *Race Differences.* Harper & Brothers, 1935, p. 183 ff.
3. Abel, L. B., "The Effects of Shifts in Motivation upon the Learning of Sensory-Motor Tasks." *Archives of Psychology,* Vol. 29, No. 205.
4. Klineberg, 1944, *op. cit.,* p. 78.
5. Klineberg, 1935, *op. cit.,* pp. 167 ff.
6. Altus, W. D., A Note on Group Differences in Intelligence and the Type of Test Employed. *Journal of Consulting Psychology,* 12:194-195, 1948.
7. Davis, W. A., and Havighurst, R. J., The Measurement of Mental Systems. *Science Monthly,* 66:301-316, 1948.
8. Klineberg, 1935, *op. cit.,* p. 184.
9. Dollard, J., *Class and Caste in a Southern Town.* Yale University Press, New Haven, Conn., 1937.
10. Davie, M. R., *Negroes in American Society.* McGraw-Hill, New York, 1949, pp. 79 and 151.
11. *Ibid.,* p. 147.
12. Klineberg, 1935, *op. cit.,* p. 186.
13. Sandels, S., "On intelligentmatningar av barn i forskolealdern enlight Terman-Merril's skala, L-foremen." *Tidskr., Psykol., Peedag.* 1:65-72, 1942.

CHAPTER 6

PERSONALITY AND CULTURE

"Let me have men about me that are fat;
Sleek-headed men, and such as sleep o' nights.
Yond Cassius has a lean and hungry look;
He thinks too much: such men are dangerous."
SHAKESPEARE: *Julius Caesar*

Since time immemorial man has tended to associate definite personality patterns with specific physical types. It matters little whether mankind is divided by physique, sex, race, or nationality, the basic tendency has always been the same. Each one of these groups is believed to have in common ways of thinking and acting, feelings and modes of expression.

PHYSIQUE AND CHARACTER

Most of us are certain that members of *other* groups are alike with regard to major psychological characteristics. When confronted with a member of a different race or nationality, we believe that we can anticipate his behavior because "we know" what type of people Negroes, or Jews, Frenchmen or Irishmen are. In contrast we see all our friends as different from each other. Whenever we meet a new individual belonging to our own group, we try to find out what kind of a person he is. We approach members of the ingroup as individuals, those of other groups as members of a "species."

One of the first steps toward the development of sound intergroup relations is to induce the prejudiced individual to look at members of other groups as individuals. In each race, nationality, religious group, there are tremendous differences in personality, very much the same as in our own group. Even if Shakespeare's belief that fat men are jolly and harmless had some basis of truth, it would still be necessary to look closely at the individual.

In view of the fact that large differences in personality exist within each group, how do we explain the tendency to lump together all members of groups other than our own intimate group? Such "stereo-typing" which exists even within our immediate environment is due first of all to the tendency to save time and effort. For example, it is much easier to have a definite opinion as to the type of creature women are and behave accordingly than to analyze and study each woman anew.

Secondly, there may actually be some differences in personality between the average man and the average woman. When Johnny jumps across the garden fence his father will probably be delighted at this boyish exuberance and show of daring. When Mary follows after him, her mother may well be annoyed about such rowdy, unfeminine behavior . . . "Little girls don't do such things." No wonder that the different upbringing of boys and girls will lead to differences in male and female personality even if biological differences were not a de-termining factor. Likewise, the average Italian may be brought up differently from the average Englishman. Where the former may be brought up to express his emotions freely, the latter is taught restraint.

Differences in personality, regardless of the groups we choose for comparison, can be entirely the result of environmental factors or may be more or less determined by hereditary factors. Let us presume, for example, that it suddenly became true that "gentlemen prefer blondes." Blondes would no longer find it difficult to obtain a husband or a position as a secretary, whereas brunettes would be in for a hard time. The consequences can easily be predicted. Blondes would be-come conceited, demanding, more or less egocentric. Having no difficulties in getting a job, there would be little reason to develop their intellectual capacities, and blondes would be dumb. The bru-nettes, to compete successfully, would have to develop personal charm, take a real interest in the other sex, develop their intellectual capacities, to make up for the "natural" advantages of the blondes. On the other hand, they might also develop inferiority feelings and perhaps a little resentment which might easily turn into aggressive tendencies. The mere difference in preference would thus lead to differences in personality, and it would not take long for the unen-lightened laymen to attribute this discrepancy in character to innate differences between these distinct physical types.

We can easily see how differences in upbringing and differences in treatment by their fellow men could produce differences in personality between Jews and Gentiles, Negroes and whites, immigrants and old Americans. Since differences in personality between ethnic and racial groups may contribute to friction, we shall have to ascertain the extent to which such differences exist, whatever their origin. But we should also like to know whether, as the prejudiced person has it, the different personality characteristics are due to hereditary factors, thus complicating the chances of mutual accommodation and assimilation between the interacting groups.

There are few fields of science where the need for objectivity is greater than in the field of personality evaluation. While most people pride themselves on being good judges of others, we have already noted the subjective nature of such judgments. Aside from prejudice, the individual's own personality enters almost invariably into his judgment of others. Aggressive persons easily tend to see all other people as aggressive. Insecure individuals tend to overrate the strength of others. Our own needs influence our perception of others. A dependent man craving affection may not find any woman sufficiently warm and affectionate. Another one, bent on preserving his independence at any price, may see an attempt to gain his interest, to establish a relationship, as an imposition, an attempt to lure him into a marriage, a sign of unwanted affection. The same principles operating in the relations between individuals operate in the relations between groups. As we shall see later, it is the power-hungry anti-Semite who tends to accuse the Jews of the desire to dominate the world.

EMOTIONAL EXPRESSIONS AS LANGUAGE

Apart from the difficulty in escaping the operation of need-determined perception, there are other obstacles in the path of an objective evaluation of the personality of members of other groups. We judge others in terms of their overt behavior and infer from their behavior as well as from their conversations what they feel, what their motives are. From self-observation, we know how we feel and what we think, when we use certain words or gestures or behave in a given way. We often expect to find in others the *same* relationship between specific words and expressions on the one hand, specific feeling and motivations on the other. This assumption is by no means justified. Some people when amused laugh heartily, while others just smile a little. Ardent declarations of love do not mean the same in the cases of Romeo and Don Juan, though the words may be identical.

Differences in expressions cannot necessarily be considered as indicative of differences in feelings, even within the confines of our own culture. It is a much more dangerous procedure when we attempt to understand members of other cultures by analogy with our own. Foreigners, unaware of the American teaching "to keep smiling regardless of how you feel" may easily come to the conclusion that most Americans are always happy and in a good mood.

Our study of personality differences has to consider the existence of different layers of personality. Only the surface level is open to direct outside observation. We can observe whether a person acts aggressively or submissively, hides or expresses his emotions. But underneath the overt expressions, we find the covert level of personality, the individual's emotions and thoughts which cannot be observed directly. Least accessible is the area of drives and motives, which determine the individual's actions. Yet in spite of this lack of direct information, we often presume that not only can we understand the motives of most people in our own society, but that we can also appreciate those of alien cultures which are oriented toward different goals and values.

In the light of the above considerations, it appears easiest to study first overt differences in personality. Many groups are accused of lacking emotional "control," of being excessively emotional. When Jews are excluded from resort hotels and fashionable clubs, the reason given is "that they are loud and excitable." When the French are considered great lovers, we assume that they inherited the "indefatigable Gallic temperament."

Apparent differences in emotional control are often the result of differences in cultural expression which can lead to more or less amusing misunderstandings. Two middle class Americans who have not seen each other for a time are apt to greet each other and express their joy at seeing each other by a hearty slap on the shoulder, an unforgivable lack of good manners, or lack of control, when seen from the point of view of the average Englishman. The same Americans will be horrified to see two adult Frenchmen kiss each other at a reunion, a sign of friendly esteem in France, of great exaggeration if not of homosexuality in America. Emotional expressions are part of the language of every culture and must be understood as such before we can make any statements concerning differences in emotion.[1] They give no adequate clue to the presence or absence of specific emotions unless we can read their meaning.

Lafcadio Hearn tells of a female Japanese servant who smilingly asked her mistress if she might go to her husband's funeral. After the funeral, she returned with his ashes in a vase and said, actually laughing, "Here is my husband." Naturally her white mistress regarded her as a cynical creature devoid of any feelings. Actually she should rather have been considered a heroine. To understand her reaction, it is necessary to know that it is against the Japanese etiquette to burden one's superior with one's grief.[2]

Apart from the problem of interpretation, it is, of course, possible to compare different groups in terms of their emotional expressivity measured with regard to speed, spread, and intensity of gesticulation.

"The Italian and the Jew will accompany their speech with a generous dose of gestures, shoulder shrugs, and hand movements, where the Englishman will be relatively immobile."[3] British Jews will express themselves differently from French Jews. Differences in emotional expression are not inherited, but learned. The member of a specific group expresses his emotions in ways customary for the culture in which he grows up regardless of his racial or ethnic origin.

IMPACT OF LIFE HISTORY ON EMOTIONAL CONTROL

Depending upon their culture, the whole range of expressions is found within each racial group. Anthropological research has discovered "highly emotional" as well as "highly controlled" peoples within each racial group.[4] While the American Negro is held to be uncontrolled and highly emotional, the Kipsigis of Central Africa are described as being opposed to noise, excitement, anger, or any display of feelings as being typical for children. They say: "Be silent till your anger has abated."[5]

Generally, in Western civilization differences in emotional expression are also related to class. Upper class children are brought up more rigidly than are the children of the lower classes. Their parents tend to stress emotional control more than those of lower status.[6] Most Negro children grow up in a lower class environment. Hence, if they show lack of emotional control, this can be partially ascribed to their milieu. The American Negro is emotional largely because he is lower class. Those who succeed in rising to the middle classes show the same outward behavior as whites of similar status.

Perhaps even more important than cultural influences are the experiences of the individual, his personal life history. Insecurity, fear, unjust treatment, all contribute to our emotionality. In comparing two ethnic groups in regard to their emotional control, we must take into consideration their exposure to emotion-provoking situations. The following autobiographical report (an excerpt from a term paper) describes the feelings of a Negro college student upon his "first" acquaintance with discrimination:

As far as we can remember, our first contact with that horrible venom, discrimination, came in my home town of Kansas City. . . . About five of us were returning home from a municipal park after a strenuous and hot afternoon of baseball. We stopped in a small candy store for a soda, and were asked rather sarcastically, "Are you boys going to take these sodas out to drink?" Of course, our answer was "No; we are going to drink them here," and the counterman became very indignant, and told us, "You niggers can't drink this pop in here, you have got to take them outside." That was a slap in the face for me, and it was evident that the rest of the boys were hurt, even at this tender age. I didn't know what to do. I was angry at first, frustrated, and then I tried to understand, and even felt sympathetic toward the perpetrator. In my mind, he was a sick man. Without further argument, we walked out, and left the counter-man holding five bottles of opened sodas. Of course, they were on him, because we didn't pay for them. The other fellows wanted to wreck the place, but I talked them out of it and explained to them it would mean only trouble.

We noted earlier that minority group members are more often subject to ridicule and humiliation than majority group members.[7] It would indeed be surprising if Southern Negroes failed to react to the intimidation, fear, and suppression to which they are exposed. Such emotional conflict is particularly strong whenever the situation of an ethnic group suddenly deteriorates. The rapid change in fortune of German Jews following the transition from relative security before Hitler to the status of a member of a persecuted minority led to a pronounced increase in emotionality.

One of the most evident changes in a negative direction is the increase in emotionality as a result of the enormous nervous tension which flows out of a constant persecution and discrimination. . . . The individual in distress gradually loses control over his body and his emotions. In cases with terrifying experiences, excitability, often combined with a constant fear of persecution, finds many external manifestations. The extreme nervous tension leads to jerky and abrupt movements, which may become habitual. One has the impression that the whole person is constantly in flight. This may even affect the posture; instead of walking straight and with long steady steps, such persons develop a quick and irregular gait, with back and head bent. . . . The constant fear of being heard results in subdued speech; in other cases, through overcompensation in the desire to overcome anxiety, in loud and endless speeches. Frequent repetitions and exaggerations serve the same purpose.[8]

For the above reasons, any deductions about the "innate" emotionality of racial or ethnic groups living in isolation as majority members and as minority group members under the more or less benevolent domination of a privileged majority, are scientifically unsound.

COMPARISONS OF PERSONALITY

Prejudiced people not only accuse the Negro and many other minority groups of being more childish, of exhibiting a deplorable lack of emotional control, they also believe in the existence of *innate* differences between racial and ethnic groups on a deeper level, in terms of the basic structure of personality. The psychologist here speaks of traits, which he considers as persistent ways of acting, thinking, and perceiving the world. The "aggressive" person not only acts aggressively, he sees a situation as provoking which does not appear hostile to the submissive person. The "introvert" person does not only tend to be withdrawn, disinterested in social life, he also is preoccupied with thoughts centering around his feelings and ideas rather than about the outside world.

As earlier with regard to the measurement of intelligence, psychologists have been interested in the development of instruments for the objective measurement of personality traits. Originally constructed for purposes of personnel evaluation, the screening out of maladjusted individuals, and the preliminary diagnosis preceding psychotherapeutic treatment, they have also been used extensively for comparisons of different racial and ethnic groups. Like the intelligence tests they can be used satisfactorily only to compare individuals of like backgrounds.

Objective studies comparing different racial and ethnic groups living within the same culture and having as much of a similar background as can be found permit us to check the veracity of the beliefs in innate differences in personality traits described at the beginning of this chapter.* With all their imperfections these studies are still more trustworthy than subjective comparisons by the layman. Prejudiced persons for example tend to call disliked groups aggressive, and explain their dislike on the basis of the alleged aggressiveness of the out-group. At the same time, they may hire a young man because his letter of recommendation describes him as an "aggressive, forward looking, conscientious, and ambitious young man." Evidently the word "aggression" has different meanings. If *we* assert ourselves, push forward in the face of obstacles, of opposition by others, aggressiveness assumes a positive connotation. If *others* assert themselves, push us aside, we call them "pushing," and the word "aggressive" acquires a more negative meaning. A survey of the literature, avoiding such

* The reader interested in the more technical aspects of these studies may be reminded that many of the studies on this subject fail to match majority and minority groups satisfactorily. There is also insufficient consideration of the different meanings of the tests for different groups. Even if we could match the comparison groups with regard to all major objective categories we still would have to deal with the differences in environment introduced by the majority and minority status of the groups themselves. If regardless of these imperfections no personality differences were discovered we may ascribe these results to the absence of innate personality differences or the tests. To the extent that the existing literature shows no differences in traits between groups matched for socioeconomic characteristics in spite of differences in prestige and status, it testifies to the considerable adaptability of human beings even under conditions of adversity.

pitfalls, fails to unearth any scientifically valid studies showing differences in aggression between Negroes and whites, Jews and Gentiles, living in the American culture.

Another trait held typically for some ethnic minorities is dishonesty. Hartshorne and May used experimental procedures to study honesty in children.[9] Comparing only children of the same socioeconomic background, they found no differences between Jewish and non-Jewish children. Their findings, however, that lower class children cheat more than upper class children, is significant in view of the fact that proportionately more Negro than white children are found in the lower class. When Murdock, in a study conducted in Hawaii, finds Japanese children to be more honest than Anglo-Saxon children, cultural differences in morality may be considered responsible.[10]

Much, of course, will depend also on the cultural definition of honesty. The Hungarian peasant migrating to America, who steals coal from the railroad yards, is not a thief in his culture where the gathering of firewood from the baronial woods was the custom. Similarly, black market buying is not considered dishonest by everyone. Occupational differences need also be considered. When through the Middle Ages Jews were permitted only to enter such occupations as money lenders, the behavior of the usurer came to be thought of as typically Jewish rather than as typical for that calling.

Negroes have been considered not only aggressive and dishonest but also have been accused of being by nature a happy-go-lucky group, as being irrepressible extroverts. We already observed how this belief fits in with the assumption of many prejudiced people that they do not suffer from discrimination, are happiest in the South. To avoid guilt feelings, the Southerner needs to believe in the myth of the happy-go-lucky Negro. Hence, he encourages behavior supporting his beliefs. Again, it is the culture and not heredity which favors the emergence of a specific personality trait. This holds true also for the Jew, who in contrast to the Negro is considered as basically introvert, as given to oversensitiveness, being overcritical, unable to let loose and enjoy himself, be a good sport.

While the results of studies using paper and pencil tests are not entirely conclusive, so far no significant differences between comparable groups of Jews and Gentiles, Negroes and whites of the *same* background have been found.[11,12,13] It cannot be emphasized enough, however, that practically all studies undertaken in this country that have showed a lack of difference in the extent of extrovertism between different ethnic groups have used college students as subjects. College students, however, usually constitute the most assimilated middle and upper class members of their group. The college man is practically trained to behave in as outgoing, sociable, and sporty a manner as he can. Almost by definition, college life is the happiest period of our life. Studies of cross sections of different ethnic groups living in the United States may be expected to show entirely different results. The average adult Jews, Negroes, or Italians live in comparative isolation, have not succeeded to an extent equal to the college student in entering the mainstream of American life, or partaking in the culture.* It may well be that the adult Jew, Italian, or Negro living in a New York slum may be more influenced by cultural differences than the college student of the same group.

CLASS DIFFERENCES IN PERSONALITY

Negroes are believed also to lack drive and ambition, and to be highly suggestible. We already noted that the low aspiration level of New York Negroes may be considered a defense against the experience of frustration since they are prevented by discrimination from getting ahead to the same extent as white men. Again, class differences are significant. Actual differences in ambition were found to exist not so much between ethnic or racial groups but rather between classes regardless of the racial or ethnic origin of their members. If the Irish or Polish or Negro unskilled worker lacks drive and ambition, it is not his race or nationality, but his upbringing, his economic situation which is responsible:

The habits of "shiftlessness," "irresponsibility," lack of "ambition," absenteeism, and of quitting the job, which management usually regards as the result of the "innate" perversity of underprivileged white and Negro workers, are in fact *normal responses,* that the worker has learned from his physical and social environment. . . . [The] terrible pressure for physical survival means that the child in the average working-class family usually does not learn the "ambition," the drive for high skills, and for educational achievement that the middle-class child learns in his family. The working-class individual usually does not learn to respond to these strong incentives and to seek these difficult goals, because they have been submerged in his family life by the daily battle for food, shelter, and for the preservation of the family.[15]

Prejudiced persons often use the low drive and ambition resulting from the combined impact of low status and discrimination in order to blame the minority member for his failure to make good. Wherever we compare Negroes and whites of the same class, differences in ambition tend to disappear.[16]

Suggestibility, too, is taken as a sign of racial inferiority, and fits

* This hypothesis is supported by the one study showing slight Negro-white differences, which used adult subjects rather than college students.[14]

in with the stereotype of the ignorant Negro who believes everything told him. An early study in the deep South comparing Negro and white school children from the same socioeconomic level finds the former slightly more suggestible.[17] This study, however, is of doubtful value if one considers that the Negroes tested had a lower intelligence quotient. Suggestibility is a function of intelligence and knowledge. The more we know about a given situation the less influenced are we by the opinions of others.

How do we reconcile our findings concerning the absence of innate personality differences between different racial and ethnic groups with the persistence of the belief in racial and ethnic stereotypes on the one hand and our conclusions concerning the impact of discrimination on minority group members on the other hand?[18] Most of the studies discussed had as subjects college students, who not only may suffer least from overt exposure to discrimination but also represent the most assimilated and prosperous section of the minority group.

The prejudiced person rarely meets only the minority college students, but rather the average more or less adjusted member of the minority group who shows the effects of prejudice and discrimination, and in the case of the first generation immigrant belongs to a different culture. Moreover, in a society which discriminates against minority groups, equal status contacts are unlikely. Most white people in this country do not have an opportunity to meet the educated middle-class Negro. They only know lower class Negroes, their maid or servant, and generalize from this experience as to the intelligence of the Negro race as a whole. Similar situations are found at the base of popular judgments concerning different types of immigrants to this country. Generalizations about the intelligence or personality of Italians derive from our acquaintance with the Italian shoemaker or flower vendor. Few persons ever realize that their Italian acquaintances are not representative for the population of Italians either in America or in Italy. The Italians who migrated during the last 60 years into this country usually came from the lower classes residing in the rural districts of southern Italy. Educational facilities there were poor, as were the general conditions of living in southern as compared to the more prosperous northern part of Italy. The better schooled Italian from the more prosperous parts of Italy stayed behind.

CULTURE AND PERSONALITY

Prejudice is influenced by intolerance of differences in personality regardless of their origin in heredity or environment. Even though we found no innate differences to exist, the prejudiced person meets members of minority groups who differ because they have been brought up in other cultures. Since our behavior is in the last analysis influenced by cultural emphasis it is important to realize to what extent cultures differ in their basic outlook toward life, their emphasis on different drives and motives.

Many people tend to assume uncritically that we are all alike insofar as we are subject to the same basic needs and desires, hunger, thirst, sex, the desire to get ahead and to accumulate wealth, all of which we consider part of basic human nature. We tend to consider *our* own motives and values, *our* way of looking at things as part of basic human nature. We look at those seeking other values, having a different outlook on life, as unnatural and misguided.

The belief in the basic likeness of human nature is correct only insofar as these needs are anchored in our physical make-up, like hunger and thirst. But there are many desires which do not spring from sheer physical necessity, for example, the wish to get ahead and rise above our fellow men. Such motives are taken over from the culture in which we live. Moreover, even basic needs such as the sex drive may be emphasized in one culture and not considered particularly important in another.

Contemporary Western civilization—particularly in the United States—is characterized by an ambivalent attitude toward sex. Contrary to China or ancient Greece we tend at the same time to overemphasize sex and to consider it taboo, imbued with shame, if not unclean. The enjoyment of sex for its own reasons is rejected. Even within our own society subtle differences in attitude are apparent, if we compare the American puritan tradition with the greater freedom of the French or Italian. Hence we cannot be surprised that groups toward whom we harbor ill feelings are often accused of being oversexed, immoral. The widespread popularity of the Kinsey report may have done away with the belief that Negroes are sexually more potent, differ in biological apparatus from whites.[19] Sex mores of American Negroes and whites were found to be identical class for class.[20] But if we take into account that most Negroes belong to the less inhibited lower classes with which the middle and upper class whites compare themselves, the origin of the belief in excessive Negro sexuality becomes apparent.

Cultural differences may not be restricted to the emphasis on one or the other drive but may represent an entirely different outlook toward life. One prominent Chinese observer paraphrases the difference between East and West by explaining that "the occidental when meeting with a difficulty tries to remove it, making a change in the external environment, an external adjustment . . . the Chinese finds it easier to make an internal adjustment, to change his soul to an attitude of acceptance."²¹ This emphasis on action rather than acceptance and resignation—again strongest in America—is related to our preference for the extrovert. To be an introvert is almost considered to be a sign of maladjustment by the layman. Our preference for the extrovert determines the upbringing of our children, and perhaps our rejection of more introvert cultures.

When we say that the Japanese are inscrutable, cold, and inhuman, we admit our failure to understand their outlook toward life, as it determines their daily behavior as well as the actions of the nation as a whole. The daily decisions and actions of a Japanese are determined by his sense of indebtedness, whereas the Westerner gives only slight attention to his debt to the world and what it has given him in terms of care, education, or even the mere fact of having been born at all:

> Virtuous men do not say, as they do in America, that they owe nothing to any man. . . . Righteousness in Japan depends upon recognition of one's place in the great network of mutual indebtedness that embraces both one's forebears and one's contemporaries. . . . Until we understand it in Japan we shall not be able to plumb either the extreme sacrifice of self with which we became familiar during the war or the quick resentments which Japanese are capable of in situations where we think resentments are not called for.²²

The devotion of the son for his mother is considered as an obligation for all she has done for him, bringing him into the world, caring for him, educating him. While the expression of such relationship resembles filial love as practiced in our society, to the Japanese its primary meaning is the debt the child owes to her. In contrast we think of love as something freely given unfettered by obligation.²³ This attitude forms the basis of the famous oriental filial piety which gives the parents such unquestioning authority over their children and is related to the almost complete absence of juvenile delinquency in the unassimilated Japanese family in America.

The Japanese concept of the family is in many aspects the complete antithesis to the attitude found in many American families that the parents owe a debt to their children and should do everything for their children without expecting anything in return. In our child-oriented culture the parents are expected to sacrifice for the children because they brought them into the world. Their interests are considered secondary to that of their children.

In some respects the European attitude toward children takes an intermediate position. There is greater emphasis on obedience and parental authority. Children are often expected to help their parents and to make life easier for them.

In some respects these differences in attitudes are related to the greater emphasis on the rights of the individual as contrasted with the rights of the group. Democratic capitalistic society stresses the right of the individual to personal happiness through self-advancement,[24] by getting ahead of others through aggressive, individual competitiveness.[25]

The emphasis on individual happiness as a major goal in life is alien to the Japanese: "The idea that the pursuit of happiness is a serious goal of life is to them an amazing and immoral doctrine. Happiness is a relaxation in which one indulges when one can, but to dignify it as something by which the state and family should be judged is quite unthinkable." This does not mean that they condemn the seeking of pleasure as such. They only feel that it should not be made the main motive. "The fact that a man often suffers intensely in living up to his obligations . . . is no more than they expect. It makes life hard but they are prepared for that. They constantly give up pleasures which they consider in no way evil. That requires strength of will. But such strength is the most admired virtue in Japan."[26]

While the concept of the sinfulness of pleasures, so prominent in Western puritan societies, is absent, sacrifice is brought about by a sense of obligation. It is not considered the supreme goal of society to bring about the greatest happiness for the greatest number of people.

DIFFERENCES IN MOTIVATIONS AND VALUES

Man in our society is expected to be happy if he succeeds and gets ahead of others by amassing material wealth, the supreme goal. Western man does not engage in acquisitive behavior solely to sustain life. Even those who have more money than they can consume do not cease in their attempt to acquire even greater wealth. Acquisitiveness has become an end in itself rather than a means to an end. The amount of wealth determines a man's status.[27] It is important to have the more expensive car, the more conspicuous fur coat.

This does not mean that in our society money is the only value which counts. The time of the arrival of one's ancestors in the United States or in the community in which one lives, counts, as does education. But to some extent it is the possession of a college degree rather than the possession of culture, or real knowledge, which adds to one's status.[28] Teachers and professors—as non-productive elements in the population—enjoy less prestige in America than in Europe. This contrasts sharply with the high status of the learned man abroad which reaches its height in the orthodox Jewish community.[29] It is easy to imagine how such differences in emphasis may lead Europeans to accuse Americans of being shallow and materialistic. On the other hand the emphasis on abstract learning, impractical argumentation as practiced in extreme form by the Talmudic scholar appears alien to the practical American.

The emphasis on wealth, acquisition, and competition was absent in medieval Europe. In a feudal society, where the individual's status was determined by birth, and which was deeply religious, subordination, the performance of good works, piety, were the supreme values. Our stress on competition was so alien to the medieval spirit that the saints of the Middle Ages were constantly afraid of the sin of conceit, feared they were not properly humble. To feel that one was better than others would have been sacrilegious, whereas our modern competitive society rather cherishes such feelings. If we compare America with less competitive modern societies like England or even more semi-feudal societies like China before communism the effect of difference in cultural emphasis on personality becomes apparent. The author of a textbook in *Psychology of Personality* declares: "In America, it is normal to show a moderate amount of self-esteem by overvaluing oneself on rating scales and questionnaires. This apparently is not true of other cultures, e.g. the Chinese."[30] In practice this may cause the British or Chinese to feel that we are conceited, or Americans to believe that the members of these cultures are hypocrites.

If we should ask a member of our society why he works so hard to succeed he may answer us that he does so in order to get ahead in life, and, perhaps as an afterthought, that he wants to have the means toward a greater enjoyment of life. Yet there seems to be some evidence that in his haste to advance himself modern man has largely forgotten how to enjoy himself, does not know how to relax and enjoy the fruits of his labor. If we compare different societies with regard to their relative emphasis on work versus leisure we find that our society more than many others is work-oriented,[31] again in part perhaps due to our puritan heritage. Contrary to Latin countries like France, retirement in America is seen as a dreaded event which is postponed as long as possible, whereas in France country middle class men often look forward to the day when they can occupy themselves exclusively with their hobby or garden, the earlier in life the better. Whereas the American takes off as little time as possible for lunch, the Italian businessman under like climatic conditions will retire to a lengthy siesta. While such behavior may perhaps be attributed by the prejudiced person to the "innate laziness" of the Italians, again cultural differences in values and motivations are decisive.

EXTENT AND TYPES OF CRIME

The last part of our discussion centered primarily around the differences in personality between the natives of different countries and cultures. But the existing differences in personality between majority and minority Americans such as immigrants from different countries are the result not only of cultural differences but also differences in class position and cultural conflict related to the minority's attempt to assimilate. The combined effect of these factors can be demonstrated by a short analysis of differences in crime and insanity among different ethnic groups.

Contrary to frequent assertions that immigrants contribute unduly to crime in the United States—an argument advanced often by politicians interested in preventing further immigration—statistical evidence indicates that immigrants tend to have a decidedly lower crime rate than old Americans (third or more generation in this country).[32] The highest crime rate is found among second generation Americans,[33] and is caused by the clash between old world standards represented by the parents and the new standards to which these second generation Americans are exposed. By and large, the first generation immigrants tend to live in the closely knit, well-organized, immigrant communities of our large cities and have little social contact with other groups. Their children, however, go to American schools and are encouraged by them to seek the company of other children living outside the immigrant ghettos. Participating in the main stream of American culture and at the same time living in a home representing old world values, they bear the brunt of the conflict. We may think here of the Italian immigrant girl whose parents believe that she should not go to mixed parties, have unchaperoned dates, but whose schoolmates follow the American pattern of courtship. The ultimate outcome of the conflict between the desire to do what her playmates do, the fear of ridicule in school, and parental punishment at home may lead to revolt against the parents and perhaps even lead the child to the bars of our juvenile courts.[34]

Such conflict will be less marked where authoritarian control is still strong as in the more traditional Japanese or Jewish family. Apparent differences in delinquency may be caused by parental attitudes toward their children's transgressions. Catholic parents often appear to consider delinquent behavior as a sin for which atonement is needed, whereas the Jewish parent may consider the same behavior as a sign of maladjustment and may seek the help of a social worker or psychiatrist rather than to bring their child before the juvenile court.

But more important here than the relative incidence of crime in different ethnic groups is the difference in type of crime. Irish immigrants to the United States have been shown to have a much higher homicide rate than native-born Americans but commit no rape and engage less often in gambling. As a result of assimilation, however, the second generation Irish already show a marked decrease in their homicide rate and a corresponding increase in rape and gambling. The absence of rape cases among first generation Irish immigrants reflects probably differences in attitude toward women, as compared for example, with the Italians, another Catholic group.[35]

This appears the more likely because the same cultural pressures are reflected in the types of mental disease found among our foreign born. Alcoholic psychosis is found far more frequently among the Irish, who at the same time have an exceptionally low rate of paresis which appears related to sexual promiscuity. These results can be interpreted only in considering the general culture pattern of each group with regard to its emphasis on specific values and motives. In comparing our two predominantly Catholic groups, we find the Irish indulging in alcohol but more inhibited in the sexual sphere, whereas the Italians are freer, less inhibited in their relation to women, and hence perhaps less given to excessive drinking. The higher rate of admissions of foreign-born whites as compared to native-born Americans probably reflects the lower economic status of the foreign born as well as the cultural conflict and difficulties of adjustment to a new country.

Table 6.   Mental Diseases of Native- and Foreign-born Whites
in New York State

Country of birth:	Total	Dementia praecox	Manic depressive	Alcoholic psychosis	General paresis
All white	97.4	25.7	13.3	6.5	9.3
Ireland	161.3	33.0	22.0	30.5	6.8
England	101.1	25.8	13.9	4.8	9.3
Scandinavia	110.4	33.8	17.0	7.9	13.2
Germany	104.0	35.7	17.5	3.8	12.3
Italy	101.7	30.4	15.4	4.3	12.2

Adapted from: *Average Annual Standardized Rate of First Admissions to all Hospitals for Mental Disease in New York State, 1929-1931*. Condensed and rearranged by author, from B. Malzberg, in Klineberg, O. *Characteristics of the American Negro.* Harper & Brothers, New York, 1944, pp. 382-387.

Just as we can not hold any one ethnic group responsible for adding more than their share to crime and insanity, it will be impossible, recent Russian attempts notwithstanding, to attribute all major contributions to humanity to a distinct racial or ethnic group. Within the orbit of Western civilization the center of the most highly developed civilizations shifted from Egypt and the Near East to Crete, Greece, and finally Rome. In the Middle Ages the centers of civilization were found first in Ireland, and somewhat later around the river Rhine. In more modern times arts and science blossomed successively in Italy, the Netherlands, England, then France and Germany. Throughout history new ethnic groups became the carriers of great civilizations. It is meaningless, hence, to claim that any particular ethnic group or nationality is superior to any other group. To prove or disprove the claim of any specific group we only need to choose another century for our discussion.

Many books have been written to show how all the ethnic groups which together constitute the American population have contributed to American culture. Yet the very difference in culture and personality of the various parts of the American population may well contribute to prejudice when the conditions for its development are present.

SELECTED READINGS

1. Davis, A., and Dollard, J., *Children of Bondage*. American Council of Education, Washington, D. C., 1940 (semi-popular; case histories of Southern Negroes).
2. Zborowksy, M., and Herzog, B., *Life Is with People*. International University Press, New York, 1952, chaps. 2 and 5 (semipopular; a description of Eastern Jewish Culture).
3. Benedict, R., *The Chrysanthemum and the Sword*. Houghton Mifflin, Boston, Mass., 1946 (semipopular; a description of the Japanese culture).
4. Brown, F. J., and Roucek, J. B., *One America: The History, Contributions, and Present Problems of Our Racial and National Minorities* (revised edition). Prentice Hall, New York, 1945.
5. Singer, H. H., "The Influence of Sudden Oppression on a Racial Minority." *J. of Social Psychology*, 10:127-145, 1939.
6. Davis, A. "The Motivation of the Underprivileged Worker" in *Industry and Society*, ed. Whyte, W. F. McGraw-Hill, New York, 1946, chap. V.

REFERENCES

1. Efron, D., *Gesture and Environment*. Columbia University Press, New York, 1941.
2. Klineberg, O., *Race Differences*. Harper & Brothers, New York, 1935, p. 286.
3. Krech, D., and Crutchfield, R. S., *Theory and Problems of Social Psychology*. McGraw-Hill, New York, 1948, p. 321.

84 *The Social Psychology of Prejudice*

4. Benedict, R., *Patterns of Culture*. Pelican Books, New York, 1946. p. 72.
5. Orchardson, I. Q., "Some Traits of the Kipsigis in Relation to Their Contacts with Europeans." *Africa*, 4:466-474, 1931.
6. Boas, F., *The Mind of Primitive Man*. Macmillan, New York, 1911, p. 151.
7. Lawson, E. H., "Arthur Brown Applies for a Job." *Journal of Social Issues*, 1:11-14, 1945.
8. Singer, G. H., "The Influence of Sudden Oppression on a Racial Minority." *Journal of Social Psychology*, 10:142, 1939.
9. Hartshorne, H. L., and May, M. A., *Studies in Deceit*. Macmillan, New York, 1928.
10. Murdock, K. A., "A Study of Differences Found between Races in Intellect and Morality." *School and Society*, 22:628-632; 659-664, 1925.
11. Sward, K., and Friedman, M. B., "Patterns of Jewish Temperament." *Journal of Applied Psychology*, 19:70-84, 1938.
12. Sperling, A., "A Comparison of the Human Behavior Inventory with Two Other Personality Inventories." *Educational Psychology Measurement*, 2:291-297, 1942.
13. Sims, V. M., and Patrick J. R., "Personality Differences between Negro and White College Students, North and South." *Journal of Abnormal and Social Psychology*, 29:181-201, 1934.
14. Hunter, M., "Responses of Comparable White and Negro Adults to the Rorschach Test." *Journal of Psychology*, 3:173-182, 1937.
15. Davis, A., "The Motivation of the Underprivileged Worker," in *Industry and Society*, ed. Whyte, W. F. McGraw-Hill, New York, 1946, pp. 86 and 89.
16. Gray, S., "The Wishes of Negro Children." *Journal of Genetic Psychology*, 64:225-237, 1944.
17. Young, P. C., "Intelligence and Suggestibility in Negroes and Whites." *Journal of Comparative Psychology*, 9:339-359, 1929.
18. Linton, R., "The Personality of Peoples." *Scientific American*, 181:11-15, 1949.
19. Kinsey, A. C., Pomeroy, W. B., and Martin, C. E. *Sexual Behavior in the Human Male*. Saunders, Philadelphia, Pa., 1948.
20. Davis, A., and Dollard, J., *Children of Bondage*. American Council of Education, Washington, D. C., 1940.
21. Klineberg, *op. cit.*, p. 116.
22. Benedict, R., *The Chrysanthemum and the Sword*. Houghton Mifflin, Boston, Mass., 1946, pp. 98 ff.
23. *Ibid*, p. 101.
24. Weber, M., *The Protestant Ethic and the Spirit of Capitalism*. Allen and Unwin, London, 1930.
25. Lynd, R., *Knowledge, For What*. Princeton University Press, Princeton, N. Y., 1939, chap. III.
26. Benedict, R., *The Chrysanthemum and the Sword, op. cit.*, p. 192.

27. Veblen, T., *The Theory of the Leisure Class*. Macmillan, New York, 1899.
28. Lazarsfeld, P., "The Information Please Program," in *Radio and the Printed Page*. Duell, Sloan and Pearce, New York, 1940.
29. Zborowsky, M., and Herzog, E., *Life Is with People*. International University Press, New York, 1952, chaps. 2 and 3.
30. Stagner, R., Psychology of Personality (ed. 2). McGraw-Hill, New York, 1948, p. 174.
31. Lynd, *op. cit.*, chap. 3.
32. Klineberg, *op. cit.*, pp. 230 ff.
33. Sellin, J. T., *Culture Conflict and Crime*. Social Science Research Council, New York, 1938.
34. Levy, J., "Conflict of Cultures and Children's Maladjustment." *Mental Hygiene*, 17:41-50, 1933.
35. Sutherland, E. H., *Principles of Criminology*. Lippincott, Chicago, Illinois, 1939.

B.   THE PROCESS OF INTERACTION

In contrast to the prejudiced layman, social scientists do not seek the causes of prejudice and discrimination in the physical and psychological make-up of its victims. They tend to interest themselves in the factors which determine the interaction between hostile groups. They are concerned with the economic and social structure of societies in which prejudice is rampant, as well as with the kind of personalities whose needs predispose them to become prejudiced.

For a long time there had been the search for the *one* cause of prejudice, as there has been the quest for *the* cause of depressions or *the* cause of wars. At present we tend to realize more and more that these major evils of society have many and mutually interrelated causes. Insufficient consumer buying power, overproduction, foreign competition, may all contribute to a depression.

The boy who was overprotected at home and prevented from making his own decisions may have gotten along fairly well in the protection of the home atmosphere. Being drafted and forced to rely upon himself he may break down. Here we call his weak character structure the predisposing factor; adverse circumstances followed by a nervous breakdown the precipitating factor. Similarly in the field of race relations, a person may look with suspicion at the new neighbor who looks and behaves differently, but there may be no outbreak of open hostility until our friend suffers reverses in his business, becomes irritated and upset. Smoldering prejudice may come into the open in the heat of a political campaign.

We often find a cumulative effect of different factors operating at the same time. Husband and wife may quarrel because the weather is humid, the boss refused him a raise, and the maid spoiled the dinner. Perhaps none of these factors by itself would have precipitated a fight but taken together they are too strong to tolerate. A race riot may break out, as in one instance, if there is some initial prejudice, competition for poor housing, a rapid turnover of the population, prejudicial propaganda, a high degree of juvenile delinquency, lack of recreational facilities, and, finally, a heat wave. None of these factors alone would have caused the riot but taken together they caused an explosion.

The different factors contributing to an outbreak of hostility are often interdependent. A high degree of population turnover and the lack of recreational facilities may contribute to juvenile delinquency. Juvenile delinquency practiced by one segment of the population will influence the level of prejudice. The heat wave makes the crowded tenements more unbearable.

We may dislike our neighbors on the right and on the left for different reasons. One of them may irritate us by running his radio too loud; the other by parking his car before our driveway. We may hate our brother for different reasons at different times. At the age of three we resent the fact that he can stay up longer, at six because he has a bike while we are not permitted to own one, at twelve because we have to wear his discarded clothes.

Although this may be a truism, the significance of these general principles in the field of ethnic relations is often overlooked. Different groups may be disliked for entirely different reasons. White Protestant residents of California may dislike the Japanese because they feel that they are working for less, the Jews because they make too much money, and the Catholics for religious reasons.

The same group can be chosen as a target of attack for different reasons during different times. In the Middle Ages the Jews were attacked as infidels, during the nineteenth century as advocates of modern mercantilism, the philosophy of laissez faire.

Finally, the same group in a given community may be disliked by different groups for different reasons. New York Negroes may object to the recent influx of Puerto Ricans because they compete for jobs and feel superior to them. The whites may feel antagonistic because they believe them to be dirty and uneducated, contributing to crime and delinquency.

It appears, therefore, that we do not only have to detect the different causes of prejudices and discrimination, but to list *all* the causes and to analyze their relative importance in different situations. For purposes of orientation the determinants of prejudice may be divided into three major groups: (1) *Economic, social, and political interests,* particularly where different groups conflict with each other; (2) *Personality structure and adjustment,* ways of gratifying needs and desires emerging from the interplay of the individual and his society; and (3) *Education and propaganda,* the intentional or unintentional indoctrination towards prejudice in home and community.

CHAPTER 7

ECONOMIC AND SOCIAL DETERMINANTS

OF PREJUDICE

"When the Spanish writers justified the exploitation of the American Indians on the grounds that they were racially distinct from and inferior to the Whites, they set a fashion which was widely followed."[1]

The origin of the racial myth can be traced historically to the necessity to justify the institution of slavery, as well as the exploitation of native populations by the emerging colonial powers in the age of the great discoveries.

Slavery is a very old institution, practiced by the Greeks and Romans. These ancient peoples, however, did not consider their slaves as inferior. Elaborate beliefs in the inferiority of non-white people were not originated before the exploitation of native populations was attacked on moral and religious grounds and held to be incompatible with Christian and democratic ideals.[2] Democratic societies, which believe in basic human rights and equality of opportunity, need rationalizations to permit them to discriminate against racial and ethnic minorities without feeling guilty. They need to believe that they deny jobs to members of other groups not because they desire them for themselves, but because the others are incapable of performing them.

PREJUDICE SERVES ECONOMIC NEEDS

The propagation of the theory of racial inferiority not only serves to soothe the conscience of the exploiting majority group but is often specifically adapted to the changing economic needs of the dominant group. It not only states that the suppressed minorities are "happy" in their situation, but explains most specifically that the inferior group cannot do the work from which they have been excluded for the benefit of the latter group. Many citizens of the Union of South Africa are convinced that their natives are constitutionally unable to perform any skilled or administrative work and will work only under the close supervision of a white overseer. In neighboring Congo where there is not a sufficient number of whites to do all the work, Negroes are believed to be able to—and actually do—perform skilled jobs and administrative duties.* This difference in outlook is vividly recorded in the impressions of a recent traveller crossing the frontier between these two countries:

> When at last we pulled out of the station the train had completely changed its character . . . the surprising feature was the fact that the engineer and firemen were Natives; a thing I had not seen before in Africa. Nor could I observe that the train itself behaved itself in different fashion to the ones I had been riding on for weeks; it did not run off the track or indulge in any quirks of an unusual nature, but rocked along in the customary speed of African express trains. . . . When it stopped and started I could detect no difference in the jolts and jerks, and the whistle sounded just the same as when a European pulled the cord. If I had not seen the engineer and fireman I would have had no reason to suspect their skins were black. An hour later we were at the frontier station at Sakania. . . . and here at Sakania was another revelation; for, excepting two or three quasi military Belgian officials, the Customs and Immigration Staff was composed of native clerks and typists—a dispensation nonexistent in South Africa. So far as I could see they appeared to be carrying on their duties like such minor functionaries everywhere.[3]

When the economic pattern of a society changes, discrimination as well as supporting prejudices will change with it. During slavery a large part of the skilled mechanical work in the South was done by Negro slaves. With Emancipation skilled jobs became highly desirable and were fairly well paid. As a result these jobs were now coveted by white artisans and it did not take long until the theory was advanced that Negroes were constitutionally unable to do the very work they had done before the Civil War.[4] On the other hand, when the scarcity of labor during World War II forced the employment of women as welders and solderers prejudices against the employment of women in heavy industry soon lessened.

During the early period of the colonization of California, Japanese farmers as well as Chinese were welcomed in large numbers because of the need for agricultural products at a time when many white men preferred searching for gold to working on the land.

* There are 2,300,000 whites and 7,700,000 Negroes in South Africa, whereas the Congo has 40,000 whites living in a country with 13,000,000 natives.

The serious overpopulation of Japan restricted the size of farms to something like three acres for the average family. As a result, the Japanese farmer developed a remarkable knowledge of soil, fertilizers, methods of land reclamation, and modes of intensive cultivation quite in contrast with the lavish expansionism of the American pioneer. By a combination of highly disciplined labor and a knowledge of intensive cultivation, the Japanese were able to enter areas of California regarded by the white man as uncultivable—sections like the Imperial Valley and the Delta country or the waste timber lands of the Northwest—and from the inhospitable soil they wrested new green fields and orchards and vineyards. A good deal of California's remarkable fertility is due to these methods of cultivation, which in some cases increased fruit and vegetable yields three and four fold.[5]

When a few decades later the whites desired to live on the land, the very success of the Japanese became the chief reason for the development of prejudice. They were no longer seen as welcome suppliers of farm products but undesirable competitors. Their frugality, ability to work hard, ambition, once considered important assets, were now advanced as the very reason for demanding their exclusion. Frugality became interpreted as a tendency to work for less and be satisfied with a lower standard of living than white Americans. We hear that members of the Oriental race can live on less than members of the white race. Ambitiousness, the desire to get ahead, is now called avarice and overambitiousness. ". . . if they asked less than the going wage, they were threatening the American standard of living," writes a California observer; "if they were successful in farming and saved enough to buy their own ranch, they were driving the whites out; if they were unsuccessful they were 'wearing out the land.' "[6]

The more direct the competition between majority and minority, and the more successful the vulnerable minority group, the greater is the amount of hostility directed toward the latter group.[7]

INDEPENDENCE OF PREJUDICE FROM CHARACTER OF MINORITY

The emergence of prejudice and discrimination under such circumstances may even be relatively independent of the characteristics of the target group, as shown by the history of immigration to the United States. Prejudice against immigrants can be found even in the colonial days. In the eighteenth century as well as today "native-born" Americans complained about "recent" immigrants.

During times of prosperity and rapid geographic expansion, efforts were made to lure immigrants into the country in order to provide cheap labor. Attacks against immigrants declined, and the newcomers were considered as valuable contributors to American life. Prejudice and discrimination rose whenever depressions hit the country.

While the economic situation of the country determined the fluctuations in prejudice and discrimination, some prejudice was always present. Socially the "alien" character of each new wave of immigrants created antagonism. Economically they formed a threat to the earlier arrivals.

Yet throughout the history of mass immigration one type of immigrants after the other arrived, became assimilated and climbed the ladder to social and economic success. After a generation or two the children and grandchildren of each immigrant group, whose own parents and grandparents had once been the targets of prejudice and exploitation, became the defenders of the American standard of living and were among those most violently opposed to the next group coming to these shores, regardless of the latter's ethnic and religious origin.

The new immigrants, unfamiliar with the ways of their new country, often unable to speak its language, were ruthlessly exploited, given the most undesirable work and paid the lowest wages. Ignorance alone cannot be blamed for this state of affairs. When the newcomers complained about their lower wages, the employers tended to accuse them of being ungrateful and threatened to use American-born workers.[8] These practices tended to arouse the wrath of native labor, who complained of unfair competition and accused the newcomer of depressing the American standard of living.

A typical example of the conflict between new and old immigration is furnished by the history of the city of Lowell, Massachusetts, which was originally inhabited by persons of old Yankee origin, until the conversion to textile industry during the middle of the last century brought in Irish and French-Canadian immigrants. During the period of the "Know Nothing" movement, these groups formed the main targets of prejudice and discrimination. But toward the end of the century a wave of new immigrants from Greece arrived which soon got into conflict with the older workers:

> Back in these early nineties the sons of Hellas began the third important migration. Their coming made the Irish and French, who had held down the mill jobs before, mad. From time immemorial Monday and often Tuesday had been held sacred as the drunk days, when an habitual Hibernian or French "hangover" retarded the mill machinery. The Greeks were free from drink and were good for work all the week, and the overseers naturally favored them because of that. This made the French and the Irish madder. From the very beginning these two dominant races attacked and ill-used the new Greek laborers and hounded them from good lodgings.[9]

The constant succession of different ethnic groups as targets of prejudice and discrimination ends with the cessation of large-scale immigration to the United States caused by the passage of restrictive legislation after World War I. Jews from Eastern Europe and Catholics from there as well as Southern Europe constituted the last large migration wave. With the exception of the perennial target, the Negro, there is no new ethnic group to take their place on the bottom of the social ladder. Coupled with the greater cultural difference of the new immigration from earlier assimilated groups, this appears to have led to a partial freezing of social cleavages, and impeded the assimilation and absorption of the last group of immigrants. To the extent that economic, social, and psychological conditions favor the maintenance of prejudice and discrimination, to that extent can prejudice against these groups be expected to continue.

It may be argued that progress in their assimilation would cause prejudice toward these groups to decline. We have seen, however, that successful assimilation of any one group depends on the extent of discrimination to which they are exposed, the extent to which society permits previous ethnic groups to become assimilated. In the absence of new target groups, it appears that many old Americans may not be willing to admit the latest arrivals to the extent to which they admitted earlier immigrant groups.[10]

IMMIGRATION AND CLASS STRUCTURE

Discrimination against new immigrants is not restricted to the United States. Wherever a new religious or ethnic group migrated into an already settled country, it found it difficult to establish itself socially and economically. When in the seventeenth century the Huguenots, as a result of religious persecution, left France to settle in Germany, they engaged in weaving and soap and glass making, occupations heretofore not found on German soil. But trouble ensued when some years later they entered into occupations which brought them into direct competition with the Germans. They, as well as the Dutch who settled during the same period in the city of Frankfurt, were forced to leave and to settle elsewhere.[11]

The history of European Jews resembles in its essential elements that of other foreign groups. From the fall of the Roman Empire until the thirteenth century, while the whole of Europe lived on agriculture, they engaged in itinerant trade and to some extent in lending money to the lords of the manor. As they did not compete with the rest of the population they lived in peace and enjoyed a high status. With the development of trade and commerce in the era of the crusades, however, they got into competition with the new middle-class and the gentry and were finally excluded from trade and restricted to usury and marginal occupations as pawnbroking or dealing in second-hand goods. In some areas of Germany the ensuing hostility led to their total exclusion, in others to severe economic restrictions and imprisonment in the ghetto. This situation lasted until the eighteenth century, when the philosophy of enlightenment, the spiritual precursor of the American revolution, led in Europe to the emancipation of the Jews and permitted them to enter into a greater and greater number of occupations, a process not completed until the end of the nineteenth century.

The Jews enjoyed a relatively better fate in Poland and other parts of Eastern Europe. Ironically enough, however, this superior position brought them into conflict with the newly rising middle class at the same time when the emancipation improved the Jewish position elsewhere, leading to their emigration in large numbers to England, France, and Germany as well as to America. Hence, when after World War I worsening economic conditions contributed to demands for the exclusion of Jews from trade and the professions, the increase in the Jewish population of the western countries caused by the influx of Eastern Jews further worsened their position.[12]

Jews had been limited to urban centers, and, as a result of occupational restrictions had developed considerable skill in trade. When during the nineteenth century the trend from the country to the cities gained momentum, the migrating rural population found in their new urban homes the well-entrenched and established Jewish traders, a situation which further reinforced anti-Semitism.

Concentrations of ethnic groups in specific occupations, in specific areas of our economic structure hence are the result of a tendency to restrict outsiders to the least desirable occupations. Even in America with its succession of ever new immigrant groups and its philosophy of assimilation and equal opportunity, we find the earliest settlers on top of the economic and social pyramid and the latest arrivals at its bottom. The excessive concentration of the "earliest" settlers in the upper strata of society, far out of proportion to their numerical representation in the population, has frequently been shown. In Connecticut people of British-American (Old Yankee) descent represent but 14 per cent of the population, but out of a list of 110 of the most prominent industrialists in the period 1900–1930, 92 were of "British-American" origin. In general, "British-Americans" tend to be found in a "position of leadership in the most consequential fields of the state's economic life. Their most serious rivals are the 'old' immigrant groups, particularly the Irish."[13] To a certain extent this abnormal distribution represents the fact that the older families, as a result of their earlier arrival, had a longer time to climb to a position of prominence. Partially, however, it also represents the result of discriminatory practices toward new arrivals.

The above findings are in direct contradiction to the widespread belief that some minority groups, particularly the Jews, exert a dominating influence in the American economy. According to the 1936 *Fortune* magazine survey, Jews do not exercise an excessive influence in American business. Of the 80,000 names in Poor's *Register of Directors* only 4.7 per cent appear to be Jewish, corresponding almost exactly to their proportion in the total population (estimated to be about 5 per cent). What is important, however, is that they do not occupy a controlling position. In the central positions of investment banking, commercial banking, and insurance, according to the same sources, their influence is negligible or nonexistent. While there is a heavy concentration of Jews in law, the most important office law business in America is "in the hands of non-Jewish firms, many of which, even though they have numerous Jewish clients, have no Jewish partners."[14] Contrary to common beliefs, they do not have a considerable influence in opinion making, newspapers, magazines, and book publishing, with the possible exception of the movies.

Industries dominated by Jews are largely marginal businesses, dealing with distribution rather than production, for example dressmaking, the scrap iron industry, retail stores, the amusement and liquor industry. The types of industries and businesses in which Jews are concentrated traditionally carried a certain element of social stigma, as well as a high risk.[15]

Most ethnic groups show similar abnormal distributions. We recall the earlier concentration of the Irish in railroading, and their present concentration in civil service, police, and fire departments. Italians are overrepresented in the building and construction industry, the Chinese in the laundry business. In most cases the occupational concentrations of immigrant groups are determined by the economic situation at the time of their arrival, the group's ethnic tradition and past history, and the operation of discriminatory practices.

But the extraordinary occupational distribution of Jews and other minority groups, which is a consequence of discrimination, itself tends to contribute to and reinforce earlier prejudices. Jews do not enter into marginal businesses in which "sharp" practices are not infrequently found because their personality is suited to these occupations. Rather, being forced into these types of businesses, the requirements of the business determine their behavior.

We have seen that it is not so much the nature of the foreign group, the ethnic minority, which determines the rise of discrimination and prejudice, but the economic situation of the country in which they reside. Economic crises, competition for scarce jobs, occur in relatively heterogeneous countries with large ethnic minorities as well as in countries having relatively homogeneous populations. In both cases we find the desire to limit the number of competitors. Social scientists, therefore, claimed that "race prejudice is replaced by class prejudice" in countries like England, France, and Spain, which have no significantly large ethnic groups.

When in modern America class barriers are less rigid than in modern Europe, we owe this perhaps not only to our philosophy of basic equality and the belief of equal opportunity for everyone, but to the existence of racial and ethnic barriers which can take the place of class barriers, i.e., the partial substitution of race prejudice for class prejudice.

Ethnic conflicts may be deliberately used to prevent a focusing of class conflicts by diverting potential hostility on the part of labor from employers toward ethnic targets. Time and again Negroes have been used as strike-breakers in industries ordinarily employing only white workers. When Negroes are in need of work and at the same time excluded from labor unions, they do not tend to feel solidarity with the white worker, and may accept these jobs only too gladly. Their use as strike-breakers may not only lead to a defeat of the strikers but also to increased bitterness of the white workers toward the colored "scabs."[16]

Similarly, where differential wages are paid to majority and minority members, usually as a result of previously existing prejudices, the very existence of such differences tends to distract from attention to class conflicts. Majority workers become preoccupied with keeping the member of the minority in his place, and tend to disregard the existing conflict between labor and management—to be content with lower wages. In the same situation the workers in a country with a homogeneous ethnic and racial make-up are more likely to become occupied with the fight for higher wages.

Individual security and prestige may rest on economic as well as social rewards. The white collar worker in American industry accepts lower wages and refuses to join unions to fight for increased economic rewards often because he is given to understand that he is in a privileged position, superior to the manual worker. His superiority is emphasized in a way designed to express his higher status by awarding him different methods of payment, different recreational and eating facilities within a plant, different ways of address. To the extent that status symbols are substituted for economic rewards, to that extent will there be a lessening of demands for the latter, a decrease of tension between the white collar worker and management, and a corresponding increase of prejudice and tension toward the manual worker.

VESTED INTERESTS IN PREJUDICE

The above discussion has led us to recognize that different groups of the population have different reasons for prejudice and discrimination; may in fact benefit by a persistence of ethnic cleavages. Discriminatory practices appear to be of definite advantage for the representatives of management in a competitive economic system.

Similarly, discrimination operates to the advantage of the property owner in slum areas. He can command higher rents from the Negroes than from the whites, because the Negro has no choice in choosing his place or residence, is forced to live in the Negro quarters. Being forced to stay within a segregated area, he is also less able to demand adequate repairs than is the white tenant, who can threaten to leave. Negroes will find it almost impossible to get better accommodations elsewhere.* To apologize for their refusal to make adequate repairs, the theory is advanced that Negroes do not know how to take care of the property. Few people realize that it is the bad state of repair and overcrowding which leads to negligent tenants.

Real estate speculators often profit from the existing prejudice by taking both whites and Negroes for a ride. The intention of Negroes to move into a hitherto white area is considered a threat by the white home owners, induces him to leave the neighborhood. Where some inroads have been made, real estate values are bound to fall. The broker then encourages the white home owners to sell even at a loss. The ensuing panic often causes a temporary drop in real estate values used by speculators to buy at this point, and later to sell to Negroes at 30 to 100 per cent above normal value.[17]

Similarly, in neighborhoods where prejudices against Jews and other minorities are rampant, gentile home owners will pay more for the privilege of living in a restricted, "high class," neighborhood. Finally, the refusal of many Gentile resort hotels to take Jews makes it possible for the owner of a Jewish resort, enjoying a monopoly on Jewish trade, to charge higher prices.

In the lower strata of society widespread discriminatory tendencies against Negroes are practiced by many unions. Differences in union policies partly reflect the prevailing ideology of the union, partly the economic situation found in a given labor market.

---

* During times of a general housing shortage white tenants are in a condition resembling that of Negroes during normal times. They are less able to enforce demands for adequate repairs and maintenance.

The racial policies of American trade unions vary from outright exclusion of Negroes by some organizations to the full acceptance of them with all privileges of membership by others. Moreover, union policies toward Negroes are somewhat fluid and subject to change if the circumstances so warrant. For example, the appearance of a rival union with a liberal racial policy may result in a reversal of the policies of its competitor which had up to that time discriminated against colored workers. On the other hand, the presence of an exclusionist union in the same jurisdiction with one which usually tolerates no discrimination may cause the latter to relax its principles for fear that it will alienate its predominantly white membership.[18]

Discrimination is found most frequently among members of the A. F. of L. and independent unions. It is particularly strong among the railroad unions, but relatively absent among member unions of the C. I. O. The reason for this difference is that the bargaining strength of industrial unions depends on their ability to enroll all workers employed in an industry. Among the craft unions, however, success depends upon the extent to which they can monopolize a certain skill.[19] When the railroad unions had to face the problem of competition by Negro workers who were paid lower wages, they had the alternatives of admitting them to their unions and demanding equal wages or of excluding them from the field. They chose the latter alternative, a method more frequently chosen in declining than in expanding industries.

Before the Civil War economic advantages favored the continuation of slavery in the South. In the Northern states the farm type of agriculture made it disadvantageous to continue the exploitation of the Negro, a factor influential in the concentration of the anti-slave movement in that section of the country. "Although slavery was legally sanctioned and tried out in all the colonies," writes Davie, "it soon became a question of latitude: it was profitable only in the South, where the plantation system, based on the production of the great staples of tobacco, cotton, sugar, and rice, could be developed. In the North, which was adapted to the farm type of agriculture, the slaves were few in number."[20]

POPULATION DISTRIBUTION

In addition to economic factors the density of minority populations also appears to be related to the intensity of prejudice. Anti-Semitism in the United States is strongest in the North East and Middle West, weakest in the South and Far West. It is greatest in the large metropolitan centers where the majority of Jews reside and competition between Jews and non-Jews reaches a maximum. Prejudice against

Negroes, on the other hand, appears most widespread in the South, where the largest numbers of Negroes reside.[21]

Prejudice against Jews is more frequent in the upper classes, prejudice against Negroes is more widespread on the lower socio-economic levels, because the former group finds itself more in competition with the Jew, the latter more in competition with the Negro.[22]

EDUCATION AND PREJUDICE

Education, as well as religion and age, were also found to be related to the relative frequency of prejudice. Within each income group, the more educated appear to be less prejudiced against members of minority groups. This may perhaps be explained as the result of their greater exposure to intergroup education, or by their greater familiarity with the American creed which inhibits the expression of prejudice. To the extent that ignorance creates fear of the unknown, to that extent may education counteract prejudicial tendencies. On the other hand it is possible that those more familiar with the American creed are more capable of giving the correct "unprejudicial" answers in response to questionnaires.[23, 24]

An attempt to correlate religion with prejudice yields, at first glance, conflicting results. A study of anti-Semitism in Denver shows Protestants to be more anti-Semitic than Catholics.[25] A study of anti-Negro attitudes in the South shows Catholics to be more prejudiced.[26]

SITUATIONAL DETERMINANTS OF PREJUDICE

The explanation for this apparent contradiction appears after a detailed analysis of the position of Catholics and Protestants on different income levels in different areas of the country. A public opinion survey conducted in New York City indicates that the lower income Protestants and the middle income Catholics tended to be more prejudiced than the upper income Protestants and the low income Catholics.[27]

The results suggest that it is necessary to consider the situation of a specific group in its environment. White Protestants in New York constitute the dominant group from both an economic and social point of view. They were the first ones to settle in the city and hence occupy positions of social and economic leadership. A poor Protestant has failed to participate in the rise of his group. The majority of Catholics, on the other hand, arrived relatively recently mainly during the last seventy years. Most of them have not been able to advance themselves socially and economically. There is nothing unusual in being a low income Catholic. Low income Catholics do not need to feel that they have been failures. They have not fallen behind the majority of the members of their religious group of Irish, Italians, or

Polish descent. The Catholic minority, which succeeded in improving its economic position, on the other hand, is engaged in a struggle for social recognition by the older Protestant groups. To achieve such recognition it would not be surprising if they tended to become more snobbish, to imitate and exaggerate the prejudices of the high status group, and look down on other minorities in order to emphasize their superiority.*

If we find that young adults between twenty-one and thirty-four years of age in this country show less prejudice than other age groups, we can understand this phenomenon partially in terms of the greater and more immediate impact of education on this group, partially in terms of their aspirations and expectations. The young adult, just starting on his career, has high hopes. He expects to succeed in living up to the American dream, to get ahead. Not everyone, however, can succeed in a competitive society. Only a limited number of people reach a higher social level. By the time our young adult passes his early thirties, he begins to realize that he may not be able to fulfill his former youthful ambitions, may never become rich and successful. The inevitable frustration resulting from the shattering of his youthful dreams may lead to bitterness and resentfulness and furnish the basis of an antagonism toward other groups. When the man past fifty has been found to be less prejudiced than the middle-aged person, we may presume that he has become resigned to his fate and seeks to enjoy what he has rather than forever trying to advance himself.

In addition to scrutinizing the situation of different majority and minority groups we need, finally, to analyze the process of interaction on the community level in greater detail. Here the size of the interacting ethnic groups becomes important. For example, an increase in the size of a minority group toward which a minimum of prejudice exists may often lead to a chain reaction. If there are only a few minority members in a community they tend to associate with the majority, partly because they do not form a competitive threat and hence create little prejudice, and partly because there are not enough members of their own group. With increasing numbers they tend to be seen more as a group, which, competing with the majority, calls forth more and more "defensive" discriminatory actions.

Moreover, there are now sufficient families belonging to their own group, for instance, Jewish refugees, or Irish Catholics. The preference of strangers to associate with members of their own group, for

---

* This relationship furnishes a perfect example of the applicability of *Gestalt* theoretical thinking to intergroup relations. It is the relationship of the group or individual to its environment, the way a specific situation is perceived, rather than the objective characteristics of the isolated unit, which determines its thinking and behavior.

reasons of security, is furthered by growing exclusionary tendencies among the natives. Increased discrimination and in consequence further segregatory tendencies are bound to follow in a vicious circle.

Much depends here not only on the growing size of the minority group (as well as on the original prejudice level and competitive factors), but also on the speed with which the population changes its composition. A slow, imperceptible change over years or decades is less likely to create a negative reaction than a sudden increase in minority population over a short period of time. Sudden change is not only more noticeable, but also leads to greater difficulties of integrating the newcomers into the community. It is obviously easier to accommodate a group of half a million immigrants distributed over a period of ten years than to accommodate the same number in a single year.

The contribution of different factors to intergroup hostility can be demonstrated best in the study of ethnic relations in a changing community. In the previously mentioned study of upper Manhattan more than 300,000 persons of different race and religion were found crowded together in a space of two square miles.[28] Overcrowding alone may perhaps have sufficed to create unrest and hostility. But unequal living conditions contributed further to envy and resentment. The Protestants and Jews living in the area generally enjoy the highest standard of living, followed by the Catholics, and finally by the Negroes. The first two groups live in fairly decent houses near the park; Catholics and Negroes dwell in the tenements away from the river. The Jews and Protestants did not earn necessarily much more money than the Catholics. But where the average white Jewish or Protestant family supported two children, the average white Catholic family had four. While the first two groups could spend considerable parts of their budget on rent, the Catholic family not only had to feed more mouths, but spend a relatively larger part of the husband's income on alcoholic beverages, leaving even less money for rent and clothing.

The Catholic families were unaware of the real causes for these visible differences in living standards. They only observed that Protestants and Jews were better housed and clothed, which they attributed to the higher earnings of the other two white religious groups, not to their smaller family size and different distribution of their budget.

PRINCIPLE OF DIFFERENTIAL CONTACT

The occupational distribution of Protestants and Jews in Washington Heights made things even worse. The Protestants work downtown where nobody sees them, their working life is unknown to their neighbors. Many Jews, however, own the small retail stores in the neighborhood, and live, so to speak, on their neighbors. While the large chain stores in the vicinity are owned by firms controlled by Protestants, this fact was not generally known. The contacts between Jewish and Catholic adults were thus contacts between businessmen and customers, rather than mere social contacts between neighbors.

Our attitudes are influenced not by the objective world in which we live, but by our perceptions of our environment. As long as the Catholics believe that the Jews are much better off because they earn more, this belief governs their attitudes and will cause envy and resentment. Similarly, when the Negroes have to pay higher rents and live in the least desirable parts of the area, their hatred tends to be directed against the neighboring whites, not the distant and usually unknown landlord, often one of the large downtown banks.

The neighborhood had not always had its present character. It was once a well-to-do Protestant and Jewish area with ample space, private homes, and spacious apartments. The Catholics moved in later and the Negroes came last. Private homes changed into apartments, and large flats were split into smaller units to make more money and to accommodate the growing population.

As usual the old settler blamed the new arrivals for the deterioration of the neighborhood. They did not realize that it is the large family of the Catholic whites, the lower income of the Negro, which force them to live as they do. They only saw that the Negro children were not taken care of, were allowed to play by themselves, but failed to recognize that this is the fault of the low Negro income which forces the Negro mother to work and leave her children alone. They only saw the consequences and resented what they saw.

Hence we find in the neighborhood two opposite forms of hostility. There is the antagonism of the "underprivileged" toward the "privileged" groups, which takes the form of envy and resentment. To the newcomer the old residents are snobbish, "uppity," greedy. The old residents, in turn, view the new arrival as "inferior," "undesirable," "aggressive." This would have occurred even if the new arrivals had been lower class families of the same ethnic group.

In spite of all the tensions generated in the neighborhood as the result of overcrowding, the differences in living standard, and the emergence of juvenile delinquency, there may have been no open outbreak of racial and ethnic antagonism if there had been no previous racial and religious prejudices which served to canalize the hostility. The observed differences in living standards and behavior fit in with earlier preconceived notions. The children, Negro or white, may have become delinquent under the circumstances regardless of whether they lived in a homogeneous or heterogeneous neighborhood. But the hostility of their parents is transmitted to them, the gang on the next block is ethnically different, and hence easier to distinguish. Therefore, the pre-existing hostility and aggression is directed toward other racial and ethnic groups.

The amount of fighting going on in different parts of the area was not the same everywhere; it tended to be greatest where the turnover of the population was greatest. Here people were most aware of the changes that occurred. Unsettled conditions were most pronounced. It always takes time for a new group to settle down and establish good relations with its neighbors. It takes time for the community to organize its resources, schools, clubs, and churches.

Although the same proportion of Jews and Catholics lived in the southern as well as the northern part of Washington Heights, fights between these two white groups occurred only in those areas where no Negroes resided. In fact, where the two white groups lived side by side with Negroes, they were often completely unaware of the existence of whites of a different religion. The less visible religious differences, so to speak, became invisible in the face of the more obvious differences in color. This never happened in areas where no Negroes lived. In the absence of the stronger color contrasts, the less conspicuous religious difference loomed larger.

If three groups are mutually antagonistic, the main conflict appears to occur between the groups demonstrating greatest visible differences. Often two groups having higher social status will join against the group of lowest status until this group is defeated or disappears. Methodists and Baptists may compete with each other, but will join forces if they get into rivalry with the Catholic church. All three may join forces to fight the influence of atheism. The same situation prevails in the relations of individuals, groups within a society or nation, and in the struggle of the nations itself. After fighting the common enemy, the victors quarrel among themselves.

This pattern, however, does not always exist. It appears to operate only where the conditions are such that a fight against a common enemy is practical, cooperation with other groups imperative. Within the country as a whole, minorities do not generally make common cause against the majority. Experience has shown that they tend to be prejudiced against each other and to keep each other in check. Only where successful educational attempts bring the common interest to the awareness of the various minorities do they unite in the fight against suppression and discrimination.

Relative differences in visibility are determined by objective as well as subjective factors. Members of societies emphasizing class differences rather than race differences may be more aware of differences in speech, clothing, manners, and other class attributes than of differences in skin color. In our society race differences are considered the most important, followed by ethnic differences centering around religion and country of origin, with class differences the least important. This cultural emphasis determines the main lines of association and segregation. Even here, however, the individual may choose to run counter to cultural emphasis, and may consider communality of interests and personality more important than the race or religion of his neighbors.

CREATION OF PREJUDICE FOR POLITICAL PURPOSES

Where circumstances favor the emergence of prejudice and discrimination these may emerge spontaneously. Not infrequently, however, we find that a group deliberately fosters the rise of ethnic and race prejudice for its own ends.

In the South "race" hatred has long been kept alive and fanned to white heat at the instigation of unscrupulous industrialists and politicians, ever ready to capitalize on baseless popular superstitions, prejudices, and beliefs, because there is no issue more useful than "race" as a political platform for securing votes. Tell the poor whites that their condition is due to the competition of the Negroes and that their very existence is threatened by the latter, and they will vote for anything to which such an issue is tied in apparent favor of themselves.[29]

Since the beginnings of time, governments have tended to divert public discontent, resulting from their own inability to solve their nation's problem, toward minority groups. In ancient Rome the blame was placed on the Christians who were held responsible for unemployment and impoverishment caused by government corruption and mismanagement. In more recent times, the Jews have often taken the blame. Hitler followed a time-honored tradition in German history in blaming the Jews for Germany's misfortune.[30]

The tendency to blame small, helpless outgroups for the evils of society, however, did not originate in the field of politics. It is found in the ceremony of the scapegoat, going back to an ancient religious custom. The Bible prescribes the burdening of people's sins onto a goat who is to be chased into the wilderness, thus freeing them of their sins. Something analogous to this custom may be discerned in such historical incidents as the burning of Joan of Arc and in our tendency to blame the other party for all the evils befalling our country. It is found not only in religion and politics, economics and education, but is a strong habit of human beings everywhere. With the description of "scapegoating," (the Biblical term has been applied to this whole group of phenomena) however, we leave the field of economics and politics, and enter into a discussion of the psychological factors in prejudice.

SELECTED READINGS

1. Myrdal, G., *An American Dilemma: The Negro Problem and Modern Democracy*. Harper & Brothers, New York, 1944, Parts I, IV, and V.
2. McWilliams, C., *A Mask for Privilege*. Little, Brown & Co., Boston, Mass., 1948.
3. Massing, P. W., *Rehearsal for Destruction, A Study of Political Anti-Semitism in Imperial Germany*. Harper & Brothers, New York, 1949.
4. Northrup, H. R., *Organized Labor and the Negro*. Harper & Brothers, New York, 1944 (technical).
5. Merton, R. K., "A Social Psychological Factor (The Self-Fulfilling Prophecy)," in *Race Prejudice and Discrimination*, ed., Rose, A. Knopf, New York, 1951, chap. 50.

REFERENCES

1. Klineberg, O., *Race Differences*. Harper & Brothers, New York, 1935, p. 343.
2. Montagu, M. F. A., *Man's Most Dangerous Myth: The Fallacy of Race*. Columbia University Press, New York, 1945, pp. 10 ff.
3. Flavin, M., *Black and White, from the Cape to the Congo*. Harper & Brothers, New York, 1950, p. 84.
4. Klineberg, *op. cit.*, p. 344.
5. Schermerhorn, R. A., *These Our People*. Heath, Boston, 1949, p. 205.
6. Strong, E. K., Jr., *The Second-Generation Japanese Problem*. Stanford University Press, San Francisco, Calif., 1934, p. 125.
7. Williams R. M., Jr., *The Reduction of Intergroup Tension*. Social Science Research Council, Bulletin 57, New York, 1947, p. 57.
8. Saenger, G., *Today's Refugees, Tomorrow's Citizens*, Harper & Brothers, New York, 1941, pp. 210 ff.
9. Burgess, T., *The Greeks in America*. Heath, Boston, Mass., 1930, pp. 141 ff.
10. Myrdal, G., *An American Dilemma*, Harper & Brothers, New York, 1944, pp. 51 ff.
11. Weinryb, B. D., "The Economic and Social Background of Modern Anti-Semitism," in *Essays on Anti-Semitism*, ed. Pinsen, K. S. Conference on Jewish Relations, New York, 1946, pp. 18 ff.
12. Handlin, O., "Prejudice and Capitalistic Exploitation." *Commentary*, 6:79-85, 1948.

13. Koenig, S., "Ethnic Factors in the Economic Life of Urban Connecticut." *American Sociological Review*, 8:193, 1943.
14. *Jews in America*, by the Editors of *Fortune Magazine*. Random House, New York, 1936, pp. 104 ff.
15. McWilliams, C., *A Mask for Privilege*. Little, Brown & Co., Boston, Mass., 1948, chap. VI.
16. Weltfish, G., "The Causes of Group Antagonism." *Journal of Social Issues*, I:7, 1945.
17. Weaver, R., *The Negro Ghetto*. Harcourt, Brace & Co., New York, 1944.
18. Northrup, H. R., *Organized Labor and the Negro*. Harper & Brothers, New York, 1944, p. 1.
19. *Ibid*, pp. 233 ff.
20. Davie, M. R., *Negroes in American Society*. McGraw-Hill, New York, 1949, p. 20.
21. "National Opinion Research Center Poll, 1946." *Public Opinion Quarterly*, Winter, 1946-47, p. 623.
22. Rose, A. M., *Studies in Reduction of Prejudice* (ed. 2). American Council on Race Relations, Chicago, Ill., 1948, pp. 63-70.
23. Allport, G. W., and Kramer, B. M., "Some Roots of Prejudice." *Journal of Psychology*, 22:31, 1946.
24. Saenger, G., and Gilbert, E., "Customer Reactions to the Integration of Negro Sales Personnel." *International Journal of Opinion and Attitude Research*, 4:57-76, 1950.
25. Parry, H., "Protestants, Catholics, and Prejudice." *International Journal of Opinion and Attitude Research*, 3:205-223, 1949.
26. Prothro, E. T., "Group Differences in Ethnic Attitudes of Louisiana College Students." *Sociology and Social Research*, 34:252-258, 1950.
27. Robinson, D., and Rohde, S., "A Public Opinion Study of Anti-Semitism in New York City." *American Sociological Review*, 10:515, 1945.
28. Saenger, G., and Shulman, H. M., "Some Factors Determining Intercultural Behavior and Attitudes of Members of Different Ethnic Groups in Mixed Neighborhoods." *Journal of Psychology*, 25:365-380, 1948.
29. Montagu, *op. cit.*, p. 81.
30. Massing, P. W., *Rehearsal for Destruction: A Study of Political Anti-Semitism in Imperial Germany*, Harper & Brothers, New York, 1949, p. 11.

CHAPTER 8

PSYCHOLOGICAL DETERMINANTS OF

PREJUDICE

Discrimination and prejudice appear to be economically, socially, and politically advantageous for the more privileged groups. They enhance and reenforce the position of the dominant majority.

Individual prejudice may fulfill a similar purpose in the psychological adjustment of a person. It may serve to build up his self-esteem, to alleviate guilt feelings, and to provide an outlet for his aggression. Prejudice can be a neurotic pattern of behavior, providing an outlet for the individual's neurotic needs. The withdrawn neurotic withdraws from other people because he is afraid to be disappointed or because he has failed to acquire the necessary skills to get along with others. His withdrawal preserves his self-esteem by hiding his fears and weaknesses. He believes that he does not like people, prefers books which are more interesting. Actually, he is unaware of the real causes of his withdrawal. But as in all cases of neuroses, the maladjusted persons pays the price. He lacks companionship, fails to develop his social skills.

When a society resorts to discrimination and prejudice, it fails to solve its real problems. We found that discrimination is most widespread in the most economically backward regions. We saw how prejudiced workers excluded Negroes and thereby defeated their own ends by encouraging their use as strike-breakers. Discrimination seems to be a shortsighted attempt to solve the problems of any one group. Temporary advantages gained by excluding an unwanted competitor group lead to a deterioration of the total consumer buying power, stifle fair competition, and fail to make adequate use of the resources of human power found in a nation. The basic needs which led to discrimination and prejudice still remain.

A similar process occurs when the individual resorts to prejudice to solve his problems. Prejudice furnishes him with a solution of his inner needs. But the solution is only on the surface. Actually, this avenue of escape is only a blind alley, and his real needs remain unanswered. It is necessary to look at the nature of the inner needs which lead one person to hate another. When people living under identical social and economic circumstances differ in the extent to which they are prejudiced, the explanation may be found in personality differences. Why does one person in an anti-Semitic country club delight in making anti-Jewish remarks, whereas another not only refrains from making remarks but tends to defend Jews?

The answer to this question must be sought in our knowledge of individual psychology. There are some common elements in the desire to keep minorities down and to kick the dog when we have trouble with our boss or with a newly acquired household gadget. When things go wrong, people become frustrated, angry, and they have a need to express their anger.

FRUSTRATION-AGGRESSION

The child who fails to get his ice cream is only temporarily blocked. The woman whose husband broke her favorite vase may soon loose her anger. More important for our purposes are the lasting frustrations which accumulate over long periods of time. The child whose parents are overstrict and at the same time withhold love and affection and the adult who waits in vain for years for a promotion due him are more seriously affected. The steady growth of hostility from such frustration needs to be released.

The release of overt hostility born of frustration is often prevented by motives or needs which counteract the desire to act out one's aggression. An upper class woman of "good breeding" may be prevented from releasing her aggression by her need to act in accordance with the standards of her class. She may fear to lose status if she lets herself go. In other cases, the release of hostility may be prevented by external factors. The frustrated child may find herself in a school where the teachers suppress any overt acts of aggression. She may be afraid of the consequences of hostility, feel weak, no match for others, and hence repress her hostile tendencies.

To generalize, when hostility is engendered by frustration, it can be directed against three different kinds of targets. The path chosen is a function of the individual's feeling of strength and the obstacles confronting him in a given situation.

1. Hostility can be expressed openly and directed against the source of the frustration. The boss scolds his assistant whose advice did not work out. Here we speak of direct aggression.

2. Hostility can be expressed openly but not directed against the

source of the original frustration. The angry assistant releases his hostility toward his children after returning home. Here we speak of displaced aggression.

3. Repressed hostility is directed toward the self. The assistant hates himself for his stupidity, or, failing to do so openly, develops a severe headache. Here we speak of aggression turned inward.

Society is not in danger when aggression is turned inward, for few if any innocent people (generally members of the intimate family or close friends) are made to suffer. Turning aggression inward makes the individual suffer without removing his frustration; it is therefore, of concern for the clinical psychologist and psychiatrist, not for the person interested in large-scale interpersonal relations. Nor does any social problem arise when the hostility is directed toward the source of the frustration, except when the hostility is great enough to lead to crimes of violence. To the extent that the direct release of aggression serves to reduce the frustration and does not lead to new frustrations, it will lead to a reduction of hostility and adjustment takes place.*

It is however, displaced aggression which concerns us here, where hostility is directed away from the real source of frustration toward other targets.[1] While displaced aggression provides a needed outlet for the individual's hostility, it does not lead to satisfactory adjustment. It not only fails to reduce the frustration which caused it, but it may lead to repressed guilt feelings for having directed hostility toward persons not responsible for the problems.

Displaced aggression occurs in a variety of circumstances. It is found whenever aggression toward the source of frustration constitutes a danger to the individual. Aggression toward one's boss may mean immediate dismissal. Displaced aggression may be found when we have ambivalent feelings toward the person who thwarted us, when we both love and hate the person who frustrates us and are too dependent on him to show (or to face) our true feelings. The dependent wife may direct her feelings of hostility toward her children rather than her inconsiderate husband.

Displacement may occur when the sources of the frustration are complex and is almost inevitable when they are unknown. The causes of an economic depression are complex and difficult to comprehend, and hence difficult to attack constructively. Yet the fear, frustration, and diffused hostility caused by the depression demand action. Aggression of any kind resolves anxiety. Since this is easiest, and least threatening for the frustrated individual, he tends to seek to attack a single cause, for example, the government or the monopolies.

Finally, aggression may be displaced when the source of our frustra-

* Such aggression may also be released on the phantasy level and even then be followed by some, though probably not sufficient, reduction of hostility.

tion is inaccessible. When the small employee of a large concern is denied a salary increase, the ensuing hostility may be directed toward the paymaster rather than toward the remote and inaccessible vice president.

Whatever its cause, displaced aggression needs an outlet. The diffuse hostility may choose an accidental target which happens to be handy, or be directed toward targets which by their very nature offer themselves as convenient. The bus driver in congested New York whose patience has been exhausted by a number of near accidents and his inability to keep his schedule may vent his hostility indiscriminately toward the next passenger who enters without change.

In a recent study, thirty young men at a summer camp who had just expressed their attitudes toward Japanese and Mexicans in response to a questionnaire, were deliberately frustrated by being prevented from attending bank night at the local theatre, and were forced instead to take a series of hard tests. When they replied to the same questionnaire after thus being deprived of their customary Saturday amusements, they tended to ascribe a smaller number of desirable and a larger number of undesirable traits to these foreigners who could not possibly have been to blame for their situation.[2]

The production of generalized hostility appears to be particularly great when the frustration is experienced as unreasonable, unjust, and unnecessary.[3] The bus driver may consider the many questions of his passengers or their failure to have adequate change as unnecessary. The camp boys felt that their detention in camp was unreasonable. The college professor may consider his failure to obtain a promotion in spite of his achievements as unjust.

All these frustrations are subjective experiences, although they have a basis in reality. Yet there is a subtle difference in all these experiences. In the first two cases, we deal with a mere need deprivation, causing no harm to the victim's self-esteem. In the case of the college professor, however, the recognition of his worth as an individual is denied, and his self-esteem suffers. The girl who remains seated while all the others are asked to dance, similarly experiences not only a mere frustration of her desire to dance, to be near men, but suffers a severe blow to her ego. Whenever deprivations are experienced as a threat to our security or our self-esteem, they are likely to lead to more intense feelings of hostility than mere deprivations of needs.[4]

THE SCAPEGOAT THEORY

When hostility is directed against a given person or group either completely or at least partially innocent of the evils which have befallen the frustrated individual or group, we speak of "scapegoating." The "scapegoat" may be held responsible for our sins, for whatever causes us anguish and discomfort. We are already familiar with the historical origin of this practice in religion, and know its use in politics. Scapegoating is an everyday occurrence, practiced by individuals as well as groups. All of us know of situations where one individual has been held responsible for the failure of a whole group, the party which flopped, the break of discipline in school. After a severe railroad accident, public wrath demands the punishment of the guilty party. Although a number of causes may have contributed to the catastrophe, such as outworn equipment, inadequate safety measures, human failure, the public may be satisfied when the "guilty" person, who was perhaps responsible for the tragedy to only a minor degree, if at all, is summarily dismissed, or brought to trial for manslaughter. Scapegoating is particularly likely when the frustrated person is partially responsible for the blamed event, but unwilling to admit this either to himself or to others.

Usually, the chosen target of displaced aggression has to satisfy a number of conditions. The scapegoat may be a person or group against whom we were already prejudiced. We find it easier to believe in the guilt of those whom we already dislike. Also, the scapegoat is very likely to be a person or group too weak to strike back when attacked. Finally, the choice of certain groups or group members as scapegoats is often sanctioned by society, and we may learn to think of a specific group as responsible for our frustrations. When we think of these conditions we can readily see that minority groups are peculiarly liable to be chosen as scapegoats. They are weak and hence in no position to strike back at the aggressor. Initial prejudices make it easy to blame them for all our troubles. And it is commonly quite the norm for a society or a segment of a society to blame certain minorities for all its shortcomings, as instanced by the Nazi slogan, "The Jews are our misfortune."

"FRUSTRATION TOLERANCE"

Frustration is a subjective experience. The same objective deprivation will have different significance for the secure and the insecure individual. It may be of no importance for one individual and constitute a major frustration for another. The husband in a happy and well-adjusted marriage takes the temporary withdrawal of the wife from her marital obligations as unimportant, accepts her statement that she is tired and not feeling too well. The insecure husband in an unhappy relationship interprets the wife's denial as a lack of love and feels rejected.[5]

Bettelheim and Janowitz have demonstrated the same phenomenon in the reactions of soldiers to army life. They cite the case of two men who underwent exactly the same objective deprivation, yet one of them experienced the situation as frustrating, the other failed to do so and took it in his stride. Interviews uncovered striking discrepancies between the objective conditions which these veterans had experienced and their subjective reactions to them. The first soldier, characterized as having a "low frustration tolerance," said, "I did no fighting, I was never wounded, I was never hospitalized," yet in reply to the question whether he "had a bad break in the army" stated:

"I decided it was impossible to get ahead with the rules the army had and the way the game was played. I couldn't do the things you had to do to get ahead. There's no use for a person to try to change things . . ."

The second veteran, who had been subjected to severe conditions of deprivation, described his experiences in these words:

"I was a teletype operator in Africa for three or four months and wasn't in combat then, but all the rest of the time I was laying wire in combat areas. We lost 80 per cent of the company. I never thought I had a chance to come out of it alive." Yet, when questioned whether he had a good or bad break in the army, he replied: "I came out lucky. I came out swell on money and passes. I didn't get any breaks, but to come back alive today is really swell."[6]

We will not be surprised to learn that the veterans characterized by a low frustration tolerance tended to be most anti-Semitic. The subjective experience of frustration rather than the actual degree of deprivation was found to be a determining factor in prejudice. Individuals to whom even the smallest obstacles appear insuperable, who cannot stand adversity, tend toward prejudice more often than individuals who, though severely handicapped, have the strength to "take it."

THE INSECURE INDIVIDUAL

These differences in reactions to different situations reflect the relative security or insecurity of the person. Insecurity itself is a major determinant of prejudice. The anti-Semitic movement in Germany was started by former World War I soldiers unable to adjust to civilian life. Like Hitler they missed the security and freedom from many otherwise normal responsibilities in army life as compared to the turbulent uncertainty of the postwar years. While the army exposed its members to danger, it also provided them with food and shelter, clothing and spending money. As long as they were in the army, they found it in many ways unnecessary to make their own decisions.

The insecure individual particularly avoids reaching decisions and shirks responsibility. In the postwar world, the individual veteran had to take care of himself and assume responsibility for his own acts. The failure of the less secure veteran to succeed in his endeavors led to increased hostility directed against the democratic government and the Jews.

The study of the Chicago veterans indicated that prejudice is related to the individual's general expectations, reflecting his security level. The anti-Semites were generally more pessimistic than the unprejudiced, they worried more about unemployment, were more likely to recall deprivations experienced during the last depression.

The more prejudiced veterans also were more likely to feel that not enough was done for the veterans. Insecure persons appear unwilling to assume responsibility; the insecure person tends to be dependent. He lacks faith in himself, doubts his ability to handle new situations.

For these reasons the insecure, dependent personality may respond favorably toward an authoritarian social order. Authoritarian societies take care of their followers in return for blind allegiance. The followers are told what to do; they do not need to make decisions or to take the initiative. In return for their submission, which forms the basis of their insecurity, the leader promises to take care of them.[7] In capitalistic democratic societies, security is vested in individual initiative and requires more secure individuals, willing and able to look after themselves.

INSECURITY IN THE MODERN WORLD

Some believe that we experience today a worldwide trend toward authoritarianism which has become increasingly noticeable even in our country. This trend is caused in part by the bewildering complexity of modern life, in part by dependence on the impersonal factors that govern it. Industrialization itself leaves less and less room for individual initiative on the part of the majority of the population.[8] The very complexity of the factors which determine our life is difficult to understand and hence adds to insecurity. The fate of the individual laborer or white collar worker is determined by the large industrial organization in which he works. Europeans as well as many Americans feel that the outcome of the present world conflict is beyond their influence, and depends on the decision of a few top men in Washington and Moscow.

The system of values prevalent in our culture also contributes somewhat to insecurity. Self-esteem is based in part on success, getting ahead in a competitive struggle, on recognition by others. We tend to feel good if others think highly of us. If they are disparaging of us we tend to feel low, perhaps without regard to the true merits of their opinions. Basically we may be the same person regardless of whether we achieve the desired promotion, but actually most of us feel different, think more highly of ourselves if we succeed.

Striving to advance ourselves, we take risks. There is always the possibility of failure. The constant struggle to keep up with the Joneses does not permit us to relax. Moreover, this attempt to keep up with others is destructive of human relations. We view others, often our own friends, as rivals and potential competitors, a fact not conducive to the development of warm human relations which form the basis of security.[9] Even if we succeed in climbing the social ladder we may be uncertain of receiving the needed recognition by members of the new group in which we desire membership.

This isolation of individuals in a competitive society tends to be aggravated further by the decreasing emotional support given by the modern family. We no longer live in an age where strong emotional ties to the members of a large family group provide security. Many of the functions of the family have been turned over to other institutions—school, business and church. The family is less apt to be a basis for status and security.

The atomization of man, judging from the social life of these patients, is highly advanced in this society. Individuals are isolated, families are isolated. There does not seem to exist a meaningful group belongingness, unless it is organized around an issue of social prestige. The country club fulfills such a function, but a function without positive content. . . . Spontaneous friendliness is hamstrung by the fact and the fear of exploitation, and human relations are consequently evaluated according to their utility. This society debases friendship for its own sake, and debases group membership for any purpose but prestige and utility.[10]

Finally, modern society tends to emphasize career and money rather than the enjoyment of one's work for its own sake. The worker on the assembly belt cannot be expected to enjoy his work, put his heart into it as did the artisan of past centuries who expressed his skill and artistic feeling in the unique piece of work he produced. Today even many professionals are not interested in their work as such but only as a means to the end of providing money, prestige, and social status. Such emphasis may easily contribute to a feeling of emptiness, and make life meaningless.

The combined effect of all these factors, stronger in some than in others, is frequently the occurrence of a general feeling of weakness and self-doubt, often of anxiety. The individual tends to become uncertain of where he stands, afraid of others, and fearful of the future. To the extent that his self-image is based on external events, his changing fortune, rather than built upon a full knowledge and appreciation of his potentialities, to that extent is he uncertain even about his identity as a person.

When insecurity is related to self-doubt and disturbed feelings of identity and belonging, a pseudo-feeling of belonging can be achieved through prejudice. Identification with a "superior" group leads to a feeling of superiority, gains the insecure person a place in society. The individual who emphasizes that he is a member of the white, Protestant, Anglo-Saxon group not only knows where he belongs but also who he is. He gains strength through his awareness of belonging to the right group, which is better and stronger than the minorities. The lower the individual's self-esteem, the fewer his accomplishments, the greater will be his need to consider the minorities as inferior in order to feel strong and superior by contrast.

The patient, a woman, "achieved an extraordinary rise in social status, emerging from the worst slum conditions of poverty and crime to gain a well paid position as an executive. She was beset by anxiety, not knowing whether she belonged to the misery of her childhood or to the luxury of her early adult life. In the course of attempts to escape this conflict she became unhappy and turned to alcoholism. This was terminated through prolonged hospitalization, but since the basic confusion of her self-image remained, she soon hit upon anti-Semitism as another and equally spurious means to escape this conflict."[11]

We found the growing depersonalization of human relations and the decline of the family related to disturbed feelings of belonging. These needs are aggravated where the insecure individual has general difficulties in establishing emotional ties with other persons. His tendency to be prejudiced appear the greater the more isolated he is and the greater his need for belonging. If the individual really felt wanted, sure of himself, he would not need such support. But feeling unwanted, unrecognized, he can overcome his isolation by emphasizing his membership in the elite. Such pseudo-feelings of belonging again represent a neurotic solution. While they restore the individual's self-esteem, they do not satisfy the real need for intimate human relations. The feelings of inferiority and loneliness are only repressed, not removed.

This need for belonging has many concrete consequences. The preponderance of lonely spinsters or men without close personal ties in the meetings of the lunatic hate fringe has frequently been noted. The more insecure and hence more prejudiced students are more likely to join prestige-endowed organizations such as fraternities and sororities.[12] Organizations such as fraternities and sororities are often exclusive, and hence satisfy the needs of the insecure. They make him feel less alone and at the same time superior to those not chosen as members.

NEED FOR CONFORMITY

The same insecurity which leads the person to emphasize group membership in a high status group and to become a joiner, also leads him to emphasize conformity. An excessive need for conformity is characteristic of the prejudiced individual and helps to explain his negative attitudes toward minorities, who are seen as nonconformists, as people who are and act different. To be a successful member of a group, it is always necessary to conform to its standards, its ways of feeling and acting. But strict conformity is less necessary for the person who feels sure of himself, has good relations with others, and is liked for his own sake. The insecure person, uncertain of whether others like him and recognize him as a group member, can assure his acceptance by rigidly conforming to the demands of the group and by proving his belonging by perfect adherence to its customs and mores.

Clinical studies of prejudiced individuals emphasize their rigid adherence to conventional middle class values. This does not mean that all conformist persons are prejudiced.[13] Their insecurity concerning their place in society leads them to guide their lives by a set of values in which they consider as "good" what is socially accepted and helpful in climbing the social ladder. Deviant behavior is considered "bad" by its very nature, because it constitutes a threat to the group and to the individual whose emotional strength rests in the group rather than in a feeling of his own ability and uniqueness. Moreover, rigid conformity also relieves the individual of the need to make his own decisions. He acts according to the prescriptions of his society, of those in authority.

While rigid conformity makes the person outwardly secure and tends to alleviate his anxiety, it subconsciously leads to resentment. Conformity is gained at the price of the suppression of all individuality, to say nothing of antisocial tendencies. To live a model life is strenuous and exacting. To the extent that self-expression, the realization of individuality, is a necessary condition for psychological adjustment, to that extent is the conformist thwarted. To the extent that he succeeds in acting and feeling like everyone else, to that extent does he defeat his very purpose in conforming, for in the very search for conformity, "Babbit" renders himself personally insignificant and replaceable. In contrast the self-esteem of the well-adjusted person rests, in part, in his awareness of being unique or different from others, of his possession of the courage of his own convictions.[14]

The conformist, therefore, tends to hate those who do not conform. Persons who are different and apparently do not attempt to conform appear provocative.[15] They are unconsciously envied, because they act in ways the prejudiced conformist would like to act and are individuals in their own right. The more the conformist submits to the demands of society, the greater his unconscious need to rebel. The nonconformist minority member hence represents the repressed tendencies of the prejudiced individual, which reminds him of his own desire to revolt and hence cannot be tolerated. The minority person, in daring to be different, appears to have the strength to act independently.

It would not be surprising if the unconscious needs of the conformists alone could spontaneously produce prejudice. There is at present in our society little occasion for such spontaneous generation of hostility toward the nonconformist minorities. Many of us are taught not only that the minorities differ but that they represent an inferior and potentially dangerous way of life. The person who is unable to tolerate nonconformity in himself and others, is thus already provided with a target for his hostility.

This insistence on conformity in the neurotic anti-Semite reveals itself in the frequent occurrence of the phrase, "If only the Jews behaved like everybody else."[16] But the hostility of the insecure and thus conformist individual toward minorities is here increased by envy. Excluded from the larger community, the members of individual minorities are forced to associate with each other for self-protection. The prejudiced person perceives such association (which through the "sour grapes" mechanism is converted into a fault) as clannishness. The Jews and other minorities are seen as secure and belonging. Contrary to the insecure and prejudiced person, they seem to enjoy strong family ties and to help each other. In spite of their apparent "inferiority," they have achieved this security without conforming. While the prejudiced person has to give up the right to express his own individuality as the price for gaining security and a feeling of belonging, the minority person seems to enjoy the former without giving up the latter.

PROJECTION OF UNDESIRABLE TRAITS

As a result of their childhood training, most people strongly condemn various types of "asocial" behavior: unbridled sexuality, destructiveness, or an uncurbed striving for power. Whenever the individual discovers tendencies toward such behavior in himself, guilt feelings emerge. As Freud has taught us, such feelings of guilt occur even on an unconscious level, when the forbidden tendencies are repressed.

Many people fail to dissolve the conflict between their hidden desires and their conscience either by giving up these desires or by yielding to them and giving up their high standards of morality. They repress their hidden desires and manage to convince themselves of their high morality by projecting the offending tendencies onto others. When the angry employee who has been unjustly accused by his boss attacks his wife after returning home from the office, he cannot safely do so without feeling guilty. In order to displace his anger from the boss toward his mate, he first needs to convince himself that *he* does not feel hostile, it is rather his wife who is inconsiderate and unreasonable. He has, so to speak, to project his own feelings onto his wife. When he returns home, he may find that she has prepared his favorite dinner, for example, steak. In this event, he may find reason for his hostility by accusing her of squandering his money. Let us now suppose that she has been thrifty and failed to satisfy his expensive taste. In this case he may say, that "After a hard day at the office, a man may expect something decent to eat." Whatever she does will be wrong because he needs to find fault with her.

Projection is apparent also in the case of the zealous moralist accusing everyone of improper actions and thoughts and engaged in a campaign to purify the city, cleanse the magazines, and remove indecent scenes from the movies. Not infrequently such zeal is the result of unconscious guilt feelings based on his own repressed sexual thoughts, his desire to commit acts which he considers reprehensible. He will accuse others of the forbidden tendencies, sexual promiscuity and lasciviousness, ruthless economic exploitation or unreasonable hostility, and persecute them for their alleged tendencies. In this manner he proves himself free from the forbidden thoughts and in thus conforming to the mores, effectively combats feelings of guilt.

At the same time, such projection permits vicarious gratification of one's forbidden desires. The moralist may find it hard to accuse the magazines or movies of indecency without first looking them over, "investigating them." Such vicarious gratification is sometimes deliberately introduced by those engaged in spreading prejudice. The notorious anti-Semitic Nazi paper, *Der Stürmer* printed in every edition pornographic pictures involving Jews. Southerners often delight in telling stories of Negro immorality.

It is of relatively minor importance whether the victim of such projection has the characteristics of which he is accused. The nature of the projection is determined largely by the repressed needs of the accuser. These needs differ from person to person and from culture to culture depending upon the type of behavior or feelings disapproved of. To the extent that we project onto minorities our own repressed desires, to that extent will the image of the minority become a replica of our own repressed self. The person who has feelings of guilt about his inordinate need for power will ascribe insatiable ambition to a minority. The individual who feels guilty about his repressed sadistic sexual tendencies will attribute these feelings to the minority. Commenting about a recent novel by Lillian Smith, a well-known psycho-analyst writes:

> *Strange Fruit* lays bare with appalling vividness the empty personal and social lives of white people in a small southern town. From the prevailing emotional aridity, they find temporary escape in hysterical religious and sadistic orgies. Feeling devoid of the capacity for the expression of genuine warmth, unconsciously they feel that the Negro has what they lack. They anxiously search for something which will give meaning to their lives through their contacts with the Negro. These contacts, however, are fraught with the terror of the forbidden. Their inflexible consciences, in seeking a victim to punish for all manner of forbidden impulses, must keep in subservience those who represent the temptation.[17]

We do not mean to imply that only the inner needs of the projecting person influence his image of the minority and determine the choice of the target for his hostility. Whenever possible existing differences will be seized upon to choose an appropriate object for one's projection. We saw earlier that sexual inhibition reaches a maximum in the middle class, and was found to be particularly strong among middle and upper class Southern women. In contrast, the freer, less inhibited life of the lower classes, where most Negroes are found, appears to them to be immoral and at the same time enviable.

While the Negro thus "invites" the projection of unconscious sexual desires, the Jewish group lends itself to a projection of desires for power and success. When the anti-Semitic literature depicts the Jews as powerful and successful, it furnishes a basis for such projection which has at least in part a foundation in reality. For reasons previously discussed, the Jewish group fared better than other recently arrived immigrant groups even though they are less successful and powerful than the dominant majority.

In addition to the envy thus generated by the Jews' success, according to at least one study, they are hated because they represent the demands of the prejudiced person's own conscience or superego.[18] In our society, failure to succeed is generally attributed to the individual himself. The presumed "ambition," "hard work," "coopera-tion" (clannishness) of the Jewish group remind the anti-Semite of his own failure to live up to the demands of his society, which have become incorporated into his own conscience. Unwilling and unable to concede such sins of omission, he rationalizes away his short-comings by blaming the Jews rather than himself or society for his failure. But unconsciously he knows better. Hence, his picture of the Jews remains an unpleasant reminder of his own inability to live up to his standards.

To defend his self-esteem the unsuccessful person also needs to believe that the Jews succeeded where he failed, not because they were better but because they used improper means, were "overaggressive." His hate for the Jews may increase if he himself would like to be more aggressive but feels either too weak, or disapproves of aggression.

While projection may be anchored to some extent in facts, it does not always require support in reality. In Nazi Germany, where the Jews constituted the only minority, both the demands of the "id" and the "superego," sexual as well as power needs were projected onto the Jews. The Jews were considered immoral as well as hungry for power. It was Hitler, the man who wanted power more than anybody else and desired to dominate the world, who accused the Jews of this intent.

The lack of a reality basis as well as the projective character of the accusations advanced against minorities reveal themselves also in the inconsistencies of the accusations hurled against them. When Jews are accused simultaneously of being clannish and intruders, success-ful and low class, we can attribute these contradictions to the am-bivalences and contradictions of the prejudiced character itself.[19] It is the prejudiced person who wants to belong and conform but at the same time to preserve his independence, who wants to be recognized as a member of the upper class, but at the same time desires to enjoy the freer expressions of the impulses permitted to the members of the lower class.

Through projection prejudiced individuals can free themselves of guilt feelings and obtain an excuse for the expression of their hostility. Having successfully projected their "shortcomings" and "ambiva-lences" onto the minority, they now have an excuse for their aggres-sion against this minority. It almost becomes a duty to hate and persecute the minorities because of *their* behavior, *their* immorality, *their* guilt.

Such aggression gains part of its energy from the fact that it is really directed against the self, in an attempt to cleanse the self of guilt. Insight into the mechanisms of projection is rare and difficult to achieve because it would lead to a recurrence of the unbearable guilt feelings which were the original cause of the repression. Only the more secure individual can admit his own shortcomings and does not need to engage in projection.

FEELINGS OF GUILT

On a deeper level, we know about the injustices we commit against the objects of our projection, know that aggression is unjustified. The dim, unconscious knowledge of our injustices may generate further guilt feelings and hence lead to further aggression against the minorities. While there is no clear-cut evidence for the operation of such a vicious neurotic circle in the case of prejudice, all neurosis tends to be self-accumulating. Indulging in defensive behavior to bolster our self-esteem makes us less able to solve our real problems and brings about the need for further defensive reaction.

The dependent son of overstrict parents will repress his hostile tendencies toward them because he fears punishment and further deprivation. He will not, however, lose his guilt feelings about his unconscious thoughts. To reassure himself further, he will outwardly be even more compliant. The need for such compliance creates further hostility, which in turn creates more guilt, a vicious circle responsible for the fact that neurotic patterns become more severe in time.

Several authors[20, 21] stress the fact that unconsciously the prejudiced person knows that he is wrong, realizes the sufferings he causes through discrimination and persecution. To alleviate his guilt feelings, he needs to believe, therefore, that the minorities are guilty and deserve the treatment they receive. In his own interest he must believe that they are not only inferior, but hostile and cunning, perhaps even aiming at his destruction. Only then can he release his aggression with umpunity. "I am going to run this Jew out of business" is a thought which may normally be accompanied by guilt feelings. If the desire to act in this manner is projected onto the Jew, it changes into "The Jews are trying to ruin my business."[22] Aggression has now become justified self-defense. The Jew deserves to be ruined because of his "unethical" business practices.

Myrdal argues that we often protect ourselves from becoming aware of the main reasons for discrimination against the Negro in order to convince ourselves that we do believe and take seriously the American creed of equal opportunity, and hence avoid feelings of guilt. The desire to ward off Negro competition for economic reasons becomes conscious as the desire to prevent miscegenation, although this rationalization is in turn reinforced by the projection of repressed sexual desires born of an inadequate psychosexual adjustment.[23]

A corollary of such guilt feelings can be seen in the frequent assertion of prejudiced and discriminating persons that the Negroes are
different, they do not feel discrimination, do not suffer, enjoy their
station in life. Another attempt to ward off guilt feelings exists when
the prejudiced person assures us that "some of my best friends are
Jews."

The prejudiced person thus lacks insight into the causes of his
prejudice as well as into his own motivations and personality generally. Prejudice is one of the main defense mechanisms designed to
prevent insight into one's own personality defects in the interest
of the preservation of our self-esteem. The generalized nature of this
lack of insight as a characteristic of the prejudiced personality has
been demonstrated by Allport and Kramer. Asking their students to
what extent they thought they had been influenced in their thinking
by their parents' attitude toward minority groups, they found the
greatest proportion of prejudiced individuals among those who stated
that they had not been influenced by their parents at all, a lack of
insight into the origin of our attitudes quite appalling for a college
student.[24]

SELECTED READINGS

1. Bettelheim, B., and Janowitz, M., *Dynamics of Prejudice: A Psychological and Social Study of Veterans.* Harper & Brothers, New York,
   1950.
2. Allport, G. W., *ABC's of Scapegoating.* Anti-Defamation League
   of Bnai Brith, New York, 1948, (popular pamphlet).
3. Allport, G. W., and Kramer, B. M., "Some Roots of Prejudice."
   Journal of Social Psychology, 22:9-39, 1946.
4. Rose, A. M., *The Roots of Prejudice.* UNESCO, Paris, 1951 (semi-
   popular pamphlet).

REFERENCES

1. Allport, G. W., *ABC's of Scapegoating.* Anti-Defamation League of
   Bnai Brith, New York, 1948.
2. Miller, N. E., and Bugelski, R., "Minor Studies in Aggression: II.
   The Influence of Frustration Imposed by the In-group On Attitudes
   Expressed toward Outgroups." *Journal of Psychology,* 25:437-442,
   1948.
3. Pastore, N., "A Neglected Factor in the Frustration-Aggression Hypothesis: A Comment." *Journal of Psychology,* 29:271-279, 1950.
4. Williams, R. M., Jr., *The Reduction of Intergroup Tensions.* Social
   Science Research Council, New York, 1947 Bulletin 57, p. 53.

5. Levy, J., and Munroe, R., *The Happy Family*. Knopf, New York, 1938, pp. 110 ff.
6. Bettelheim, B., and Janowitz, M., *Dynamics of Prejudice*. Harper & Brothers, New York, 1950, p. 67.
7. Lazarsfeld-Jahoda, H. M., and Zeisel, H., *Die Arbeitslosen von Marienthal*. Hirsel, Leipzig, 1932.
8. Fromm, E., *Escape from Freedom*. Farrar and Rinehart, New York, 1941, chaps. IV, V, and VII.
9. Horney, K., *The Neurotic Personality of Our Time*. Norton, New York, 1937, chap. II.
10. Ackerman, N. W., and Jahoda, M., *Anti-Semitism and Emotional Disorder*. Harper & Brothers, New York, 1950, p. 90.
11. *Ibid*, pp. 29 ff.
12. Levinson, D. J., and Sanford, R. N., "A Scale for the Measurement of Anti-Semitism." *Journal of Psychology*, 17:339-370, 1944.
13. Adorno, T. W., Frenkel-Brunswik, E., Levinson, D. J., and Sanford, R. N., *The Authoritarian Personality*. Harper & Brothers, New York, 1950, p. 385.
14. Fromm, *op. cit.*, pp. 185 ff.
15. Ackerman and Jahoda, *op. cit.*, p. 34.
16. *Ibid*, p. 35.
17. McLean, H. V., "Psychodynamic Factors in Racial Relations." *Annals of the American Academy of Political and Social Science*, 244:164, 1946.
18. Bettelheim and Janowitz, *op cit.*, pp. 157-159.
19. Ackerman and Jahoda, *op. cit.*, pp. 56-58.
20. Myrdal, G., *An American Dilemma*. Harper & Brothers, New York, 1944.
21. Weltfish, G. "The Causes of Group Antagonism." *Journal of Social Issues*, 1:7, 1945.
22. Brown, J. F., "The Origin of the Anti-Semitic Attitude," in *Jews in a Gentile World*, ed. Graeber, I., and Britt, S. H. Macmillan, New York, 1942, pp. 124 ff.
23. Myrdal, *op. cit.*, pp. 59 ff.
24. Allport, G. W., and Kramer, B. M., "Some Roots of Prejudice." *Journal of Psychology*, 22:19, 1946.

CHAPTER 9

THE AUTHORITARIAN AND THE

DEMOCRATIC PERSONALITY

In the last chapter, we attempted to show how different psychological factors contribute to the development of prejudice. Research conducted in the last ten years has established that prejudiced and relatively unprejudiced individuals differ in basic philosophy and outlook toward life, their feelings about others and themselves, and their relation to other people.

Not all persons showing prejudices against one group or the other necessarily demonstrate the personality patterns of the prejudiced individual, nor should we expect that this type of person would become prejudiced if he lived in a society where prejudice was relatively rare and not sanctioned by the culture. The type of person described here may be said only to be predisposed to being prejudiced, to find in it an answer to his problems.

THE CONCEPT OF THE AUTHORITARIAN PERSONALITY

The description of this personality type goes back mainly to the work of Erich Fromm. His study of the history of western civilization led him to the postulate of a distinct personality, the "authoritarian" (or sado-masochistic) character.[1]

Societies like Hitler's Germany emphasize submission to an absolute authority. The development of the democratic personality, on the other hand, is encouraged more by democratic forms of society, and found to be characterized more by equalitarian tendencies and self-sufficiency. Both types of personality, however, are found, though with different frequency, in authoritarian as well as democratic societies.

The authoritarian person is basically a weak person, who relinquishes his personal initiative and gains strength by submitting to a "wise" and powerful leader. His weakness, as we shall see, may be the result of the upbringing he received as a child. It may be caused, as we have already seen, by living in a world that he finds too difficult to understand and that makes it safer for him to rely on those who profess to know. In countries with an authoritarian form of government, the actual powerlessness of the individual may further the development of the authoritarian personality. In more democratic countries differences in childhood upbringing may be more important.

The people in authority must be regarded as both all-powerful and all-wise because they must be regarded as protectors by those who feel weak and hence submit. If they lacked these capacities, one could not rely upon them. Moreover, such submission becomes more palatable if the persons in authority are seen as greatly superior in every respect. These needs of the insecure and bewildered individual explain the blind adoration which the German authoritarian person felt for the leader. In a similar vein, the authoritarian American feels that his parents can do no wrong no matter how harsh and strict they are. Their emphasis on discipline is considered to be in the interest of the person who obeys.

The authoritarian personality hence sees the world divided into the strong and the weak; the idea of equality is basically alien to him. His weakness will prevent him from questioning the authorities because such doubt would endanger his own security. The authoritarian personality will uncritically obey the mores and conventions of his society because they are supported by the authorities and therefore are right. It is the democratic person whose feeling of strength permits him to question the authorities and to decide for himself what is right or wrong.

His own weakness makes the authoritarian person consider the world as a dangerous place, a place in which security can be found only in strength, in the ruthless elimination of one's enemies.

The authoritarian person lives in a world . . . pictured by him as a sort of jungle in which man's hand is necessarily against every other man's, in which the whole world is conceived as dangerous, threatening, or, at least challenging, and in which human beings are conceived of as primarily selfish or evil or stupid. One's safety lies in one's own strength and this strength consists primarily in the power to dominate. If one is not strong enough the only alternative is to find a strong protector . . . Once granted this world view, everything that the authoritarian person does is logical and sensible. . . . To speak of love, kindness . . . would be senseless and unrealistic.[2]

The authoritarian sees the world in terms of dominance and submission, divided by sharp cleavages of social status and power. The individual on the higher level is there by virtue of his innate superiority, those on lower levels because they are inferior. A person is considered either totally superior or totally inferior.

In sharp contrast to the authoritarian the democratic personality believes in the basic equality of all men. He recognizes that everyone has his good and bad sides, is superior in some aspects and inferior in others. Status lines are not rigid but fluid and subject to change as a result of individual effort. He may obey the temporary leader because the latter may have more knowledge and experience for the time being, not because he has more power. Fundamentally, he feels equal to those higher up in a highly mobile society.

Convinced of his own worth, and viewing the world as a friendly place in which he is the master of his own destiny, the democratic individual feels secure and need not submit to blind authority. Here is no rigid adherence to conventional mores, no blind obedience, but flexibility and openness to change. Feeling strong, he does not need to suppress others in order to assert himself. Human relations are seen as a give and take relationship with emphasis on warmth and affection rather than on a struggle for power. In contrast, the authoritarian person considers love and sympathy as signs of weakness. To the extent that he cannot really conceive of a relationship between equals, he views love and affection as crippling ties which make him dependent.

The authoritarian personality is predisposed toward prejudice. Such predisposition originates in his failure to recognize the basic equality of men regardless of their station in life, and his need to feel superior to at least some people as well as his inability to feel affection and sympathy. His basic concept of the world as a dangerous place in which security can be found only in submission and conformity, make him susceptible to the development of prejudiced attitudes.

These theoretical formulations were made concrete by a group of psychologists at Berkeley, who demonstrated, through extensive research, that at least in this country most prejudiced persons show the characteristics of the authoritarian personality.[3] Beginning with the development of a series of reliable tests for the measurement of anti-Negro attitudes, anti-Semitism, and prejudice against ethnic groups in general, as well as tests designed to measure political attitudes, they next constructed scales for the measurement of basic personality patterns and outlook toward life. Finally, through detailed clinical interviews and projective tests, they studied the conscious as well as the unconscious aspects of the personality of their subjects. These tests were subsequently administered to hundreds of subjects, students of the local university, as well as prison inmates in San Quentin, members of midde class civic organizations, and working class men and women.*

The preliminary results showed that intolerance is usually not an isolated attitude directed toward one or the other group, but a generalized way of looking at people, a state of mind. The authoritarian person is against all out-groups, Jews and Negroes, Mexicans and Japanese, labor and the British. The choice of the specific target may be partially a function of the individual's environment, depending on whether he lives in a community which stresses anti-Semitism or anti-Negro feelings, or whether personally he is more in competition with one rather than the other group. But the chances are high that the person who is intensely anti-Semitic is also intensely anti-Negro.[5] †

The authoritarian personality also tends to be politically conservative rather than liberal, to favor the status quo. But his conservatism is not based on a genuine belief in equality of opportunity and freedom of enterprise. The "Americanism" of the "pseudo-conservative" authoritarian as opposed to genuine conservatism stresses the empty expression of patriotic slogans and conformity of thought.[6] Pseudo-conservatism steers away from individualism and equality of opportunity and moves in the direction of a "rigidly stratified society in which there is a minimum of economic mobility and in which the 'right' groups are in power."[7]

A similar relationship between conformity and prejudice manifests

* The technically inclined reader may be interested in the statistical findings. The correlation between the "F" or "fascism scale" (measuring degree of authoritarianism) and the "E" scale, measuring prejudice against different ethnic groups, was .77 for all groups combined for the most advanced form of the scales (Form 40). The correlation between the "A-S" scale, measuring anti-Semitism, and the "F" scale was somewhat lower (.53) The authors interpret the high but not perfect correlation between the F and E scales as follows: "This correlation does not mean that 'E' and 'F' for all practical purposes measure the same thing. A correlation of .775 means that about two thirds of the subjects who score in the high quartile on the one scale, score in the high quartile on the other, and that there are practically no reversals, i.e. cases in which a subject is high on one scale but low on the other. Surely there are some individuals who have the kind of susceptibility to fascist propaganda with which the F scale is concerned, but for one reason or another tend to inhibit expressions of hostility against minority groups . . . there are other people who rather freely repeat the cliches of ethnocentrism—perhaps in accordance with the climate of opinion in which they are living—without this being expressive of deep lying trends in their personality."[4]

† The correlations between anti-Semitism and anti-Negro sentiment on some attitude scales were as high as .74.

itself when we find a higher proportion of prejudiced individuals among those who attend church regularly and follow a conventional pattern of religion. It is important for them to belong to a church. They often adhere merely to the outer form but fail to be deeply religious. Their religion is without meaning, is an attachment to form rather than to substance. The genuinely religious and patriotic person tends to be relatively unprejudiced, the conformist intolerant.[8, 9]

MEASUREMENT AND MAIN CHARACTERISTICS OF THE AUTHORITARIAN PERSONALITY

The most important result of the California research, however, is the statistical demonstration that prejudice shows a high correlation with the outlook toward life typical of the authoritarian personality. Study after study tended to verify their findings regardless of the area of the country in which the survey was undertaken, and regardless of whether the subjects studied belonged to the dominant majority or a minority group.[10]

In a poll of a cross section of the population of a large metropolitan center in the southern part of the Middle Atlantic seaboard, all subjects were asked to express their agreement or disagreement with a series of questions designed to classify them in terms of their basic personality structure. Those who accepted these statements and hence subscribed to an authoritarian philosophy of life tended to favor discrimination more often than those who disagreed with them, i.e., the more democratically inclined individuals.

The first statement emphasizes the authoritarian belief in the hierarchical division of the world into two opposed groups, the strong and the weak. The second emphasizes the stress on discipline and obedience rather than love and affection. The authoritarian pattern is most clearly expressed in the third question. Democratic persons may have stressed understanding or knowledge as most important in leaders. While the fourth statement brings out the emphasis on conventional mores, the fifth permits the expression of potential aggressive sadistic tendencies in the reader.

Having indicated their agreement or disagreement with the items designed to ascertain their personality all subjects were next asked a series of questions designed to ascertain their attitude toward minority groups in terms of the extent to which they would endorse discriminatory practices. If one classified all those subscribing to two or less of the statements listed above as democratic, and all those agreeing with four or more statements as authoritarian in character, very few highly prejudiced individuals (17 per cent) were found among the

Table 7.   Relationship between Authoritarian Beliefs and Prejudice
in an Eastern Metropolitan City

Personality test items		Low prejudice (%)	High prejudice (%)
There are two kinds of people in the world, the weak and the strong	Agree	65	88
	Disagree	35	12
The most important thing to teach children is absolute obedience to parents	Agree	61	88
	Disagree	39	12
Any good leader should be strict with people under him in order to gain their respect	Agree	57	76
	Disagree	43	24
No decent man can respect a woman who had sex relations before marriage	Agree	38	61
	Disagree	62	39
Prison is too good for sex criminals—they should be publicly whipped or worse	Agree	38	58
	Disagree	62	42
Character structure			
Nonauthoritarians (persons accepting two or less statements)		83	17
Authoritarians (persons accepting four or five statements)		47	53

Unpublished study, Department of Scientific Research, American Jewish Committee.

democratic personalities. Among the authoritarian personalities, however, as many as 53 per cent showed a high degree of prejudice.

The finding that not all persons possessing an authoritarian character structure are highly prejudiced verifies our earlier assertion that personality is not the only factor determining prejudice. Also, a highly authoritarian person living in a genuinely democratic setting may not adopt prejudiced attitudes—perhaps partly because he is not exposed to prejudiced attitudes and partly because in doing so he would become alienated from his group. To go against the stream is difficult for the person who needs to conform. We are justified in saying only that wherever two different individuals live in the same environment, the authoritarian personality is more likely to show prejudiced attitudes than the democratic personality.

From a practical point of view, the genesis of the authoritarian personality is of great importance. If we know what determines the emergence of this type of personality we may be in a better position to advocate techniques which prevent the development of personality characteristics harmful to society as well as to the individual. Before discussing what is known about the antecedents of the authoritarian personality, we may do well to review in summary fashion its main characteristics as they emerged from the preceding discussions.

1. The authoritarian personality is characterized mainly by repressed feelings of weakness and rejection.

2. The world appears to him as a jungle, in which everyone is the enemy of everyone else. People are out for themselves, and not basically interested in others.

3. The authoritarian personality hence emphasizes strength and toughness as supreme values, considers love and sympathy as signs of weakness. Security can be obtained only through domination or submission, not love and cooperation.

4. The ensuing distrust of others is coupled with the absence of secure emotional attachments, disturbances in his feelings of belonging. He is unclear about his role and place in society.

5. In line with his own feelings of weakness, the authoritarian personality overrates the power of some and exaggerates the weakness of others. He divides the world into the weak and the strong, born leaders and born followers.

6. Doubt in his ability to carry things through to their successful completion leads to unwillingness to accept responsibility for his own deeds, avoidance of taking the initiative.[11]

7. Lack of ego-strength, expressed in more or less unconscious doubt about his own worth, is coupled with high dependency needs, the desire to lean upon and submit to a strong person or group.

8. In more democratic societies, submission to the dictates of the group, blind conformity, takes the place of submission to a strong leader. Such submission occurs at the expense of individualistic self-expression.

9. Protests against the leader in authoritarian societies, violation of the group rules in democratic societies, are experienced as powerful threats to the security of the weak individual, which is based on submission.

10. The reaction to such submission, the giving up of individuality, leads to the generation of strong hostile tendencies which need release. While the individual admires and praises the authorities on which he is dependent (leaders, the family, the group) he secretly hates them because they are testimony of his own weakness and surrender.[12]

11. The ensuing hostility has to be displaced because the authoritarian personality cannot afford to attack those on whom he is dependent.

12. Hostility tends to be displaced toward those who are weak and nonconformist, often against the minority groups.

GENESIS OF THE AUTHORITARIAN PERSONALITY IN CHILDHOOD

The fundamental weakness of the authoritarian personality is in part attributed to a stern, disciplinarian childhood in which love and affection are missing to a marked degree. In extreme cases, anti-Semitism was found to be related to parental rejection with ensuing damage to the development of security and self-esteem in the child.[13]

The parents of the most prejudiced children tended to be greatly concerned with social status and prestige, conformity and the external rules of proper behavior. It was important to them that their children associate only with the right type of people.[14]

Any display of emotions was frowned upon, considered low class. The contrast between the strict, punitive upbringing of the children who in later life were highly prejudiced as compared to the more permissive and warm treatment of the less prejudiced is highlighted in these descriptions of their fathers:

"My father died five years ago—he was very—I've judged him with so much prejudice. I thought he was so strict . . . actually he was just the opposite . . . not the least demonstrative . . . he disapproved of any show of emotion of any kind." (*High prejudice*)[15]

"He would hold me back in . . . Never let me play if I'd done something wrong . . . If I did anything wrong during the day he would spank me at night." (*High prejudice*)[16]

"What was your father like?" "He was a very kind man, gentle, was always very good to us, that is, as much as possible under the circumstances. . . ." "Was he strict about some things?" "Not very. He liked us kids a lot. . . ." (*Low prejudice*)[17]

The suppression of feelings in the early childhood of the more prejudiced led to the development of a demand for conformity related to a pronounced inability to enjoy the pleasurable aspects of life:

Analysis revealed that early in life this patient had started to repress all emotion. His mother was a dominant woman whose rigid religiosity banned all feelings of ease and relaxation. Not even laughter was permitted in her house, and under her influence, emotionality and sex became symbols of evil.

As a boy, the patient lived as though pleasure and "goodness" were incompatible. Pleasure was reprehensible and he decided in favor of goodness.

We noted earlier how such a person tends to hate and unconsciously to envy those who are allowed to express their emotions.

But the repression was incomplete, and impotence, as the manifestation of the unsuccessful repression, was revealed in analysis to be accompanied by deep-seated anxiety about the threat of injury in sexual relations. Jews, who supposedly have the same abilities—persistence, shrewdness, intelligence—which the patient valued in himself, presented a source of deep irritation because they had apparently resolved the false conflict which had governed his life. To him, they had the courage to be emotional, uncontrolled, and yet, somehow, "good." The injury to his self-esteem implied in this comparison was too strong to be faced. Therefore he defended himself by hating the Jews, and by an insistence upon conformity.[18]

The success of parental indoctrination in shaping the general outlook of the child became apparent in another study where the most prejudiced and least prejudiced children were asked to define the perfect boy. The former tended to define the perfect boy as being "polite," "having good manners," "being clean," whereas the latter tended to mention more often "companionship" and "being fun." The trend toward outward conformity in the prejudiced child finds expression also in their more frequent endorsement of statements like:

"There is only one right way to do anything."
"Appearances are usually the best test."
"One should avoid doing things in public which seem wrong to others even though one knows that these things are really all right."[19]

The authoritarian children accepted the emphasis on discipline to such an extent that they described the perfect father in terms of the punitive and restrictive aspects of parent-child relations rather than in terms of love and understanding:

"He spanks you when you are bad and does not give you too much money. . . ."
"When you ask for something he ought not to give it to you right away. Not soft on you, strict."[20]

These differences in emphasis in childhood are reflected in the relations between parents and children. The relatively unprejudiced child "is more likely to be treated as an equal" and given "the opportunity to express feelings of rebellion or disagreement."[21] He thinks of his parents as companions. The prejudiced child tends to view his parents more as punishing disciplinarians, more or less strict masters. The first type of child learns at home the equalitarian and individualized approach to people, the second the authoritarian and hierarchical way of thinking.

The authoritarian child submits to the demands of a harsh and strict parent because of fear of punishment. The originally forced submission to parental authority, however, leads later in life not only to a continued demand for autocratic leadership, but to an acceptance of and glorification of a system of strict discipline and punishment.

German children as well as parents consider as their favorite reading a well-known German children's book *Struwwelpeter* (written by Heinrich Hoffman, in 1847), in which the parents are considered as absolute authorities. This book is marked by examples of extreme punishment for disobedience. The girl who plays with matches against her mother's orders, burns to death. The boy who refuses to give up thumbsucking is visited by a stranger who cuts off his thumbs.[22]

The authoritarian obeys initially because he is forced to do so. The more democratically educated child obeys because he received compensatory love and affection in return for compliance to parental demands. Such compensatory love permits stronger identification with the parent facilitated by the emphasis on companionship and hence permits a greater interiorization of parental values.

The authoritarian child of authoritarian parents obeys because of strong external pressure, and still continues to do so after he has grown up. Parental ideals have not become part of his inner make-up, there is less self-control. Wherever society relaxes its controls, sanctions the release of hostility, the authoritarian person acts out his stronger aggression. The democratic personality contains his hostility not only because he possesses greater tolerance for frustration but also because such restraint is part of his inner make-up. The authoritarian personality is controlled by the environment, the genuinely democratic personality by himself.[23] The latter acts in accord with the ideals of his society because he adopts and genuinely cherishes them, not because he is afraid of punishment from the outer world. In keeping with this theory a study of the character structure of German anti-Nazis working in the underground during World War II indicated an exceptionally close and comradely relationship between father and son in their early childhood.[24]

MENTAL RIGIDITY AND LACK OF ORIGINALITY

The habit of the prejudiced person of seeing the world in terms of black and white, good and bad, strong and weak, appears to go back to a specific way of thinking typical of the authoritarian personality. While the authoritarian and democratic personalities do not differ in intelligence, the former's thinking is characterized by greater rigidity and a lack of the capacity of abstract thought. They tend to generalize too rapidly and too broadly. If they have been trained to solve a school problem in a particular way, they find it difficult to shift to another, perhaps better, method. They are puzzled by ambiguous situations, prefer clear-cut issues. When there are positive and negative aspects to an issue, they become bewildered.

This difference in approach to abstract logical problems in the thinking of the prejudiced and unprejudiced person has been shown not only for adults,[25] but was apparent in the thinking of seven-year-old children.[26] It is easy to see how such rigidity of thinking encourages the tendency to classify people in terms of broad categories, such as ethnic or class groups, whose members are considered as basically alike. It discourages awareness of and concern with individual differences. Jews are either good or bad, women emotional or calculating.

The authoritarian person also tends to be less productive intellectually, less original and less responsive emotionally.[27] Such lack of creativity stems in part from the discouragement of independent thinking in the authoritarian child early in his life. It is typical of all completely authoritarian societies, whether fascist or communist in form.[28]

The emotional deprivation of the authoritarian personality probably does result not only from inhibitions caused by his strict upbringing, but is the result also of the devaluation of emotional expression by the parents. Authoritarian regimes generally emphasize the Spartan approach to life, value duty and obedience over love and affection. They de-emphasize the right of the individual to happiness and self-expression.

The emphasis on power also interferes with the capacity to enjoy life. While sex is important to the authoritarian person, it is experienced as overpowering or submitting, and is dissociated from affection. This is not surprising if we consider that the authoritarian person has received less affection and is therefore less able to give it. We also noted that he has been brought up to consider love and affection as weakness. Sex thus often becomes a device to subjugate others, to manipulate people. Similarly, the emphasis on success with its corollary stress on duty even interferes with the genuine enjoyment of one's work. It is easy to see how the lack of gratification derived from major areas of life contributes to frustration and hence aggravates hostility.

Psychoanalysts have emphasized the fact that the person whose energy is employed in keeping rejected needs and desires repressed has less energy for constructive activities. The authoritarian child whose emotional needs are curbed by parental emphasis on conformity, their stress on externalized social values, and whose needs for self-expression are thwarted, is not only frustrated but has to put forth a considerable effort to keep these "undesirable" tendencies in check. His lack of creativity[29] is due not only to parental disapproval of nonconformist behavior, but the sheer lack of available "energy."

SPLIT BETWEEN CONSCIOUS AND UNCONSCIOUS LEVEL

As a result of the impoverishment of his emotional life, as well as of his strict upbringing and enforced submission to parental demands, the authoritarian child develops considerable resentment against his parents. Whenever children are forced to obey blindly, told what to do without being given a reason, and perhaps without receiving loving approval for obedience, hostility is likely to develop. Such hostility needs to be repressed not only because of the fear of retaliation but because the authoritarian child tends to be greatly dependent upon his parents.

His dependency is rooted partly in his feeling of weakness, related to parental emphasis on the consequences of disobedience, as well as the crippling of his ego by lack of opportunity for independent decision. The concept of the world as a dangerous place in which only one's own group is considered right and in which other groups are considered not only as different but bad and dangerous, enhances such insecurity.

As a result we find in the authoritarian personality a pronounced cleavage between the conscious and unconscious levels. On the surface, the authoritarian personality is conforming, moralistic, and respectable. Underneath the surface, the authoritarian personality shows aggressiveness and infantile forms of sexuality.

In contrast, whatever hostility toward the parents exists among the democratic personalities it tends to be acted out openly. The democratic child who is brought up to be independent, to think for himself, and who is loved for himself and not as a reward mainly for his compliance to parental demands and expectations, is less dependent and can afford more openly to criticize his parents. In later life, he shows less emphasis on conventional morality for its own sake, and this in turn is related to a more mature conception of sex as a blend of physical desire and emotional responsiveness relatively free from aggressive tendencies.

SOCIAL FACTORS IN THE EMERGENCE OF THE PREJUDICED PERSONALITY

While much present research emphasizes the role of early childhood upbringing for the development of the prejudiced authoritarian personality, it tends to underemphasize the role of social factors. A recent study of a cross section of adults in a New England community indicated that while differences in "authoritarianism" distinguished prejudiced and unprejudiced individuals in the upper classes, it appeared that social disorganization was more frequently related to prejudice in the lower classes.[30] In the lower class, the prejudiced people tended to feel that the community was unresponsive to their needs, that life was unpredictable, meaningless, and futile. The response to social disorganization, however, may well be a consequence rather than a cause of initial personal maladjustment. We should bear in mind that individuals of identical social status vary considerably among themselves in degree of prejudice.

A comparison of students in California and a Southwestern community finds the latter both more prejudiced and more authoritarian in character structure.[31] Both prejudice and a more rigid pattern of childhood upbringing may conceivably result from the greater emphasis on status, on material rather than spiritual values in the Southern subculture.

When some societies show a marked absence of racial prejudice, whereas others reach great heights of racial intolerance, we do not necessarily assume that their members must belong to different personality types. We have seen how a combination of historic and economic factors may lead to a rise of prejudice and discrimination in a given society. Such prejudice, once aroused, is handed over to the children of future generations by their parents. Along with many other beliefs and sentiments, attitudes concerning different races and ethnic groups are taught. To the extent that a given degree of prejudice is typical of a culture or subculture, to that extent can we speak of "normal" prejudice, "normal" anti-Semitism, or "normal" anti-Catholic feelings in the individual.

Insofar as children accept uncritically the standards, beliefs, and attitudes of their parents, whether they deal with the nature of democracy, communism, God or the devil, men or women, to that extent is it possible that they may show anti-Semitic beliefs and yet be well adjusted.[32] Only when children, and perhaps adults, show prejudice in excess of the amount prevalent in their culture—or rather the specific subculture in which they live—may we expect to find personality deviations. As has been shown, countries such as France and the United States differ in the extent to which they harbor anti-Negro sentiments. What may be considered normal anti-Semitism in a lower class Bostonian may constitute excessive anti-Semitism for a middle class citizen of San Antonio. It is not the absolute degree of anti-Semitism as much as the relative deviation from the group norm which is related to personal maladjustment.

The medieval citizen who feared witches and demons when everyone believed in them may nevertheless have been well adjusted. The denizen of the enlightened modern world afraid of witches is highly suspect of being paranoid and subject to psychiatric interest. Likewise, a Southerner hating and fearing Negroes to the same extent as his fellow citizens may be psychologically well adjusted, whereas a Northerner or even more a South American who is as prejudiced as the average Southerner are more likely to be maladjusted. He differs from his less prejudiced neighbors.

There are, however, some objections against this point of view. Recent research has shown us that already among fairly young children the less adjusted are more prejudiced. More serious is the objection that the well-adjusted adult does not blindly accept the dicta of his environment. He is capable of forming his own judgment, correcting false beliefs through experience, can test the reality. It is hence argued[33] that the well-adjusted person may be more prone to correct the erroneous beliefs which he had absorbed earlier in life.

However, our knowledge of social perception casts some doubt on the assumption that the environment can be defeated easily. We shall see how our preconceived attitudes affect our perception. If a culture tells its members that a demon may appear to them while praying, they are more likely to have visions than if they live in a society having no such notions. Moreover, if everyone, or at least most people around us, disagree with our ideas or beliefs, we tend to believe quite easily that we are wrong and the majority is right. Lastly, we have seen how the institution of discrimination lends some support to prejudiced beliefs insofar as discriminatory action brings the victim under a disadvantage leading to the appearance of undesirable characteristics. The type and limitations of contacts between prejudiced individuals and their victims in a highly prejudiced society makes a rectification of prejudices difficult. A society which practices segregation and discrimination does not provide us with the opportunity to see minority members under normal circumstances at work and at play.

There is, finally, however, another consideration bearing on the relationship between prejudice and personality. It has been shown that some societies permit an easier adjustment than do other societies. They are less complex, characterized by fewer contradictory demands, and perhaps less competitive. While little is known about cultural differences in their relation to prejudice and personality it may well be that some societies which permit an easier adjustment generate less need for displaced aggression. They do not require that the individual bolster his shaky self-esteem by indulging in prejudice. Hence, the difference between the levels of prejudice found in different societies—defined here as the "normal" prejudice of these groups —may in itself reflect differences in their capacity to permit sound adjustment. In addition such differences may be related also to the methods of childhood upbringing they practice.

But racial and ethnic prejudice is only one outlet for the individual's neurotic needs. Different cultures may canalize these needs in different ways. The tradition of a society, expressed in the education of its young as well as in its mass media of communication, determines whether or not the maladjusted individual, and perhaps society itself, will take refuge in prejudice.

SELECTED READINGS

1. Adorno, T. W., Frenkel-Brunswik, E., Levinson, D. J., and Sanford, R.N., *The Authoritarian Personality*. Harper & Brothers, New York, 1950.
2. Ackerman, N. W., and Jahoda, M., *Anti-Semitism and Emotional Disorder: A Psychoanalytic Interpretation*. Harper & Brothers, New York, 1950.
3. Fromm, E., *Escape from Freedom*. Farrar and Rinehart, New York, 1941.
4. Levy, D., "The German Anti-Nazi," *American Journal of Orthopsychiatry*, 16:3, 1946.

REFERENCES

1. Fromm, E., *Escape from Freedom*. Farrar and Rhinehart, New York, 1941.
2. Maslow, A. H., "The Authoritarian Character Structure." *Journal of Social Psychology*, 18:403, 1943.
3. Adorno, T. W., Frenkel-Brunswik, E., Levinson, D. J., and Sanford, R. N., *The Authoritarian Personality*. Harper & Brothers, New York, 1950.
4. *Ibid.*, pp. 263 ff.
5. Bettelheim, B., and Janowitz, M., *Dynamics of Prejudice*. Harper & Brothers, New York, 1950, p. 151.
6. Merton, R. K., *Mass Persuasion*, Harper & Brothers, New York, 1946, p. 101.
7. Adorno *et. al., op. cit.*, p. 182.
8. Allport, G. W., and Kramer, B. M., "Some Roots of Prejudice." *Journal of Psychology*, 22:25, 1946.
9. Adorno *et al., op. cit.*, pp. 220 ff.
10. Christie, R., *A Study of Authoritarianism and Prejudice in a Negro Sample*, unpublished.

11. Hartley, E. L., *Problems in Prejudice*. Kings Crown Press, New York, 1946.
12. Gough, H. G., "Studies of Social Intolerance." *Journal of Social Psychology*, 33:237, 1951.
13. Ackerman, N. W., and Jahoda, M., *Anti-Semitism and Emotional Disorder*. Harper & Brothers, New York, 1950, p. 45.
14. Adorno *et al.*, *op. cit.*, p. 383.
15. *Ibid.*, p. 360.
16. *Ibid.*, p. 373.
17. *Ibid.*, p. 360
18. Ackerman and Jahoda, *op. cit.*, p. 36.
19. Frenkel-Brunswik, E., "A Study of Prejudice in Children." *Human Relations,* 1:303, 1948.
20. *Ibid.*, p. 301.
21. *Ibid.*, p. 302.
22. Private communication from Prof. Henry Meyer.
23. Bettelheim and Janowitz, *op. cit.*, chap. VII.
24. Levy, D. M., "The German Anti-Nazi." *American Journal of Orthopsychiatry,* 16:507-515, 1946.
25. Rokeach, M., "Generalized Mental Rigidity as a Factor in Ethnocentrism." *Journal of Abnormal and Social Psychology*, 43:259-277, 1948.
26. Kutner, B., *Patterns of Mental Functioning Associated with Prejudice in Children*. Paper read at the American Psychological Association Meeting, Chicago, 1951.
27. Reichard, S., "Rorschach Studies of Prejudiced Personality." *American Journal of Orthopsychiatry,* 18:280-286, 1948.
28. Orwell, G., *Nineteen Eighty-Four*. Harcourt, Brace, New York, 1949.
29. Reichard, *op. cit.* 280-286.
30. Srole, L., *Social Disfunction, Personality and Social Distance Attitudes*. Paper read before the American Sociological Society, Chicago, 1951.
31. Christie, R., and Garcia, J., "Subcultural Variation in Authoritarian Personality." *Journal of Abnormal and Social Psychology*, 46:457-469, 1951.
32. Radke, M., Trager, H., and David, H., "Social Perceptions and Attitudes of Children." *Genetic Psychology Monographs,* 40:327-447, 1949.
33. Ackerman and Jahoda, *op. cit.*, pp. 3-8.

Chapter 10

LEARNING AND EXPERIENCE IN THE

GENESIS OF PREJUDICE

Each culture not only impresses upon its children specific rules of manners and behavior, and sets the goals for which its members will strive, it also determines their attitudes toward people. In the middle ages, the Christian inhabitants of Europe were taught to hate and fight the heathen. In more modern times, with the development of nationalism, hostile attitudes were cultivated toward members of other nations, a phenomenon largely absent in earlier times.

THE LEARNING OF ATTITUDES

Within each society different attitudes develop toward different groups and are passed on to the following generation. Each society teaches its young whom to admire, whom to emulate, whom to despise and avoid. Americans of the present generation, for example, tend to admire the heroes of the sport and entertainment world.[1] They tend to emulate the hard working businessman, and, parenthetically, respect mother more than father. They look down on politicians and foreigners, unless the former are highly successful and the latter distinguished visitors rather than immigrants. They avoid and look down on Jews and Negroes to a greater extent than do the inhabitants of most other countries, but show less class prejudice than Latin-Americans, who, on the other hand, are relatively free of race prejudice.

The thesis advanced here is that race and religious prejudice constitute part of the cultural norm, part of the world in which we live and which we take more or less for granted and do not ordinarily question. To the average Hindu, cows are sacred animals; to us, they are food. Their children grow up in an atmosphere in which cows are worshipped; ours in a world in which they are considered friendly

139

animals providing milk and butter. Likewise, American children are by and large brought up in a world in which one judges others by the color of their skin. They are taught to look down on people speaking with an accent or those who believe in the Jewish religion.

Differences in personality may account for deviations from the average prejudice of the culture, while the cultural norm itself may be determined by economic, social, and historical factors.[2] The prejudices of the vast majority of the population are to a considerable extent, however, determined by learning, the acquisition of the cultural norm. Contrary to the opinions of many prejudiced persons, "racial" prejudices are not the result of "innate, instinctual" aversions between different races, do not originate in negative experiences with members of "inferior" groups.

Children acquire prejudice early in life, a fact which has led many lay people as well as scientists to ask whether prejudice itself, or at least the tendency to view people of different skin with fear and suspicion, is not inborn. Such a question, of course, could not arise in countries where racial prejudice is absent.

The fears of young children, writes an eminent child psychologist, "may be influenced to a considerable extent by the example of their parents, whose display of fear not only suggests to the child that there is danger but also may have the effect of weakening the child's confidence in the protection which the parent can afford.[3] We may surmise, therefore, that whenever parents are afraid of members of different races, or any other group of people, the child will take over these fears as soon as he can identify its members.

If children are often afraid of unfamiliar or strange objects and people, it follows that where children of different racial and ethnic backgrounds are brought up together and the element of unfamiliarity is thus absent, no such fear will develop. Study after study has shown that children of nursery age who are brought up together play together without the slightest hesitation, provided their parents are free of prejudice.[4] The different color of the Negro child may perhaps appear to the white child as an object of temporary curiosity. From the child's point of view other differences such as differences in sex, age, height, strength, clothing, are much more relevant and appear much more important than differences in skin color. They affect what he can do and not do, what others can do to him and what they are permitted to do. Differences in skin color will become important to him only to the extent that adults stress such differences, attach importance to them, and treat the child in accordance with his observation of such differences.

ACQUIRING PREJUDICE IN CHILDHOOD

While there is, therefore, no reason for the spontaneous development of prejudice in the young child, it can be shown that young children in our culture will develop some racial prejudices as early as four years of age, which will continue to grow throughout their childhood. More than fifteen years ago the development of prejudice in children was shown in a study by Horowitz involving several hundred children in New York, Georgia, and Tennessee.[5] While all Southern children attended segregated schools, some of the New York children went to mixed schools, others to schools in which no Negro children were found. All children submitted to a battery of tests. In the "Ranks" test the children were asked to rank the photos of four equally handsome white and eight Negro faces in *order of preference* by being asked, "Pick out the one you like best, next best, next best," and so on until all were rated. In the "Show Me" test, the children were asked to pick out all the children whom they wanted as companions in twelve different situations, as, for example:

1. Show me all those you want to sit next to you in a street car.
2. Show me all those you want to be in your class at school.
3. Show me all those that you want to go home with you for lunch.

The results indicated that by the age of five most white boys tested demonstrated a preference for their own race rather than the Negroes, and often verbalized their feelings. The *tendency to exclude* Negroes from scenes of everyday life tested in the "Show Me" test developed somewhat slower.

The gradual increase in prejudice among the children tends to discredit the instinct theory of prejudice which says that children have a natural aversion against those of other races. This theory is behind the belief of the adherents to the Nazi doctrine of race, that the true Nordic child would cry at the sight of a Jew. Similarly, many Southerners believe in the instinctive aversion of whites toward intimate contact with Negroes.

If such "instinctual" aversion on a physiological basis would exist, it should either be ready at birth or express itself suddenly during a specific stage in our development as a result of the maturation of the underlying physiological processes. As Horowitz points out, no such sudden break in the development of prejudice has been observed. Moreover, if we assume the existence of such an instinct, it would be difficult to reconcile this assumption with the absence of race prejudice in many modern and ancient societies. In spite of the existence of our alleged instinct, upper class white babies in the

South did not seem to object to colored wet-nurses. The preponderance of racial intermixture in the United States clearly indicates the absence of an instinctual aversion against sexual intercourse with Negro women on the part of white men. The instinctual aversion seems to be aroused only against their marriage to Negro women. While Southerners have an aversion toward eating with Negroes, such aversion does not seem to extend to being served by Negro waiters.

In the light of the above evidence, it appears safe to attribute such aversions to learning. This does not mean that such strong aversions may not really exist. Our emotions are influenced by learning. Americans in general view with utmost distaste some food which the Chinese consider as delicacies, such as aged eggs and earthworms. They can equally easily be taught to react emotionally toward certain kinds of contacts with Negroes which are socially disapproved.

Prejudiced individuals may claim that hostile attitudes result from negative experiences with minority group members. The findings of the Horowitz study of the rise of prejudice in children, make it highly unlikely that negative experiences with Negroes could have been a factor in the genesis of race prejudice. Those New Yorkers who had been in contact with Negroes had the same attitude as those who had none or little contact. When the author concludes, "it seems that attitudes toward Negroes are now chiefly determined not by contact with Negroes, but by contact with the prevailing attitude toward Negroes,"[6] he bases his statement on the absence of any differences in prejudice between children in segregated and mixed schools. Only the latter had an opportunity to make negative experiences with Negro children. In general the children going to white schools did not even live near colored neighborhoods.

Together with all other attitudes, toward cleanliness and food, toward religion or education, children acquire attitudes toward people from their parents. To some extent there is direct indoctrination. The children are often specifically instructed not to play with Negro children:

First-grade girl: "Mamma tells me not to play with black children, keep away from them. Mamma tells me, she told me not to play with them. [Why not?] Mamma doesn't want me to."

Second-grade girl: "Colored children. Mother doesn't want me to play with colored children, cause they colored men. Might have pneumonia, if you play with them. I play with colored children sometimes and Mamma whips me."[7]

Parents often insist that they did not teach their children not to play with members of minority groups, insist that they had never done anything to influence their children, who were spontaneously discriminating. But their children tend to tell us another story:

Mother: "T . . . always played with other children. Yes, I used to tell her not to play with some. Just told her, never gave her any reasons. She never played with Negro children. I didn't have to tell her *that*."

Child (third-grade girl): "White girl. Colored people have dirty houses. They're dirty. Mother told me not to play with them because sometimes they have diseases and germs, and you get it from them. I had a colored girl friend who worked for Mother, she was a nice clean girl. I liked her but Mother didn't want me to play with her, but I told Mother she was all right."[8]

FORGETTING OF EARLY INDOCTRINATION

Such acquisition of racial prejudice through direct teaching tends to be forgotten later in order to permit the occurrence of the belief that we have an instinctual aversion against intimate contact. We are dealing here with essentially the same psychological process observed in toilet training. Modern child psychologists noted that the young child at the onset of toilet training is greatly interested in his feces, plays with them, has no feeling of shame about the process of elimination. Later on in life, he is taught privacy, taught to be ashamed of anal processes, taught not to play with his feces. Having learned the socially approved behavior and attitudes, he acquires an interest in the repression of the memory of his former "asocial" behavior. If he would recall what he had done earlier, he would be forced to think of himself as dirty, shameless, depraved. Hence, the memory of early anal interests or of early masturbation becomes repressed.

Similar processes are likely to occur in the learning of prejudicial attitudes. If we would recall our early childhood behavior, we would be forced to think of ourselves as deviant, as behaving in a socially disapproved fashion. Moreover, once the prejudiced person admits that he has acquired prejudice through learning, doubt in its justification may easily arise. One may have learned the "wrong attitudes." It will certainly be difficult to maintain the theory of natural aversion between races if it is necessary to teach one's children to keep away from members of "inferior" groups.

IMITATION OF PARENTAL AND SOCIETAL PREJUDICE

While prejudice is sometimes acquired through direct learning, it appears more than likely that it is most often taken over indirectly without any direct attempt by the parents to teach their children. Young children tend to imitate their parents, copy parental behavior. The imitation of parental ways is rewarded by a smile or a word of approval. Their utter dependence makes children sensitive to every subtle nuance of parental behavior, the way parents talk to each other, friends or relatives, superiors or members of minorities. From the child's point of view, parents "know" the world. What they are doing is "right." The Southern boy cannot fail to be aware of the difference with which his father greets and addresses a white man and a Negro. The New York girl brought up in an atmosphere in which her parents tell jokes about Jews and living in a restricted neighborhood, "notices" that Jews are "inferior" people. The extent to which the particular prejudicial patterns found in the immediate environment of first- and second-grade school children are taken over has been demonstrated in a study of 250 Philadelphia school children from different neighborhoods.[9] The prejudices of children in given areas closely resembled the prejudices and racial tensions found in the neighborhood. An unpublished study of the relationship between the prejudices of mothers and their children in upper Manhattan[10] showed a close correlation between the type and extent of parental and children's prejudices.

The same children who absorb prejudice in the home and their social environment generally are also exposed to the teaching of democratic principles, particularly in school, and educated against discrimination. The resulting conflict does not usually reach awareness level but is resolved often by playing with children of a different race and religion in school and maintaining prejudiced attitudes and behavior outside. They have learned that it is all right in the school situation, indeed desirable, to play with everyone, regardless of his race or religion. But they also learned that one does not invite Negroes, or perhaps children of a different religion, to one's home. The young child, lacking a well-integrated over-all system of attitudes, thinks more concretely of specific types of behavior appropriate for specific situations. In his attempt to gain the approval first of his parents and later on that of important adult persons as well as his peers, he conforms with the requirements of the situation.*

When prejudices become more highly crystallized somewhat later in life, friendships with members of other ethnic groups become rationalized. But the belief in the "good Jew," the "white Negro" are already found in rudimentary form among second-grade children:

* To some extent, such differences in the behavior of children reflect differences in parental attitudes. The same parent who is opposed to the more intimate association with minority members at home or even at the neighborhood playground, may favor "mixing" in schools as in keeping with democratic principles of education.

"I like any kind—Catholic, Jewish, or any kind. Any kind of Protestant. Any kind of people except bad people like Germans and Japs."

"Because as long as they're still Americans, it does not matter what kind they are."

"I like any kind of kids. My boy friend is Jewish, but I like him, he is nice. He spends all his money on me. He is a nut spending all his money on me."[11]

As earlier in the home situation, direct teaching of prejudice in school or outside the home does not necessarily occur. The prejudiced teacher, even where he preaches democracy, communicates his real feelings to the sensitive child in subtle gestures or tone of voice in talking to Negro children, and in other patterns of preference. The child at the age of eight or nine has already learned that adults often say one thing and mean another, act and speak differently. He has learned to gauge the real feelings of those around him.

Where children go to mixed schools and are taught democratic values and the belief in the equality of different ethnic groups, prejudiced attitudes and behavior are to some extent curbed. This is not the case where children are segregated by race. The white child knows that his school excludes Negroes, and is aware that they are excluded because they are considered inferior. Segregation here appears as the officially sanctioned expression of the inferiority of the excluded group, discrimination obtains the seal of official approval.*

REINFORCEMENT OF PREJUDICE THROUGH MASS MEDIA

Prejudices originally acquired from the child's environment in an attempt to conform to the prevailing beliefs and behavior patterns, can be reinforced through the mass media of communication. In Nazi Germany, the mass media of communication were used extensively to foment race hatred. In the United States, they serve mainly to reinforce already existing prejudices and stereotyped beliefs. Even in this country, however, there are some publications which intentionally propagate race hatred, the best known perhaps, being Father Coughlin's now extinct *Social Justice*.

The lunatic fascist fringe in this country tried to gain power by blaming the minorities for all existing evils. Its leaders—before the war often identified with the Hitler movement—are men like Gerald K. Smith, Joseph McWilliams, and General George V. H. Mosely.

* It is a different matter when people are segregated for specific reasons not related to beliefs in the greater desirability of the one and the undesirability of another group, where segregation is based on voluntary decisions of both sides. Parochial schools of all denominations are based on the desire for a thorough religious education and not on the assumption that members of other religions are inferior.

A typical example of this technique is contained in the introduction to a pamphlet attacking the Dies Committee for protecting the Jews and attacking patriotic citizens:

"Information of What to Expect when the Great Congressional Probing Racket Reaches into Your Home City and you are Subpeonaed like a Suspected Criminal for Daring to Love and Defend Your Country against Millions of Politically-Protected and Depression-Working Jews."[12]

This type of pamphlet as well as the small organized meetings held by these so-called patriotic societies reach only a small number of highly prejudiced individuals and fail largely because they attack any person or organization which does not fully agree with them, from the utmost left to the conservative right. In the absence of a major economic and political crisis and in a country with strong democratic traditions, they have little chance of influencing large numbers of people.

More effective in reenforcing existing prejudices is the treatment of minorities, particularly the Negroes, in the press. We already noted that criminal acts committed by Negroes often identify the race of the perpetrator, both in the North and South. Until relatively recently, however, Southern papers in particular refused to report on heroic deeds, scientific inventions, and artistic performances by Negroes. In a similar vein, a veterans' crime wave was "created" in the press during the summer of 1946. When other news displaced these crime reports, public awareness of veterans' crimes disappeared, although there was no change in the contribution of veterans to crime between spring and fall.

Unintentional support of prejudice is often provided by the mass media of communication. Until relatively recently American movies tended to show Negroes only as servants, jazz singers, or comical figures. Caricatured versions of Negroes in radio include Rochester in the Jack Benny program and Aunt Jemima in a well-known commercial advertising wheat cakes. Many Americans weary of propaganda and hence on the defensive against open attempts to influence their thinking, may still be influenced by the perpetuation of stereotyped versions of minorities in media of communication which are ostensibly designed to entertain.

During World War II, the American War Writers Board asked a team of researchers from Columbia University to analyze the content of approximately 200 short stories appearing in the four most popular magazines for such unintentional bias.[13] Having identified the ethnic origin of the characters appearing in the scripts, the authors counted the number of "majority" and "minority" heroes and ascertained their character, goals, and occupations. They discovered that while close to 40 per cent of our national population are members of minority groups less than one out of ten short story characters were members of these groups. More important, however, while Americans were usually shown as members of the more desirable occupations, bankers, businessmen, teachers, the ethnic minorities pursued lower class occupations, were peddlers, small businessmen, or workers.

Table 8. Occupations of Majority and Minority Characters
in American Short Stories

Occupation	Americans (%)	Anglo-Saxons and Nordics (%)	Ethnic minorities* (%)
High occupations	59	29	20
Middle occupations	19	23	20
Low occupations	11	27	36
Illegal and suspect occupations	1	2	15
Members of armed forces	10	19	9
Number of characters	602	52	66

* Ethnic minorities include Negroes, Jews, Irish, Italians, and all other ethnic groups except Anglo-Saxons and Nordics.
Table adapted from Berelson, B., and Salter, P. J.: "Majority and Minority Americans: An Analysis of Magazine Fiction." *Public Opinion Quarterly,* 10:183, 1946.

Moreover, it was taken for granted that a member of the dominant group was upper class, whereas an explanation was usually considered necessary if a member of the minorities had achieved high status. But the most significant fact was the overrepresentation in the stories of minorities in the illegal and suspect callings and their underrepresentation in the armed forces. Such unfavorable description of minorities in mass fiction is likely to reenforce existing popular stereotypes concerning the excessive contribution of minorities to crime, as well as to create the impression that minorities did not contribute an equal share to the war effort.

The authors also found that whereas majority characters are usually described as complex personalities, as individuals, minority characters are often described in stereotyped fashion:

The amusingly ignorant Negro: Rosemary is a generously upholstered maid who cackles and rocks back and forth from her rounded hips. Her golden eye teeth reveal themselves in an affectionate smile, her flat feet toed out at a forty-five degree angle, her bulgy body solid enough but looking perilously safety-pinned together. She leaves a note for her mistress: "I taken the gray evening dress like you said. Will leave it at the diars on my way home tonite. I allso taken some of your lonjourney and your lecktrick because I got to do some wash on my other job. Will bring the ion in the morning."
The sly and shrewd Jew: Jew Jake, the manager of a troop of barn-

storming stunt flyers, shows greater concern for money than for the safety of his employees. He has an ungainly and corpulent figure, and rubs his hands in a familiar and excited gesture.

The emotional Irish: Ellen, an Irish cook, is overwhelmed by her sight of the new baby. Ellen, who being a Celt, was easily moved, flew out of the kitchen, saw a fraction of David's face, and burst into tears, a flood of tears.[14]

Most short stories deal with love and adventure. When we settle down to read these stories we want to be entertained by stories of love and adventure successful in spite of all obstacles. We participate vicariously in the stories and admire the heroes with whom we identify. But goals like love, romance, adventure, the bringing to justice of murderers and cattle thieves, were found typical only for Americans and Nordics. The other minorities pursue what the authors call "head" goals in opposition to the more desirable "heart" goals. They are after power or money. As we have seen earlier, differential contact already leads the majority person to see minorities such as Negroes and Jews in connection with business, not when they are engaged in leisure time activities, adventure and love. Hence, apart from the fact that the reader prefers the lover to the businessman, the short story reinforces the already well-ingrained belief in the mercenary nature of Jews, the criminal character of Italians, the emotionality of the Irish.

It is often argued that the writer of fiction, the movie director, has the duty to represent reality as he finds it. The point is *not* that there are no lazy Negroes, jolly Irish, mercenary Jews. As a result of cultural differences and discrimination these characteristics might conceivably be more widespread among these groups than among other groups in our society. We criticize here only the tendency to select for presentation in the content of the mass media the undesirable characteristics rather than the desirable characteristics of the minority group members, those which correspond with the stereotyped beliefs of the culture, in contrast with the generally favorable presentation of majority group members. We object toward the tendency to present from the great variety of personalities found in each group those which reflect these beliefs, oppose the tendency to present the minority individual not in all his unique complexity but as a mere shadow, a stereotyped picture of the group.

SOCIAL PERCEPTION

At this point one may raise the question to what extent stereotypes contribute to prejudice? There can be no doubt that our stereotyped beliefs influence our prejudices. If we meet a Frenchman at a party but do not know his origin, we look at him with a more or less open mind. But our perception changes, narrows down, when someone tells us that he is French. We may expect him to be charming but insincere, and definitely dangerous to women. "We know what type of people Frenchmen are," because we have learned so from early childhood.

And we are not going to be disappointed. Our perception tends to highlight those aspects of his personality which tend to conform with our stereotypes. We tend to overlook or to forget those traits which do not conform with our beliefs. We may even distort what we see and hear in the direction of our beliefs, because we have an inner need to verify them.

If we believe that Jews are "aggressive" and "loud" we are bound to note all acts of aggression by Jews, note if they speak loudly, and say, "Aha! Typically Jewish." If a member of our own group acts in a particularly obnoxious and loud manner, we may say instead, "Drunk," or "Must have trouble with his wife," or "The poor fellow has diabetes." But we remember when Jews we met were loud and obnoxious. We forget when they were subdued and quiet, if for no other reason than that we may not recall their behavior as "Jewish" because it does not fit in with our beliefs. Similarly the person who believes in fortune tellers cannot easily be cured by experience. He recalls all the instances where the fortune teller "was remarkably right," but tends to forget all unfulfilled predictions.

The effect on perception of attitudes in general and stereotypes in particular has been shown in a number of experiments.[15] In one such experiment, the unsuspecting subjects were presented with a picture showing a white man holding an open razor blade and standing next to a Negro in a New York subway. Sometime later they were asked to recall what they had seen and they recalled having seen a white man threatened by a Negro holding a razor.[16]

The operation of selection and distortions in our perceptions caused by prior beliefs and attitudes explains why our experience with minority group members against whom we harbor prejudices are somewhat unlikely to change our prejudices, may, in fact reinforce them. Let us presume an anti-Semite meets three Jews at a party, an outstanding, well-mannered scientist; a crook; and a completely color-less third member of the group. The crook proves to him his original belief that all Jews are crooks, whereas the scientist may be considered an exception. The third Jew is viewed as particularly dangerous, because "he hides his true color under a harmless exterior."

A person who is friendly toward Jews reaches a different inter-pretation upon meeting these three men. The Jewish scientist is seen as an example of the brilliancy of the "race." He considers most Jews are average individuals as shown in the person of the nonentity. This time the "crook" is seen as the exception. We hear that there are "bad eggs" in any group. The same objective situation tells a different story to different individuals, in accordance with their preconceived notions and pre-existing attitudes.

To test this effect of preconceived notions on ethnic identification, several hundred students in three Eastern universities were given a series of facial photographs. While all subjects were shown the same persons, one third of the subjects were shown a few persons within the photographed group wearing glasses, another third saw photographs where the individuals shown were decorated with glasses and a stiff derby hat. The remaining subjects saw the same faces without any accessories.

Most anti-Semites believe that Jews are intellectuals or business men. They also think that glasses are more often worn by intellectuals, derbies by business men. Hence the same faces were considered as Jewish more often when equipped with glasses than when seen without, and most often when glasses and a hat were worn. Moreover, anti-Semites were more likely to identify the spectacle wearers as Jews than their less prejudiced fellow college men.[17]

EFFECT OF STEREOTYPES

The pattern of stereotypes prevalent in the United States includes the notion that Jews are intelligent and ambitious; Italians unintelligent and deficient in character. The typical Anglo-Saxon type is believed to exceed all other groups in beauty. To test the effect of these preconceived notions on the perception of the character of different ethnic groups, thirty photographs of pretty but otherwise not easily identifiable girls were shown to a number of Columbia and Barnard students. The students were then asked to rate each photograph in terms of "general liking," "beauty," "intelligence," "ambition," and "character." Two months later the same photographs were shown again, but this time surnames and first names were attached to the pictures. Five girls were given Jewish names such as Rabinowitz and Finkelstein, five Italian names like Grisolia and Fischetti, five Irish names such as O'Brien and O'Shaughnessy, and fifteen names taken from the list of the signers of the American Declaration of Independence, such as Adams and Clark. Care was taken to match the photographs in each group with those in any other group for all the characteristics in which they were rated.

When the second ratings were compared with the first rating, it was found that particularly the Jewish and Italian girls, and to a minor extent the Irish girls also, had lost in beauty. The Jewish faces now

looked to the subjects more intelligent and ambitious, the Italians and
the Irish had lost their intelligence to a considerable degree, and
together with the Jews, their character. The Italian and Irish girls
appeared to look not quite as entertaining as did the Jewish girls.
But, most important, the girls designated as Anglo-Saxon now looked
decidedly more beautiful, entertaining, and possessed most character.[18]

The results of these experiments make it evident that the prejudiced
individual sees minority members in ways designed to affirm and
strengthen his biases. This raises the question of whether stereotyped
beliefs constitute a major cause of prejudicial feelings, or are more
likely to reenforce and strengthen pre-existing prejudices rather than
to contribute to antagonistic feelings.

Many people have taken it for granted that *false beliefs* concerning
other groups are at the roots of prejudice. If this assumption is true,
it would follow that the removal of false stereotyped notions might
reduce unfavorable attitudes.

We have seen earlier that children take over prejudices directly
from their parents. Under the influence of their parents in general and
society in particular, their feelings toward different ethnic and social
groups develop before they have clear-cut notions concerning the
nature of the out-groups. Stereotypes follow rather than precede the
formation of hostile, antagonistic sentiments, and hence cannot be
held responsible for the formation of prejudice in childhood.

A recent study[19] shows that we often hold the same stereotypes
about people whom we like as we do about groups we dislike. Both
Italians and "women" are considered "emotional." Yet only the
former are criticized for being "emotional." Apparently what is right
and proper for one group is not necessarily the correct behavior for
another group. Emotionality in women is desirable, but not among
Italians.*

But how do we explain the fact that both anti-Semitic and tolerant
individuals considered ambition, intelligence, aggressiveness, and a
materialistic outlook as typical for "Jews" as well as "Americans"?
If shrewdness and aggression, materialistic and mercenary attitudes
are considered as typically "Jewish," it is somewhat surprising to find
the same traits attributed even more often to American businessmen
than to Jews.

While the more anti-Semitic students were more likely to accuse
the Jews of being aggressive, ambitious, intelligent, materialistic, they
were also more likely to consider Americans as possessing these
characteristics. What is more important, they were more likely to

* In comparing the "characteristics" of different nationalities or ethnic
groups, we usually have the men of the group in mind.

approve of these so-called "Jewish" characteristics in general when asked to indicate their attitude toward the desirability of these personality characteristics. For example, more anti-Semitic than "unprejudiced" respondents considered aggressiveness a good characteristic to have. And more anti-Semites than unprejudiced people believed that Jews, and paranthetically, they themselves, were aggressive.

The clue to this apparent puzzle lies in the fact that aggression in an American businessman is considered a desirable virtue. The aggression of a Jewish competitor, however, becomes an undesirable trait, and is no longer the same type of aggression. If I push my way into the subway, such behavior appears from my point of view a perhaps desirable action. I can get in only by getting others out of my way. If other people "push" me, it is a different matter. They are "inconsiderate," "nastily aggressive," "thinking only of themselves." If I already dislike the person who pushes me, or have a prejudice against the group to which he belongs, I easily presume that his motives are ugly, and see such behavior as "typical of his kind." To generalize, a specific type of behavior described in a stereotyped way is likely to assume a different meaning when attributed to a disliked group than when it is attributed to our own group. The agents of the enemy are "spies," our own agents operating in his country are "secret agents." Moreover, the desirability of a specific trait may change in terms of the situation of the group in society. Submission may be considered a positive trait for the slave, a negative trait for the master.

Many believe that the stereotypes held about Jews, Negroes, and other minorities, if not completely correct, contain an element of truth, or have at some time in the past been correct. We have seen earlier that many of the beliefs concerning the inferiority of ethnic groups other than our own were incorrect. While we found no innate differences between different ethnic groups, we nevertheless found differences in personality and behavior as a result of cultural differences and environmental pressure, notably of discrimination itself.

But those who argue that stereotypes contribute to prejudice are not concerned so much with correct beliefs concerning intergroup differences. They are concerned rather with false beliefs and stereotypes, incorrect and derogatory ideas about other groups. Most of the stereotypes used in support of hostility have indeed been found to have no basis in fact. Moreover, it can be demonstrated that these stereotypes themselves are an outgrowth of the interaction between different groups even where these groups are exactly alike.

Two groups of boys in a summer camp who came from the same

economic and ethnic backgrounds were pitted against each other in competitive and mildly frustrating situations involving such athletic activities as a tug of war in which each member of the winning group was given a prize. The victory of one group, therefore, constituted a threat of deprivation for the other group. The two groups had a few days previously been separated by going on separate hikes, having separate bunks, in order to encourage the formation of tightly knit groups. After the victory of the one group who called themselves "Bulldogs" over the other, the "Red Devils," arrangements were made to further frustrate the losers. Half of the cakes and ice creams provided for the victory fête were broken by the experimenter and the situation arranged in such a way that the losing group arrived first in the mess hall. The losing "Red Devils," who had already expressed their resentment about their defeat in no uncertain terms, were now able to act accordingly, which they did by immediately carrying the fresh and unbroken pieces to their own table. This unfriendly behavior led to a storm of resentment among the late arriving victors, who accused the others of being "dirty bums," "rotten jerks," "punks." The losers, in turn, had previously rationalized their defeat by accusing the winners of tampering with the rope, being "dirty players" and "cheaters." As the result of their experiences, the two homogeneous groups developed spontaneous stereotypes in spite of the absence of any group differences within the short period of two weeks.[20]

Stereotyped beliefs concerning members of other groups, whether generated spontaneously or acquired through learning, are unlikely to contribute decisively to the development of prejudice. It seems that in general they furnish only the rationalizations for a previously existing hostility, which in turn may be acquired through learning, may be the result of social or economic factors, or finally be the outgrowth of specific personality needs. Each factor may operate either alone, or in conjunction with the other determinants of prejudice.

The existing stereotypes tend to reenforce prejudice, strengthen it by making it appear reasonable. To the extent that stereotyped notions about the dangerous nature and viciousness of the other group create additional fear, they may occasionally increase a pre-existing hostility. Insofar as our stereotyped beliefs influence us to see the minority groups as inferior and threatening, to that extent do they contribute to the maintenance and preservation of prejudice.

SELECTED READINGS

1. Trager, H. G., and Radke Yarrow, M., *They Learn What They Live.* Harper & Brothers, New York, 1952.
2. Berelson, B., and Salter, P. J., "Majority and Minority Americans: An Analysis of Magazine Fiction." *Public Opinion Quarterly,* 10:2, 1946.
3. Razran, G., "Ethnic Dislikes and Stereotypes: A Laboratory Study." *Journal of Abnormal and Social Psychology,* 45:1, 1950.
4. Allport, G. W., and Postman, L., *The Basic Psychology of Rumor.* Henry Holt, New York, 1945.

REFERENCES

1. Lowenthal, L., "Biographies In Popular Magazines," in *Reader in Public Opinion and Communication,* ed. Berelson, B., and Janowitz, M. Free Press, Glencoe, Illinois, 1950, pp. 289-298.
2. Sherif, M., *An Outline of Social Psychology.* Harper & Brothers, New York, 1948, pp. 7-10.
3. Jersild, A. T., "Emotional Development," in *Manual of Child Psychology,* ed. Carmichel, L. Wiley & Sons, New York, 1946, p. 765.
4. Newcomb, T. M., *Social Psychology.* Dryden Press, New York, 1950, p. 576.
5. Horowitz, E. L., "The Development of Attitudes Toward the Negro." *Archives of Psychology,* No. 194, 1936.
6. *Ibid,* p. 5-43.
7. Murphy, Murphy, and Newcomb, *Experimental Social Psychology.* Harper & Brothers, New York, 1937, p. 371.
8. *Ibid.,* p. 372.
9. Trager, H. G., and Radke Yarrow, M., *They Learn What They Live.* Harper & Brothers, New York, 1952.
10. Shulman, M., and Saenger, G., "Some Factors Determining Intercultural Behavior and Attitudes of Members of Different Ethnic Groups in Mixed Neighborhoods." *Journal of Psychology.* 25:365-381, 1948.
11. Radke, M., Trager, H. G., and David, H., "Social Perceptions and Attitudes of Children." *Genetic Psychology Monographs,* 40:414, 1949.
12. *Martin Dies' Political Posse.* The Pelley Publishers, 1939.
13. Berelson, B., and Salter, P. J., "Majority and Minority Americans: An Analysis of Magazine Fiction." *Public Opinion Quarterly,* 10:183, 1946.
14. *Ibid,* p. 180.
15. Proshansky, H. M., "A Projective Method for the Study of Attitudes." *Journal of Abnormal and Social Psychology,* 38:393-395, 1943.

16. Allport, G. W., and Postman, L. J., "The Basic Psychology of Rumor." *Transactions of the New York Academy of Sciences,* series II, 8:61-81, 1945.

17. Abramson, G., *The Effect of a Stereotype on Judgment of Group Membership.* New York University MA Thesis, 1949.

18. Razran, G., "Ethnic Dislikes and Stereotypes: A Laboratory Study." *Journal of Abnormal and Social Psychology,* 45:7-27, 1950.

19. Saenger, G., and Flowerman, S., "Stereotypes and Prejudicial Attitudes." *Human Relations,* to be published fall 1953.

20. Sherif, M., "A Preliminary Experiment Study of Intergroup Relations," in *Social Psychology at the Crossroads.* Harper & Brothers, New York, 1951, pp. 388-426.

PART III. WHAT CAN BE DONE ABOUT PREJUDICE AND DISCRIMINATION

CHAPTER 11

APPLYING THE LESSON: STRATEGIC PRINCIPLES

IN THE FIGHT AGAINST PREJUDICE

Our knowledge of the causes of prejudice furnishes us with cues for action. But it only provides us with suggestions concerning the methods best suited to reduce prejudice and discrimination. Their effectiveness can be evaluated only in their actual application accompanied by research.[1] While subsequent chapters will take up our experiences with different types of programs used in combating prejudice, we shall attempt here to draw conclusions from our insight into its causes.

ELIMINATING FALSE BELIEFS

Our probing into the origins of prejudice and discrimination has shown us that these do not originate in any hereditary inferiority of its victims. Much of the so-called "inferiority" of racial and ethnic minorities exists only in the eyes of the prejudiced observer. Yet we found at the same time a real inferiority, related partly to the inferior social status of the minorities, and partly to the discrimination that prevented the adequate development of their talents and personalities.

Many of the "undesirable" traits of minority members, as for example aggression or oversensitivity in relations with members of other groups, were found to be reactions to prejudicial treatment. Minorities appeared conspicuous also because of their different culture. Together, these differences make the minority members stand out as the potential targets of hostility for those insisting on conformity with their own norms of behavior and appearance.

The belief in the innate inferiority of minorities can be attacked through education, provided that we should find the correction of these beliefs to be of major importance in reducing prejudice. It may perhaps be more important to remove the actual differences resulting from the handicap under which the minorities live, which antagonize the prejudiced. A reduction of discrimination and a resulting increase in social status of the minorities would lead to at least a partial disappearance of these differences.

Here it may help if particularly the more influential members of the community at large could be educated to understand that whatever differences are found, they can be explained in part as the result of differential treatment. Even the more educated often consider the behavior of the minority a "natural consequence" of the "type of people they are." Robert MacIver tells us of a conversation with a highly cultured, anti-Semitic lady:

"Well, why don't they behave like other people?" "Would you behave like other people," he asked, "if you had been born in a ghetto or had lived from your childhood in a society where you constantly met with exclusion or frustration? If they don't behave like other people your anti-Semitism is one of the reasons why they don't."[2]

It has often been said that the minority members should change their ways and get rid of their undesirable characteristics in order to become more acceptable. To the extent that such behavior really exists this appears at first glance a reasonable demand. But since many of these "undesirable" characteristics are defenses against discrimination protecting the minority member from greater harm, it would at best be difficult to erase them.

Moreover, our researches into the causes of prejudice and discrimination have made it quite clear that the major share of the work toward an improvement of intergroup relations must be carried by the majority. Their desires to exploit minorities economically and socially, as well as their neurotic needs, were responsible for conflict. Changes in the behavior of the minority would not remove these primary motives behind prejudice. The majority sets the conditions under which the minorities live and grow. Nevertheless, in spite of all these difficulties the minorities can, to a limited extent, do their share. Together with the majority, they can work on improving conditions leading to prejudice. They can to a limited extent adapt their behavior to the demands of the majority. Our knowledge of majority needs may make it possible to train minority members to meet the challenge. They can be trained how to react best in the face of personal exposure to prejudice.

For example, the majority member who despises weakness may be antagonized by signs of weakness in minority group members because they remind him unconsciously of his own weaknesses. Hence he may conceivably be impressed by a show of strength in the minority which has pride in its own achievements and insists on its rights. If the minority person fails to see his own value, the majority member may take this as a reaffirmation of his own belief in their worthlessness.

On the other hand, to the extent that the majority member needs to be dominant and feels that his values are superior, he may be more satisfied with submission to his demands, recognition of his superiority. Much will depend on the situation and the social, economic, and psychological needs of the prejudiced individual.

ASSIMILATION AND CULTURAL PLURALISM

The above considerations make it obvious that prejudice and discrimination can best be attacked by eliminating the basis of the differences between groups, through assimilation of the minority groups. If it becomes progressively impossible to distinguish the majority and the minority groups, hostility will have to be channelized in another direction, and tension between groups will disappear. The opposite approach would attempt to make people more tolerant, make them accept existing differences rather than trying to reduce them.

Assimilation and cultural pluralism are theoretical opposites. In practice they are often combined, although the one or the other approach may be stressed. German Jews, before Hitler, attempted to solve anti-Semitism through complete assimilation, with the exception of the maintenance of some of their religious customs. The American attempt to completely absorb all immigrant groups into the main stream of American life represents the same idea. The United States is seen as the "melting pot" of nations.

Cultural pluralism is stressed in Switzerland, which emphasizes the differences between its three major ethnic groups, the Germans, French, and Italians. The Swiss child growing up in a particular part of Switzerland is taught not only to appreciate the distinct culture of the inhabitants of other parts of Switzerland, but to consider such variety as a valuable asset worth preserving.

The approach chosen in a particular country depends to a considerable extent on the traditional attitude of the dominant majority group. While minority group attitudes need also to be considered they depend more or less on the attitudes and behavior of the majority, constitute a reaction to the beliefs and expectations of the latter group. Americans by and large expect their immigrant groups to assimilate, to give up their foreign mores, values, manners or speech, and ways of clothing. With the exception of the preservation of religious differences, immigrants are expected to assimilate and thus to disappear as a distinct cultural group. The immigrant groups themselves desire to take over the ways of the dominant group. This process of assimilation is a natural phenomenon. All individuals moving into a new environment adapt themselves more or less consciously to the folkways of a new society if for no other reasons than for the advantages gained by such adaption.

To the extent that immigrant groups lose their identity and merge with the majority of the population, prejudice and discrimination constitute a passing phenomenon. But adjustment to any new culture is at best a difficult task, requiring a great deal of time, often one or two generations. In the meantime prejudice and discrimination directed against the millions of immigrants residing in our country cause real suffering. Moreover, prejudice and discrimination slow the process of assimilation, lengthen the period in which minority groups tend to associate with members of their own group as protection against a foreign, bewildering, and often hostile culture.

While amalgamation is considered the approved way of solving the problem of our foreign white immigrant groups, Americans are opposed to the assimilation of the "racial" minorities, Negroes, Orientals, Mexicans, and Indians. They insist on keeping their racial minorities separate. But even if social and economic integration were encouraged, complete absorption is impossible because of visible physical differences. This does not mean that a reduction of prejudice and discrimination against members of "racial" minorities would not reduce existing differences in personality and skills, habits and customs, and hence reduce prejudice.

To the extent that we do not desire to erase existing differences or are unable to do so, and to the extent that assimilation even where it is feasible takes time, to that extent must we rely on the creation of tolerance for difference. Apart from crude necessity the preservation of ethnic differences may even be considered to have a decided aesthetic value. It would indeed be a drab and colorless world if we succeeded in erasing all cultural differences, make everybody look, think, and speak alike, eat the same food, and wear the same clothes.

Cultural pluralism involves more than teaching people to tolerate those people who act, speak and look different. We must learn to recognize different types of behavior and appearance as equal, to enjoy variety. This goal is desirable not only in terms of our objective of achieving better intergroup relations at home. A world power like the United States cannot afford to antagonize the sensitivities of the citizens of other countries who differ in culture and race by practicing discrimination and prejudice.

Unfortunately, cultural pluralism, the recognition and approval of differences, is psychologically more difficult to accomplish than is the approach toward the elimination of prejudice and discrimination through assimilation. This difficulty is vested in the insecure individual's desire for conformity as well as his need to bolster his self-esteem, his need for a scapegoat as well as his desire to gain personal advantage through discrimination. The attempt to create tolerance for difference requires a more secure and better educated population than the attempt to reduce prejudice through assimilation.

ATTACK ON PREJUDICE OR DISCRIMINATION

In fighting prejudice and discrimination between different groups we are dealing with two entirely different phenomena even though they usually appear together. Prejudice, we recall, is a state of mind, whereas discrimination involves direct action detrimental to the group at which it is aimed. While prejudice tends to lead to discrimination it does not do so in all situations and under all circumstances. The prejudiced person may not express his real feelings in a tolerant community. As he is not very secure, he may not dare to oppose public opinion. On the other hand a group may become less prejudiced yet continue to practice discrimination in an area where such behavior is sanctioned by society.

Different techniques may be used to fight prejudice and discrimination. Prejudice may be attacked through education or by establishing contact between hostile groups. The educational endeavor can take different forms. To the extent that stereotypes and false beliefs reinforce prejudice, the eradication of prejudicial material from the mass media of communication may be helpful. We may teach to parents and children the truth about minorities. Considering the relatively small contribution of stereotypes and false beliefs to the development of prejudice one may on a priori grounds doubt that this approach will be very effective.

Another type of education tries to establish better intergroup relations by teaching the individual to think and see for himself rather than to rely on hearsay. The individual acquires skills in dealing with others, becomes socially well adjusted. To the extent that this type of education succeeds in solving some of the psychological problems of the individual which lead to prejudice, it may reduce prejudice.

Prejudice, we noted, is acquired early in life. Our earliest impressions of the world are the most important. It follows that education against prejudice cannot be started too early, before childhood attitudes have a chance to become deeply ingrained.

Later in life education against prejudice may emphasize the fact that prejudice often works against our own interests. Where economic motives lead to prejudice and discrimination, one may explain that in the long run discrimination fails to make the individual or his society more prosperous. Similarly, where prejudice is a crutch for the neurotic individual, mental hygiene may demonstrate to him how it fails to solve his own adjustment problems.

The reduction of prejudice through education is usually a long and difficult task. Particularly within limited areas it may often be possible to eliminate discrimination without prior attack on prejudice. The manager of a factory may be motivated by a labor shortage to hire Puerto Ricans or Negroes even though he knows that he himself and his workers are prejudiced. The passage of a law against discrimination in education may force the biased college administrator to admit minority students.

In general, it is often easier to control people's behavior than to influence their feelings. Whenever possible, the attack on discrimination should receive priority since it alleviates suffering and leads to the appearance of conditions advantageous for the reduction of prejudice.

In practice situations arise where it is impossible or perhaps disadvantageous to attack prejudice and discrimination simultaneously. The Southern teachers cannot abolish segregation or usually not even openly attack it but they can attempt to reduce anti-Negro prejudice among their students. During wartime labor shortages, we may have no time to re-educate prejudiced personnel officers in industry, but we can induce them to abolish discriminatory practices by persuasion or coercion.

REDUCING INTERGROUP HOSTILITY

The core of prejudice and discrimination was found to lie in the hostility of the prejudiced toward other groups. Attempts to reduce intergroup tension can aim either at reducing hostility, channelize existing hostility in other directions, or suppress the outward manifestations of hostility. Where hostility can be traced to social and economic frustrations, the prevention of unemployment, a reduction of existing social and economic inequalities, adequate provisions for advancement would lead to a reduction of hostility. When hostility is rooted in personal maladjustment, a reduction of anxiety, of feelings of isolation or worthlessness, to name but a few, would lead to a reduction of hostility toward other groups.

Racial and ethnic tension would be reduced also by a re-direction of existing hostility without a reduction in the actual level of hostile feelings. Such rechannelization of aggression must not necessarily be destructive, a mere substitution of one evil for another one. It may well be possible to divert aggression into socially useful channels.

Finally, one may attempt to suppress hostility without either reducing its intensity or diverting it into other channels. The fear of punishment may deter the person bent on overt aggression, a major objective of our system of law. Legal means can be used to suppress discrimination. From a psychological point of view this approach is perhaps the least constructive, aggressive tendencies cannot easily be repressed in the long run without harm either to the individual or his society. Hostility born of fear and frustration demands an outlet.[3]

PRIORITIES IN THE FIGHT AGAINST DISCRIMINATION

Prejudice has many facets, discrimination is found in many areas of life. Those interested in fighting prejudice and discrimination can often choose the area of intergroup relations on which they wish to concentrate. Such decisions may in practice depend often on the skills of the person engaged in fighting prejudice and its manifestations, the situation in which he finds himself, the authority he possesses. As a teacher he may be better equipped to correct false beliefs and to combat prejudices. The clergyman may stress the equality of man before God, the incompatibility of prejudice and Christianity.

We found that prejudice is more often general than directed toward one or the other group only. This alone suggests that it is better to fight prejudiced thinking and perception per se rather than trying to remove specific prejudices directed against any one group. Such procedure will save us from being accused of partisan interests, and will make it a fight for democratic and religious principles rather than for special groups. While most people are motivated most strongly by self-interest, we should not underestimate the appeal to democratic and religious ideals, in which we have been strongly indoctrinated.

The fight against discrimination can concentrate on the field of employment or education, may aim at the abolition of segregation in housing, or attempt to bring about political equality. Within a given area of discrimination various aspects can be emphasized. In the field of education we may fight for the abolition of segregation in elementary schools, for the provision of equal school facilities for Negroes, or for the admission of Negroes to institutions of higher learning. We may be interested in higher salaries for Negro teachers or better schools for our minorities.

A simultaneous attack on all areas of discrimination may under certain circumstances lead to unmanageable reactions of a prejudiced community which identifies its own economic, political, and social interests with the maintenance of discriminatory practices. Much depends here on the number of people affected by a reduction of prejudice and the extent to which it forces them to change their social and economic habits. The greater and more all encompassing the change, the greater the threat to the prejudiced individual and his society.

Changes which affect only a small number of people may sometimes be easier to initiate than those affecting a larger number. One person may be willing to work with a Negro but not live close to him. Another individual may not object to living side by side with a Jew but does not want him to work in his firm. Whatever the case the threat would be felt more if the individual were forced to give up two discriminatory practices simultaneously rather than one at a time.

CONCENTRATION ON AREA OF LEAST RESISTANCE

Attack on discrimination should therefore be concentrated in areas of life where the least resistance is likely to occur. It may be easier to improve the employment conditions and wages of Negroes in the South than to lift segregation. At the same time whenever several possibilities are open we should use the type of approach most likely to have the most far reaching consequences. We noted earlier that changes in any one area of discrimination tend to spread to other areas. Job discrimination leads to a lower income followed by a lower standard of living for the minority. The lower standard of living is followed by lower education, which further lowers the earning capacity of the minority, and hence aggravates discrimination. The resulting lower standard of living raises in the majority demands for exclusion of the "dirty" minority children and increases demand for segregation in schools.

The opposite happens if we reverse the cycle. Improvement in the education of minorities will increase their earning chances. This in turn will improve their living conditions and make it easier for their children to be accepted in majority schools. Better education and an improvement of living conditions has changed their behavior and outward appearance and in the long run weakens the resistance to their acceptance by the majority group.

Unfortunately, however, the chain of events can be set in motion more easily in a downward direction than in the direction of improvement. Discrimination appears in the interest of the upper caste or classes, in the interest of the prejudiced, and is seen by them as a "natural" consequence of minority inferiority.

Moreover, an improvement of the economic conditions of a minority does not immediately lead to an improvement in other areas of life.[4] Some time elapses until it is reflected in a better education. Again, the better education may not be immediately reflected in greater political interest and participation. Learning takes time. The rise in living standard also will not immediately be reflected in the mores of the group.

Most important, it will require time for the majority to become aware of and accustomed to the changed appearance and standards of the minority, particularly since such perception is counteracted by earlier beliefs. If we always thought of a specific group as uneducated or aggressive we will not immediately accept a change at face value but consider the change as transitory or refuse to believe what we see.

Particularly at the beginning, improvements are often challenged. Any sudden change appears alarming to the individual and may lead to an increase in tension. This is true particularly for the more prejudiced individuals whose security is based on the status quo. If progress is attempted at too great a speed, adjustment of the majority to a new situation may be too difficult and resistance may increase beyond the point where progress can be made. These factors lead to the advocation of a gradual approach, a step by step elimination of prejudice and discrimination. Unfortunately, believers in prejudice and discrimination have often used this argument as an excuse for unnecessary delay, for obstructing progress altogether.

To gauge accurately the speed with which progress can be instituted we need to analyze past experiences in the abolition of discriminatory practices. It is likely that there is an optimum pace for any innovation, at which it can proceed without leading inevitably to resistance.

Such optimum pace exists not only in the field of intergroup relations, but in the general field of interpersonal relations. The psychoanalyst, endeavoring to change the thought and habit pattern of his patient, has to proceed at a given speed. If he goes too fast, the anxiety of the patient may become unbearable, the accumulated resistance will make his efforts futile. The patient may not be ready to try a new pattern of life. On the other hand, if the analyst proceeds too slowly he prolongs the period of treatment unnecessarily, wastes time and money. A similar problem confronts the social reformer, who cannot go ahead faster than the public is willing to follow him.

The optimum speed of progress depends on the total situation, the needs and feelings of the participants as well as the forces—often contrasting—to which they are exposed. Because of the need for manpower and the strong emphasis on genuine democracy the economic advancement of minorities can proceed faster during war than during peace. Resistance against re-education or the abolition of discrimination will be greater where the individual needs his prejudice to bolster up his ego or is economically insecure. Where the individual or the group harbor democratic equalitarian sentiments, progress may proceed faster than where such feelings are absent.

INEVITABILITY OF CONFLICT

Regardless of the method used in the re-education of prejudice and discrimination a certain amount of conflict and tension is often unavoidable, particularly in the early stages of the fight. The child educated to respect and appreciate minority members may get into conflict with his prejudiced parents. The employment of Negroes or women in a firm which hitherto discriminated against members of the race or sex may lead to resistance among prejudiced workers who resent the additional competition.

The appearance of conflict and tension is typical during change of any nature. The psychotherapist cannot break the neurotic patterns of his patient without causing temporary and often intense suffering. Most of us will undergo an operation to regain our health. Yet nobody would question the wisdom of these measures in view of their long range benefits. Similarly social progress is inevitably accompanied by temporary dislocations and tensions. Slum clearance uproots families, the invention of new machinery or the development of new industries temporarily throws people out of work.

Those interested in the improvement of race and ethnic relations must expect the emergence of conflict. They are not primarily interested in the avoidance of conflict at any price, but in the improvement of existing conditions. Conflict, an increase in tension, is of a temporary nature. The accomplishment of the goal will finally lead to a lower level of conflict and tension than existed prior to the initiation of the attempt to reduce prejudice and discrimination. In the long run both majority and minority benefit.

The methods used to initiate progress in intergroup relations will, of course, aim at keeping conflict during these early stages at a minimum. An indirect approach here may prove preferable to the direct approach. We must attack the causes rather than the symptoms. We are unlikely to prevent overeating in the obese person by asking her to refrain from eating or trying to force her to eat less. A better approach consists in removing the causes of overeating; e.g., insecurity in social relations, or fear of the other sex. It is necessary first to explain to her the disadvantages of overeating, the extent to which this practice prevents the person from functioning properly and from making friends. Further progress can be made when the person is made to feel more secure and self-confident.

If we desire to reduce prejudice and discrimination we should perhaps not so much emphasize the evils of prejudice and discrimination, as the advantages of the democratic approach. One may want to make clear that the abolition of discrimination saves money, combats crime, helps the individual and his community. Most important, however, one may want to try to undermine the conditions leading to prejudice and discrimination. We may attempt to alleviate economic insecurity and frustration, or work toward a better psychological adjustment of the prejudiced individual.

But before we can enter into a concrete discussion of the various methods used to reduce prejudice and discrimination, the reader should be warned once again against the frequently made mistake of searching for the best method, the cure-all. As in medicine or politics there is often no *best* method, no cure-all. Different methods prove advantageous on different occasions. We need to know why a specific person or group is prejudiced, consider the specific causes before we recommend a particular remedy. Education and mental hygiene, the establishment of favorable contact between hostile groups and the initiation of social progress, the employment of legal means and the institution of economic and political progress will have to be analyzed in the light of the above principles.

SELECTED READINGS

1. Williams, R. M. Jr., *The Reduction of Intergroup Tensions: a Survey of Research on Problems of Ethnic, Racial, and Religious Group Relations*. Social Science Research Council, Bulletin 57, New York, 1947.
2. MacIver, R. M., *The More Perfect Union*. Macmillan, New York, 1948 (on the strategy of fighting prejudice and discrimination).

REFERENCES

1. Chein, I., Cook, S. W., and Harding J., "The Field of Action Research." *The American Psychologist,* 3:2, 43-50, 1948.
2. MacIver, R. M., *The More Perfect Union,* Macmillan, New York, 1948, p. 66.
3. Williams, R. M. Jr., *The Reduction of Intergroup Tensions.* Social Science Research Council, Bulletin 57, New York, 1947, chap. III.
4. MacIver, *op. cit.,* p. 71.

CHAPTER 12

PROPAGANDA AGAINST PREJUDICE

The world in which we live is made up not so much of our own experiences but of what we are taught to believe. Many "facts" which we "know to exist" are by their very nature outside the realm of our own experience. We read about people we have never seen and in all probability will never see. We hear about the causes of war and peace, prosperity and depression, and may have to take the word of the experts concerning the facts and their meaning. We are taught what is good and desirable, what is bad and harmful. We are taught with what type of people we should associate and for what reasons we should do so. The influence of education on our beliefs and our behavior is found everywhere and at any time. Our parents are our first teachers. Later the school takes over. When we are older we continue our education by reading and listening to those whom we believe to be in the possession of knowledge.

PROPAGANDA AND EDUCATION IN THE MODERN WORLD

Political, religious, and social thinking has been spread by education throughout the ages. What is new is the widening of our horizon through the unprecedented growth of the mass media of communication, which coincides with the growing closeness of people and nations everywhere. The medieval peasant knew little of what happened in foreign lands, nor did these events have much influence on his own patterns of life. People lived in smaller and more isolated groups and did not often meet members of different communities. The growing economic and political interdependence of the world together with greater mobility of population has changed this. But while we have become more interested in others, more of our life space has become remote from personal intimate experience. This gap has been filled in by the growing development of the mass media of communication, radio and television, newspapers and films, posters and magazines, with which we spend a considerable part of our time.

It has been filled with an enormous extension of formal education for all groups of our population.

The continuous barrage of education and propaganda to which modern man is exposed can be used for good or evil. Its capacity to dominate our thinking and behavior is particularly great where the educator or propagandist enjoys a monopoly as in authoritarian countries. Propaganda played a decisive role in fanning smoldering anti-Semitism to the white hot flame of hatred of the Jew. It determines the prejudiced attitude and distorted picture the average Russian has of America. No wonder, therefore, that education has been considered one of the major weapons in the fight against prejudice and discrimination.

Before we can fruitfully discuss the different methods of education used in the fight against prejudice, it will be necessary to clarify different meanings of education. Education is often considered as synonymous with the imparting of facts and information. This holds true for much of lower and even higher education, and also for many attempts to reduce prejudice by correcting the erroneous beliefs intolerant people hold about ethnic and racial minorities. Until relatively recently, education against prejudice in schools and through the press consisted largely in telling people that not all Jews were communists or bankers; or that Negroes were not by nature lazy and dirty. It shares this approach with propaganda, which tends to be distinguished from education by its purpose of persuading and winning adherents to a point of view. By itself propaganda is neither good nor bad. It can be used in the service of the truth as well as of falsehood, operate in the interest of the propagandist or his audience.

While the assimilation of facts is an integral part of all education, true education tries to impart an attitude of an open mind as opposed to a blind acceptance of hearsay and rumor. It teaches the individual to appraise critically the various contradictory opinions to which he finds himself exposed, to attempt to evaluate the trustworthiness of the source and the type of evidence. True education encourages the pupil to check the alleged facts with his own experiences wherever possible, and to look at all sides of a complex problem. It is one of the main aims of education to teach people to think logically and to avoid generalizations from insufficient evidence. The truly educated person learns to be wary of subjective influences. He should be taught to become aware of the ways in which his own expectations and desires color his perceptions.

Education against prejudice cannot succeed on the intellectual level alone. We have seen that young children learn first how to feel about others and that only later do they acquire the rationalizations which society provides to justify prejudice and discrimination. Education against prejudice, therefore, should consist in changing feelings as well as beliefs and it should promote better intergroup relations by teaching the individual how to get along with people whatever their personality or social background.

As we have seen, a prejudiced individual may be prejudiced simply because he was taught to hate another group. Such a person is easier to re-educate than the individual whose prejudices serve emotional or economic needs. The relative ease of the educational process here depends also on the extent to which prejudicial beliefs and practices are prevalent in his immediate environment. All people are dependent on the good will of those around them and will resist the acceptance of beliefs and practices which bring them into conflict with their surroundings regardless of the nature of the issue. It is more difficult to convert a Democrat to become a Republican if he lives in a neighborhood where most people are Democrats than if he lives in an area where most people belong to the Republican party. It is difficult also to attempt to persuade a person who derives economic and social advantages from his adherence to prejudicial beliefs to give up his intolerant beliefs and practices. In general, the greater the external and internal pressures operating on the individual in the direction of the maintenance of his prejudicial beliefs, the more difficult will it be to re-educate him.

Mildly prejudiced people whose prejudice is not buttressed by neurotic needs, can be re-educated more easily than the violently prejudiced individuals. It is easier to educate prejudiced people in groups which oppose prejudice and discrimination than in those which sanction it. Fortunately for the educator there are more mildly prejudiced than highly prejudiced individuals.

REACHING THE PREJUDICED

Granted that re-education should aim rather at the conversion of the large number of people with mild prejudices than at the more difficult task of re-educating the more intensely prejudiced, we are still confronted with the task of reaching those who can be educated, as well as the selection of effective educational methods. In this chapter we shall concern ourselves with mass education only, and leave the more thorough type of emotional re-education for later.

How can we reach these masses? Can the prejudiced people be approached by books and pamphlets, or through radio and television? While the so-called mass media reach a large audience most people do not pay much attention to radio and television, soon forget what they heard or saw.[1] The constant stream of exposure to ever-varying propaganda throughout the day, makes it unlikely that the single anti-prejudice message reaches its target and gets the attention of the person for whom it was intended. Only a large volume of educational material devoted to the reduction of prejudice is likely to compete successfully for attention.

The mass media are controlled by private enterprise and interested primarily in making money. Educational campaigns conducted by agencies devoted to the fight against prejudice are enormously expensive. More money is available to bolster the sale of cars or food than for the sale of good will. Yet during the last ten years an increasing number of movies such as *Gentleman's Agreement,* or *Tomorrow the World* have been shown to nation-wide audiences.

But generally the owners of mass media tend to be weary of such experiments; they are afraid of losing money as well as the good will of the prejudiced part of the audience. Films promoting the cause of the Negro not only may antagonize prejudiced Northern audiences but run the risk of being banned in the South. Radio stations are likely to prefer so-called noncontroversial programs, they fear to antagonize any sizable section of their potential audience. A solution may lie in the direction of government sponsored education on the national, state, or community level, as for example the government sponsored weekly program *Immigrants All, Americans All,* broadcast weekly during the last war.

The problem consists not only of reaching the masses of prejudiced citizens, but of getting their attention. Studies in the field of public opinion have shown that people tend to listen only to ideas agreeing with their opinions. Republicans, by and large, listen only to Republican campaign speeches; Democrats expose themselves only to Democratic speakers.[2] The radio program *Immigrants All, Americans All* was devoted each week to the contribution of another nationality group to America. Audience research indicated that when the program dealt with Italians, the great majority of its audience consisted of Italians; when the Irish were discussed mostly Irish people listened. While such experience may seem to be extreme it is unlikely that persons prejudiced against Negroes will knowingly attend the movie *Colorblind* or read a pamphlet on facts about race. Prejudiced people are more interested in reading about "Negro crime" and "Jewish corruption."

The problem of getting the educational message to its intended audience has been effectively solved in the field of advertising. Few people would buy a magazine solely devoted to advertisements, but prefer one which offers adventure and love stories mixed with advertisements. Hence, our educational material should be included in magazines which people read because its content is of interest both to the prejudiced and unprejudiced. Even then the prejudiced person may read the love story but omit the article dealing with prejudice. The production of stories which appeal to the prejudiced individual but at the same time contain the educational message solves this problem. The advertiser here speaks of the "attention getting appeal" as contrasted to "sales appeal." A whisky ad may get attention by showing an attractive woman, but lead to buying by stressing the low price of the advertised product.[3]

Many prejudiced persons listened to the love story of two Jewish refugees escaping the Nazis during World War II not because they were interested in Jews but because they were interested in love and adventure, as well as in Kate Smith, the narrator. This method works well if it appeals to the special interests of a specific audience. During World War II the leadership of the United Automobile Workers in Detroit was interested in combating race prejudice because it was detrimental both to the war effort and to the unity of the union. It inserted into the union paper a continuous cartoon strip *The Story of Labor,* which showed how race hatred interfered with work, and throughout the history of labor had made it possible to defeat organized efforts to obtain higher wages.

How difficult it is even under such ideal circumstances to reach the whole public is demonstrated by a readership survey of this cartoon undertaken by the Columbia Bureau of Applied Social Research. Only about 50 per cent of the union membership actually got their paper, 23 per cent read it regularly, 14 per cent read the cartoon strip, and 10 per cent finished it. It becomes obvious how great an effort has to be expended to reach the prejudiced public even under ideal conditions. What is not known is the extent to which the prejudiced Southern automobile workers, who were to be educated, were exposed to pro-prejudice propaganda such as Father Coughlin's newspaper *Social Justice,* or the campaign speeches of the mayor of Detroit exploiting the race issue.

Since we found it unlikely that the prejudiced individual would voluntarily listen to education, another solution may be to force him to listen. The "captive" audience par excellence is the school or college student, the soldier in the army, the church-goer. Recent years have seen a considerable increase in the number of programs presented to schools and colleges. Should courses in race relations be made compulsory, for example, in the crucial field of teacher education? The argument has been advanced that little learning takes place if the students are forced to take a course. On the other hand where such courses are optional—as in the majority of our colleges—usually only the unprejudiced students will attend.

ELIMINATING PRO-PREJUDICE PROPAGANDA

Attempts to achieve a favorable balance in the battle between democratic and prejudicial ideas aim not only at increasing the exposure to democratic material but also at decreasing exposure to prejudicial material. The American Council of Education examined textbooks in schools and colleges with the object of eliminating all misinformation about racial and ethnic minorities, from false statements about racial differences down to the use of derogatory terms such as "swarms" or "hordes of immigrants."[4] Pressure has been exerted on newspapers to avoid "race slanting" such as the mentioning of sex crimes by Negroes under headlines featuring emotionally loaded words. The effect of reporting "sex crime waves" with racist overtones had been shown dramatically in 1945 when the "Chicago press printed daily round-ups of actual, attempted, and alleged sex crimes under headlines featuring the words 'rape' and 'terror' and with repeated and prominent use of the race label."[5] "Newspaper crime waves" actually led to "race strikes" in two Chicago schools. Race labeling is particularly dangerous where, as in the South, it is combined with an almost complete absence of reports dealing with Negro contributions and achievements. Fortunately, in some cities pressure from public spirited citizens groups has succeeded in erasing such practices. In Columbus, Ohio, for example, the editors of the three daily and two Sunday papers agreed to rule out race labeling.

Of similar importance here are attempts to prevent stereotyping of ethnic groups in the mass media of film, radio, and magazines. We have seen how the choice of minority characters as criminals reinforces popular misbeliefs. The caricaturing of minority characters, particularly of the colored races, in children's comic strips as well as in radio programs, is still fairly frequent. It is important that the white audiences see Negroes presented as normal, average citizens, not only as comedians, athletes, and servants. Again pressure from civic minded groups could probably persuade the communications industry to eliminate individually or by mutual agreement such undesirable characterizations.[6]

CHOICE OF THE EDUCATOR

To be effective education must not only reach its audience, attract and keep attention, it must be understood and accepted as true. Acceptance depends in part on the choice of the educator and sponsor of antiprejudice propaganda. The ideal educator is a person close to us, a member of our own group, in whom we trust, who enjoys prestige and authority. Children can best be taught by their parents. Teen-agers usually believe what their teachers say. Advertisers know the effect of prestige suggestion, the dictum of the movie star or base-ball hero concerning the merits of his particular brand of cigarette or soap. Studies of voting behavior have shown the importance of the opinion leader who yields greater influence in swaying public opinion than radio or the press. Within one's own circle one listens to the persons whom one trusts and assumes to be well-informed about the issues at stake: the boss or union leader, a minister or doctor. Opinion leaders carry greater weight than papers or radio speeches, more is learned and accepted in the intimate face-to-face contact than in the impersonal contact between reader and reading material. Educational campaigns directed toward opinion leaders may have often a greater effect than direct propaganda.

Much intercultural education is sponsored by good will organizations such as the Urban League, the Anti-Defamation League, or the National Conference of Christians and Jews. Do opinionated people tend to accept messages involving attempts to influence their attitudes from protagonists of these ideas whom they dislike or do they learn only from people with whom they identify and believe to be on their side?[7] Educational attempts sponsored by minority organizations may be considered by prejudiced people as purely partisan, motivated by self-interest, and hence not to be believed. This would suggest that camouflage of the real sponsorship may be recommendable. Such disguise had been one of the main rules of psychological warfare as practiced by the Nazis, who insisted that native organizations had to carry the fight in enemy countries. Their real Nazi origin had to remain a strict secret.

Similarly, fascist organizations in this country carried their fight against minorities under the mantle of democracy, Christianity, motherly love. Unfortunately for those fighting intolerance, the tendency of communist organizations ostensibly working for the welfare of the workers or farmers against race prejudice and anti-Semitism, has led particularly in reactionary and prejudiced circles, to attempts to brand all educational attempts directed against prejudice as communist inspired and conducted.

While the above considerations seem to advocate camouflage or the actual use of prestige-endowed conservative organizations such as the American Legion, or of popular writers or sport stars, the effect of such procedure is minimized because the prejudiced person often assumes that such education is disseminated or distributed by minority groups:

"A prejudiced respondent," interviewed after seeing a cartoon designed to reduce prejudice by Bill Mauldin, "sharing the general esteem in which this popular soldier-cartoonist is held by ex-GI's, said that he had re-

garded Mauldin as a 'regular guy' but he supposed that if you paid a
man enough you could get him to do anything; this respondent believed
that the material he saw was being distributed by a 'bunch of New York
communists.' "[8]

Needless to say such assumptions are usually shared only by a
minority of the readers, presumably the most prejudiced and the
most difficult to influence. To admit that people whom they like
would have a basically different attitude to the one they hold would
be a threat to their self-esteem. They cannot admit that "respectable"
persons favor minorities. The great bulk of mildly prejudiced people
are more likely to acknowledge that the fight for minority rights and
against prejudice is a legitimate task of any democratically inclined
group, majority or minority. Partially as a result of ethical considerations, few defense agencies at present tend to cover up their origin.
This does not mean, however, that sponsorship by persons and
agencies with which the prejudiced person identifies and whom he
trusts, may not carry greater weight.

DRAMATIC VERSUS RATIONAL APPEALS

More important than the question of the sponsorship of educational
campaigns is the type of appeal and the content of the message. Any
person familiar with election campaigns or advertisement is aware of
the superiority of the emotional, dramatic, over the cold intellectual
appeal.[9] Intergroup relations are determined to a greater extent by
emotions than our choice of a political candidate or merchandise,
hence the emotional appeal holds greater promises than the rational
in combating prejudice and discrimination.

We should, however, vary the approach in accordance with the
educational level and specific prejudices of the audience.

Isn't it true that the Jews crucified Jesus? is a question that troubles
some. It is a question that cannot be answered by science, but when I
asked several Roman Catholic priests, Jewish rabbis, and Protestant
ministers how they would answer it, they all agreed on the following
points. Perhaps you can add others:

Pontius Pilate pronounced the death sentence.

Roman soldiers carried it out.

Some Jews did participate in bringing Jesus to trial but not all Jews.
We must remember that the disciples and the prophets were all Jews, and
that Jews wrote most of the new testament. There is no evidence in the
Bible that more than a handful of Jews desired the death of Jesus. We
cannot blame a whole people for the misdeeds of a few.

Ellis Jensen, a leader in the field of intercultural relations, has pointed
out: "The Athenian Senate by a bare majority condemned Socrates. Are

we right in condemning the Greeks for killing Socrates? A few Southerners conspired against Lincoln. Is it correct to say that the Southerners
killed Lincoln? Leon Czolgosz, of Polish parentage, killed McKinley.
Did Polish Americans kill McKinley? Modern Jews by no stretch of the
imagination can be held responsible for the acts of a few Jews sixty
generations ago."[10]

The above excerpt from a pamphlet may not only fail to affect
those whose prejudice was not buttressed by similar arguments but
may even give additional rationalizations to prejudiced people who
had not thought along these lines. While recommendable for its attempt to teach the fallacy of generalizations holding a whole group
responsible for the misdeeds of a few of their members, it probably
would not be understood by persons on a very low level of education.

We need to distinguish here between educational material directed
toward the general public and material designed for a specific group.
In trying to reach the former we must be able to offer some food for
thought for everyone. This may not only lead to fairly general types
of arguments, but implies that the educational material includes many
thoughts with which the reader is already familiar and does not need
convincing. To point out the "obvious" may lead to annoyance.
Within the great flood of material the most important arguments may
be lost. Pamphlets addressed to specific groups, as for example the
previously mentioned labor cartoon series, have the advantage of
being able to concentrate on the central problem of its audience.

CONTENT OF THE APPEAL

In general, a limited number of topics have been emphasized in
the content of educational material:

1. Clarification concerning racial and ethnic differences:
   a. There are no important, fixed, and biologically determined
      differences between various racial and ethnic groups.
   b. Existing differences are culturally determined and the result
      of group interaction.
   c. Differences are small or altogether absent.
   d. Differences between groups are smaller than individual differ-
      ences within each group.
2. Contributions of different racial and ethnic groups to the common
   culture.
3. Prejudice and discrimination work against our self-interest and
   prevent us from achieving our own goals.
4. Prejudice is undemocratic.
5. Prejudice is un-Christian, creates suffering.

The attempt to show the errors of popular thinking concerning racial and ethnic differences is likely to be the least efficient since it offers little motivation to change basic attitudes. Misguided educators have often emphasized the likeness of different racial, ethnic, and religious groups. They emphasized that with the exception of certain superficial characteristics all people are basically alike. But the unsophisticated, prejudiced individual sees that people are different.

These so-called superficial differences are vital to him not only because he may "need" his prejudices but because they constitute the marks of classification emphasized by his culture. He "knows" what counts. Hence it is necessary to discuss the meaning and origin of differences, whether biological or cultural; to explain their origin. The point can be made clear by examples which are less likely to arouse emotions. One may want to show that the comparatively small number of female scientists and artists results not from the innate inferiority of women, but is caused by differences in upbringing and the lack of opportunities for education.

Attempts to show the contributions of different ethnic groups represent perhaps the oldest and most widely used approach to intergroup education. Prominent in textbooks on the high school as well as college level, it has recently been stressed in comic strips and posters. Many readers may have seen posters of the three heroic chaplains, a Catholic, a Jew and a Protestant, going down together with their sinking ship to save the lives of other men. Similarly, the contributions of scientists from all over the world to the development of Atomic energy has been stressed: Fermi, the Italian; Oppenheimer, the Jew; Lisa Meisner, the refugee; Nils Bohr, the Dane.

One of the more promising approaches is the stress on an enlightened self-interest. The more educated adult may be capable of understanding the effect of creating disunity on international as well as domestic affairs. They may be made to see how racial and religious cleavages, the emphasis on white supremacy, play into the hands of Russian propaganda abroad, leads to unrest and delinquency at home. Workers can be taught to see the disadvantages of racial discrimination for labor unity and advancement.

ANSWERING PREJUDICED REMARKS

Another widely used technique is the appeal to patriotic motives branding prejudiced behavior as un-American. There is some evidence that the appeal to democratic motives is more likely to succeed than the appeal to fairness showing that there are good and bad people in any group.

A study designed to measure the effect of replies to anti-Semitic remarks made in real life situations compared public attitudes before and after exposure to different types of answers. Persons overhearing anti-Semitic remarks showed a small but measurable increase in prejudice. When someone replied to the original remarks the attitudes of the group either returned to its previous level or showed a slight improvement. It did not even matter whether the answers to the prejudiced remarks were made by a member of the majority or a minority person. Considering that our attitudes are built upon innumerably small and large incidents and experiences, it can be seen why the authors of the study recommend that it is always important to answer prejudiced remarks wherever they occur.[11]

A typical scene used in a study to test audience reaction shows the anteroom of a veterans' bureau where several men wait to be called into the office. The door opens and the secretary comes to the threshold and asks:

Secretary: Who is next?
　(Two men stand up and exclaim simultaneously.)
Goldstein and Jones: I am.
Secretary: Well, I don't know for sure who is next. It's so hard to tell with so many fellows coming and going. Suppose this gentleman (Pointing) comes in now and another interviewer will be ready for you in a minute. May I have your name, please?
Goldstein: My name is Harry Goldstein.
Secretary: This way, please, Mr. Goldstein.
　(Goldstein exits with secretary. The other man turns to resume his seat and exclaims disgustedly so that the others cannot help hearing him.)
Jones: He was not next. Goldstein, huh? Another Jew who won't wait his turn. Who do they think they are anyway? (Mutters)

Up to this point each of these incidents staged unknown to the audience proceeded in the same manner. From now on, however, different answers were given to the prejudiced remarks:

1. *Democratic ideology:*
Baker: Take it easy, bud. I wouldn't say that if I were you. Maybe you were next and maybe you weren't. The secretary wasn't sure.
Jones: Ah-h. These Jews are alike. They always try to get away with something. I'd like to . . .
Baker: That's no way to talk. Look, we're both veterans. Suppose we had picked on some guys in our outfit because they weren't just like us? What kind of an army would we have had if we had always been fighting among ourselves?
Jones: What business is it of yours?
Baker: What kind of a country would we have if we didn't stick to-

gether? We'd be suckers for someone to make trouble. When a guy
was wounded he didn't ask the stretcher bearer his religion.
Jones: Are you a Jew-lover?
Baker: No, I'm not a Jew-lover, but I'm not a Jew hater either. I don't
hate any group. It took all kinds of people from lots of races and
religions to make America what it is and in a democracy we ought to
be fair to everybody.
  (Secretary returns and speaks to Jones.)
Secretary: It's your turn now. May I have your name.
Jones: My name is Jones.
Secretary: Go right in, Mr. Jones.

In contrast to the democratic appeal, arguments emphasizing individual group differences were less effective:

Baker: Take it easy, bud. I wouldn't say that if I were you. Maybe you
were next and maybe you weren't. The secretary wasn't sure.
Jones: Ah-h. These Jews are all alike. They always try to get away with
something. I'd like to . . .
Baker: That's no way to talk. Look, we're both veterans. Some fellows
in your outfit must have been regular. Weren't some of them Jews?
And how about the goldbrickers? Were they all Jews? Of course not.
Jones: What business is it of yours?
Baker: I'm only saying that you find all kinds of people in any group.
Bright and dumb, tall and short, nasty and nice. Supposing he did jump
ahead. That doesn't prove anything at all about Jews.
Jones: Are you a Jew-lover?
Baker: Well, I like some Jews and some I don't like. I try to judge each
fellow on his merits and not to lump them all together.[12]

The greater effectiveness of the patriotic-democratic appeal probably rests on the fact that the more prejudiced individual is also the
pseudo-patriot, whose patriotic emotional sentiments were aroused.
The rational approach pointing to "individual differences," is likely
to be least effective within the context of a short time exposure to a
cartoon or poster. The prejudiced person recognizes "white Jews"
and realizes that there are undesirable members of his own group.
But he considers the good Jew an exception, believes that most of
them are "pushers," considers most members of his own group nice
and unaggressive.

We are equally pessimistic about the appeal to sympathy. Empathy
requires close contact under favorable circumstances, a prolonged
educational effort. We usually tend to feel sympathetic only toward
those we like, no matter how little. Appeals to sympathy, therefore,
must attempt not only to show the sufferings of the minority but also
to make them more lovable.

A poster exhibited in buses and trolley cars showed a pretty boy crying because he had apparently been told that he is not an American. His answer, *"I am SO an American,"* was followed by the words: *"YOU BET, Sonny . . . No matter what your race or religion! FIGHT Racial and Religious Hate."* One of the factors weakening the effect of such posters is the appearance of the main character as the typical American boy, who does not resemble the "stereotyped" version of the "typical Italian" or "Jew." The prejudiced person may well feel that he would not dislike minority members if they all looked like the "cute little boy" on the poster. There is nothing wrong with little Jewish boys or girls. They are not his competitors. The trouble is that they inevitably grow up to become big "aggressive and mercenary Jews." On the other hand, the presentation of the Jew as he is envisaged by the prejudiced individual may serve to reinforce his prejudices. The solution here lies in hitting a happy medium which the prejudiced person is still able to recognize as a minority member.

CONDITIONS OF EFFECTIVE PROPAGANDA

We are now in a position to analyze the dynamic factors which determine the effects of propaganda. Its success is determined first of all by its ability to attract and hold the attention of its audience. Next, propaganda must get the message across, lead to understanding. Finally, it must sell the message so that it is accepted and may result in a change of attitude. I may enjoy a film trying to propagate democratic thinking and stay to the end without understanding its implied message, much less learning from the movie. Understanding, in turn, requires prior attention, which depends on its ability to gratify some of our inner needs. We must become involved in the action and identify with the characters.

The successive steps leading to successful propaganda can best be illustrated by the analysis of a radio short entitled the *Old One Two* produced by the Institute for Democratic Education. This is the story:

A family from the Middle West moves to a large metropolitan center in the East. Before being sent to his new school, the son is told by his father to take care of himself: "The children here are different," "not our kind of people." Willie, the son, understanding the implications of his father's words, soon succeeds in offending almost all his schoolmates who happen to come from various minority groups, Italians, Jews, Negroes, etc. He refuses to have anything to do with them. Finally he manages to lose his sole remaining friend, John Davis, whom he had considered pure Anglo-Saxon. He makes a remark about the "Polacks" and it turns out that Johnny is of Polish origin.

A solution approaches when Willie's mother accidentally passes the school-yard and finds her son left out and playing by himself. In a subsequent interview with the teacher she is told that his isolation is the result of his having attacked and fought all other children as the result of what he has been taught by his parents. Returning home, the mother succeeds in persuading a reluctant father to admit the errors of his ways. A happy ending is found when the father invites all the children to a baseball game.

The play succeeds in attracting and holding attention because it satisfies needs common to all children. Vicarious gratification of the need for aggression is provided in the person of Willie. Children with strict parents may enjoy scenes which show fathers to be wrong and admitting that they erred. Many liked the fair and loyal Johnny who, right or wrong, sticks to his friend, but fights when offended. All children were interested in the baseball games described in the story.

The success of the story in selling its message depends primarily on the extent to which the children identify with its hero and take a stand against the villain. Positive identification with the hero makes it possible to accept what he stands for. We are not likely to take over the attitudes of people whom we dislike.

Identification may be related to many factors—for example to class differences in values and outlook. Lower class children in our story tended to identify more with the villain, whereas the middle and upper class children listening to the play identified with its hero Johnny. Lower class children tended to consider "aggression" a supreme value, whereas middle class children put greater emphasis on fairness and loyalty. Hence, middle class children were more likely to learn from the hero.[13]

The fact that a specific piece of propaganda has succeeded in involving its audience emotionally does not yet mean that the script will be understood. The difficulties involved in achieving this goal have been demonstrated dramatically in an attempt by the army to create good will toward our allies during the last war. Millions of soldiers were exposed to a series of indoctrination films dealing with the background and course of the war. One of them, *The Battle of Britain* showed how the heroic stand of one thousand British Royal Air Force flyers staved off the threatened invasion of England. While the film succeeded in attracting attention it failed to change attitudes toward England. Those most prejudiced against England remembered best a very short scene showing the landing of lend-lease supplies in a British port, which lent itself to the interpretation that it was mainly the American contribution that saved England.[14]

A similar case of such "selective perception" was found in the reactions of a civilian audience to the movie *Don't Be a Sucker*, designed to demonstrate how the Nazis gained power by driving group against group, and how similar forces are at work here. Each part of the audience tested understood and accepted the part of the message which had a bearing on its own welfare, but failed to pay attention to those parts of the story which dealt with other groups. The Catholics were impressed by the part of the movie dealing with the persecution of Catholics under Hitler. The Protestants recalled best the section of the film which dealt with attacks against the Protestant church, the Jews those scenes dealing with the persecutions of the Jews.[15]

Most people are interested mainly in events which have a bearing on their own welfare. They do not like to be confronted with information which tends to contradict their attitudes, challenges basic beliefs supporting their feelings. If we dislike the British we do not want to see them as courageous or selfless. One prefers to forget, or better, not see how much they did for themselves and for the common cause. The prejudiced Protestant cannot easily admit that Hitler's attack against the Catholics was as unjustified as his attacks on the Protestants.

Resistance to propaganda expresses itself frequently in an unwillingness to *understand* the message expressed in the educational material. We tend to react to propaganda by either accepting or rejecting it. But sometimes we avoid taking a stand, prefer not to face the implications of ideas opposed to our own. In this case we are not being forced either to defend ourselves or to admit to error.[16]

"*Evasion*" through lack of understanding occurs whenever the person is unable either to reject or to accept the message without getting into conflict. The prejudiced individual may know on a deeper level that his prejudices are wrong but find himself unable to give them up. He may need a scapegoat. He may be unable to adopt a more tolerant point of view because such change would bring him into conflict with his prejudiced friends whom he does not dare to antagonize. In societies educating its members in prejudice *and* democratic beliefs the understanding of messages branding prejudicial behavior as undemocratic would confuse and disturb the biased individual.

In an effort to combat prejudice a series of cartoons showed prejudicial behavior as unattractive and inconsistent, self-defeating as well as undemocratic. The "hero" of the series was Mr. Biggott, a desiccated, sickly looking old man of somewhat ridiculous appearance. In the first series he is seen standing before the village honor roll protesting the inclusion of so many foreign names. A second series shows him refusing a blood transfusion unless the donor has "pure, American blood." He successively refuses Jewish, Negro, finally all blood except that coming from a Mayflower descendant. Mr. Biggott acts decidedly unpatriotically if not treasonously in the first series, and against his own interest in the second.

Subsequent interviews indicated that the understanding of the meaning of the cartoons depended upon the degree of prejudice of the onlooker as well as upon his concern with the dangers of prejudice. Only 27 per cent of those who were worried over the effects of prejudice in the United States and were fairly unprejudiced failed to understand the message. But as many as 77 per cent of those who were not only prejudiced but failed to see that prejudice constitutes a danger to our national welfare misinterpreted the message.[17]

Resistances of this kind are found already in childhood. Complete understanding of the message was the rule among the unprejudiced children listening to the *Old One Two* story. In contrast, practically all highly prejudiced children either failed completely or at least in part to understand the implied message, even though the prejudiced and unprejudiced children were equally intelligent. We recall that the main theme of the play dealt with the conflict between the prejudiced boy Willie and the other school children, caused by the former's prejudicial actions. It reached a climax in the fight and subsequent argument between the villain and Johnny, the loyal, tolerant hero. Yet in spite of the emphasis on the conflict and the reasons for the fight many of the prejudiced children, when asked to recall the story, managed to omit the conflict.

Others distorted the story in line with their prejudices. They either made the villain a member of a minority—"only minority group members can behave that badly"—or blamed Johnny for the fight—displaced the aggressive act from the majority to the minority member. In some cases the conflict is observed but the children manage to overlook its real cause or tend to allot blame to both sides.

Resistance to understanding must be considered a defensive mechanism designed to protect the prejudiced listener's self-esteem.[18] Understanding of the message constitutes a threat to his self-image. The prejudiced members of the *Old One Two* or the *Biggott* audience cannot keep their self-respect and identify with the villains in the stories, who behave undemocratically or are altogether ridiculous. Such identification is particularly difficult for the *Biggott* audience. Mr. Biggott not only behaves in a prejudicial and undemocratic fashion but is drawn as old-fashioned and ridiculous. The prejudiced person looking at the cartoons knows himself to be different. It might have been better to show the evils of prejudice without making the prejudiced person altogether detestable and too different from the average prejudiced individual.[19]

THE BOOMERANG EFFECT

We must also avoid the opposite extreme of making the prejudiced villain too desirable lest the audience sympathizes with the prejudiced individual rather than his victim. When propaganda reaches the opposite effect from the one intended, we speak of a boomerang effect. The movie, *Tomorrow the World,* dealt with a Nazi boy adopted by a well-to-do Connecticut family. In keeping with Nazi ideology the villain here attempts to drive a wedge between his foster parents by telling them lies about each other, attempts to inveigle his school class against their Jewish school teacher, leads it to gang up on a Polish boy. In the end, he is saved and converted through the efforts of his foster sister, who is almost killed in the attempt.

Interviews of a prejudiced adolescent audience indicated that they preferred the Nazi boy with whom they tended to identify themselves, because he had the guts to revolt against parental authority, one of their secret desires. Because of his ultimate conversion they considered the Nazi as the hero and were apparently more impressed and intrigued with the bad boy who finally sees the errors of his ways than with a character like the sister who has always been good and moral. The audience felt that the villain could not be blamed because he only acted in conformity with parental teachings, with what he had learned before coming to America.[20]

One may also suspect that the showing of cruelty against a weak victim attracts rather than repulses many prejudiced persons. Prejudiced individuals were found often to suffer from repressed hostility channelized against minority groups. In showing the effects of persecution on its victims we permit vicarious gratification of the very same sadistic impulses, bring hidden desires to the surface. There also is the yet unproven possibility that to the extent that the prejudiced individual disapproves of prejudicial actions, the implied suggestion that he is not any better than the cruel perpetrators of discriminatory and hostile acts, may tend to make him feel guilty. To avoid guilt feelings, he prefers to project guilt upon the minorities and hold them responsible for their being persecuted.

The prejudiced personality was found to be weak and in need of majority support. If he is shown how the minorities are persecuted, he also learns that others share his feelings and act as he would like to act. The mass persecution of minorities, so to speak, sanctions his own feelings: "so many people cannot be wrong." Hence it is perhaps better to accentuate progress in the fight against prejudice and for democratic ideals, to show public agreement of the necessity and desirability of fighting prejudice. The prejudiced person, we recall, needs to conform more than the unprejudiced, to get on the bandwagon.

LIMITATIONS OF MASS PROPAGANDA

In view of the great difficulties encountered in reaching a prejudiced audience, in making them listen and understand anti-prejudice messages, one may question the value of mass propaganda against prejudice. Some researchers report that single films such as the pro-Chinese film *Son of Gods*[21] or *Gentleman's Agreement*[22] created a more favorable attitude toward the Chinese or Jews. The movie about the Chinese, however, was shown at a time (1933) when Americans were not very hostile toward the Chinese. The slightly more favorable attitude created by the movie *Gentleman's Agreement* was apparently of short duration.

Even where change occurs it appears to be restricted to a reduction in stereotyping or the imparting of information about minority groups. Education may lead to mere verbal learning rather than the acquisition of deeper lying, more tolerant attitudes. Much intergroup education, though not necessarily all, only succeeds in teaching children, as well as adults, to give the right, "democratic" answers on attitude questionnaires.

On the other hand some experts[23] suggest that the effect of mass propaganda can be counted not only in terms of the conversion of the prejudiced. It may strengthen the attitudes of the unprejudiced and make them more resistant to prejudicial propaganda. Prejudiced persons confronted with anti-prejudice mass propaganda may become more aware of the prevalence of opinions going counter to their beliefs and hence more reluctant to act upon their prejudiced attitudes. Mass propaganda is providing pro-tolerance forces with ammunition as well as motivation to act in the direction of their conviction. Exposure to such propaganda may give them the impression that public sentiment supports them rather than the enemy. Their subsequent greater activity in public discussions at work or in the circle of their friends may then influence the "fence sitters," those who do not feel strongly about the issue of prejudice and are ready to jump in either direction.

Finally, the study of propaganda has taught us that while a single unit of propaganda may have no or little effect, the combined effect of several units of propaganda, an educational campaign, is greater than the effect of the sum of the different units of propaganda. But no matter how small or large such effect may be, its total effect will be limited, mainly because it fails to answer the emotional needs of the prejudiced person, and can be avoided or resisted. Only where education is "real" education, emotional reeducation, can substantial progress in the fight against prejudice be expected.

SELECTED READINGS

1. Flowerman, S. H., "Mass Propaganda in the War against Bigotry." *Journal of Abnormal and Social Psychology,* 45:1, 1950.
2. Cooper, E., and Jahoda, M., "The Evasion of Propaganda: How Prejudiced People Respond to Anti-Prejudice Propaganda." *Journal of Psychology,* 23:3-14, 1947.
3. Citron, A. F., Chein, I., and Harding, J. S., "Anti-Minority Remarks, A Problem for Action Research." *Journal of Abnormal and Social Psychology,* 45:1, 1950.
4. Lee, A. M., "The Press in the Control of Intergroup Tensions." *Annals of the American Academy of Political and Social Science.* 244:144-151, 1946.

REFERENCES

1. Flowerman, S., "Mass Propaganda in the War against Bigotry." *Journal of Abnormal and Social Psychology,* 42:431, 1947.
2. Berelson, B., "The Effects of Print upon Public Opinion," in *Print, Radio and Film in a Democracy,* ed. Waples, D. University of Chicago Press, Chicago, Ill., 1942.
3. Burtt, H. E., *The Psychology of Advertising.* Houghton Mifflin, Boston, Mass., 1938, chap. V.
4. *Intergroup Relations in Teaching Materials.* American Council on Education, Washington, D. C., 1949.
5. Lee, A. M., "The Press in the Control of Intergroup Tensions." *Annals of the American Academy of Political and Social Science,* 244:144-151, 1946.
6. *The Radio Listener's Bill of Rights,* Anti-Defamation League of Bnai Brith, New York, 1948.
7. Flowerman, *op. cit.,* p. 433.
8. Bettelheim, B., Shils, E. A., and Janowitz, M., unpublished study.
9. Hartman, G. W., "A Field Experiment on the Comparative Effectiveness of 'Emotional' and 'Rational' Political Leaflets in Determining Election Results." *Journal of Abnormal and Social Psychology,* 31: 99-114, 1936.
10. Alpenfels, E., *Sense and Nonsense about Race.* Friendship Press, New York, 1946.
11. Citron, A. F., Chein, I., and Harding, J., "Anti-Minority Remarks: A Problem for Action Research." *Journal of Abnormal and Social Psychology,* 45:99-126, 1950.

12. Selltiz, C., *et al.* "The Acceptability of Answers to Anti-Semitic Remarks." *International Journal of Opinion and Attitude Research,* 4:389, 1950.

13. Saenger, G., *Factors Determining Audience Reaction to Controversial Material.* Paper delivered at the meeting of the World Association for Public Opinion Research, Tunbridge Wells, England, 1951.

14. Hovland, C. I., Lumsdaine, A. A., and Sheffield, F. D. "The Orientation Film: The Battle of Britain," in *The American Soldier, The Social Psychology of World War II.* Princeton University Press, Princeton, 1949, vol. III, chap. 2.

15. Cooper, E., and Dinnermann, H., "Analysis of the Film 'Don't Be a Sucker': A Study in Communication." *Public Opinion Quarterly,* Summer, 1951, pp. 243-264.

16. Cooper, E., and Jahoda, M., "The Evasion of Propaganda: How Prejudiced People Respond to Anti-Prejudice Propaganda." *Journal of Psychology,* 23:15, 1947.

17. Kendall, P. L., and Wolf, K. M., *The Personification of Prejudice as a Device in Educational Propaganda.* Bureau of Applied Social Research, Columbia University, and American Jewish Committee, New York, 1946, mimeographed.

18. Cooper and Jahoda, *op. cit.,* p. 15.

19. Kendall and Wolf, *op. cit.*

20. Saenger, G., *Audience Reactions to Controversial Material: A Study of the Effects of Anti-Prejudice Propaganda.* Unpublished study.

21. Peterson, R. C., and Thurstone, L. L., *Motion Pictures and the Social Attitudes of Children.* Macmillan, New York, 1933.

22. Rosen, I., "The Effect of the Motion Picture 'Gentleman's Agreement' on Attitudes toward Jews." *Journal of Psychology,* 26:525-536, 1948.

23. Srole, L., *Private Communication.*

CHAPTER 13

THE DYNAMICS OF RE-EDUCATION

The limitations of the approach through mass propaganda originated largely in its inability to meet the needs of the prejudiced person. The adoption of tolerant behavior toward ethnic and racial minorities would have brought the individual into conflict with his immediate environment. To the extent that prejudice caters to the psychological needs of the prejudiced person, to that extent must successful re-education enable the prejudiced person to live at peace with himself and his environment.

RE-EDUCATION AND PSYCHOTHERAPY

Attempts to re-educate the prejudiced individual whose prejudices arise from personality factors resemble in many, though by no means all respects, the task facing the psychotherapist trying to help a maladjusted person. Neurotic patients can often be cured through gaining insight into the nature of their problems, through realization of the reasons for their behavior.

The ambitious man who thwarts his own progress by making derogatory remarks about others and acts in a generally hostile way toward them may be made to realize that his actions are the result of repressed feelings of inferiority. He makes others small in order to feel bigger himself. If he complains that nobody loves him, he must be made to understand that they perhaps only react to his failure to give of himself. He acts selfishly because he unconsciously feels he has nothing to give.

He must be made to realize that he feels that others are better and hates them for their superiority as well as their unwillingness to do enough for him. But since such insight is damaging to his self-esteem it will be avoided at any price. Hence the patient usually fails to gain insight by himself, may need the support of the therapist who can reassure him of his own worth and help him to build up his ego. In a similar manner, a build-up of the prejudiced person's ego makes it

190

easier to re-educate him and permits him to gain insight into the functions of prejudice in his own personality. His increasing self-esteem lessens his need to blame others for his own shortcomings.

In the psychotherapeutic process we often have to contend with much anxiety and more or less repressed hostility. These may even be temporarily aggravated when the patient begins to gain insight into his repressed feelings of which he is ashamed and prepares to adopt new and unfamiliar patterns of behavior. To be robbed of one's defenses is a painful process which is resisted. Progress may be blocked until there is an opportunity for the release of aggression, for "catharsis." Advances can often be made only after the hostility arising against the analyst and the world generally is sufficiently expressed and hence diminished. We do not see things easily if we are angry and feel under attack.

Successful intergroup education as well as successful psychotherapy must permit the individual to see himself and the world around him in a more realistic fashion. It, too, will lead to expressions of hostility directed perhaps toward the teacher as well as the minorities. After we release our hostility, after we become able to approve of ourselves and to live with ourselves, we are able to get out of our neurotic isolation and better understand others and get along with them.

Progress in psychotherapy takes times and patience as well as a skillful therapist. How long it will take depends on the severity of the illness as well as the obstacles which the patient faces. The situation again is similar for re-education against prejudice, except for the perhaps even greater role of environmental factors. The greater the extent to which prejudice is based on personality factors, the more unfavorable the social and economic conditions of the prejudiced, and the more prejudiced his environment, the more difficult and long lasting will be the process of re-education.

ROLE OF THE SCHOOL

Perhaps the most ideal place for such re-education though by no means the only one is the school. Scout groups, churches, recreational centers may easily perform a similar function, but usually occupy a smaller amount of the child's time. School gets the prejudiced person when he is still young and easily influenced, when economic and social factors do not play as large a role as in adulthood. The school can integrate democratic living and democratic education, provide an atmosphere where democratic living is the norm and the person is not rewarded for being prejudiced. It can strengthen the personality of the child and thus lessen his need to have recourse to prejudice now and in his later life.

The effectiveness of school education in human relations depends on the provision of adequate organization and leadership. School administrations must identify themselves with the fight against prejudice and discrimination, express their belief in democratic practices, and openly plan for the reduction of prejudice and discrimination within the limits of their power.

Unless the school administration is oriented in terms of intergroup education, really believes in it rather than pays mere lip service to the ideals of democratic education, not much progress is to be expected. In assessing school policies, we need to know the guiding philosophy of the school, whether the school board is liberal or conservative and supports democratic efforts in intergroup relations.[1] An exhaustive study of seven major school systems by Brameld revealed that administrative policies in American school systems range from a "direct, forthright attack upon minority problems, through a twilight zone of uncertainty, to an opposite policy almost completely opposed to direct attack of any kind."[2]

Even where the central administration is convinced of the necessity of a vigorous attack on the problem, administrators in lower echelons are in a position to sabotage an effective program of re-education. In one of our largest manufacturing cities with a population of more than one million inhabitants, which possessed a good philosophy of intergroup education on the top administrative level, about one half of all school "principals believed that the best answer to the question of how to deal with the interracial issue is 'Don't bring it out.' "

Such sabotage is often rationalized by educators who say that no real problem exists in their community or neighborhood: They explain that a program of intergroup education would only bring the problem to public attention, "make children aware of racial and ethnic differences" and thus "do more harm than good." Apart from the fact that the children in such communities usually tend to be aware of ethnic cleavages and consider others not only as different but as inferior, a good program can never do any harm. It not only clarifies the extent and causes of existing differences, but also teaches the child to evaluate differences in a positive and more favorable light.

Opposition to intergroup education often renders the whole program ineffective by adopting educational programs which fail to bring the problem out into the open. A favorite technique here is the concentration on the "contributions" approach, particularly when the various minorities are discussed in terms of their past history and contributions rather than their present situation and problems. Prejudice is not tackled by discussing the biblical history of the Jews or the contributions of the Germans to the War of Independence.

Administrative failure to institute a promising system of intergroup education may be due to the desire not to get into conflict with the more or less prejudiced community or its leaders. In most communities school boards are made up of conservative business or professional leaders, usually adherents to the status-quo.[3] They are dependent upon the taxpayer, the community.[4]

No educator can accomplish much against the opposition of the community on which he is financially and politically dependent. An educational program which is too progressive for the prevailing climate of opinion may be doomed to failure. This does not mean that educators should be afraid to initiate progress. Ideally, educators should be leaders rather than followers. While the good leader will not move at a pace faster than his followers are willing to, it is his task to initiate change. In practice, even unprejudiced educators are often afraid to promote a vigorous program of intergroup education even within the framework of the possibilities existing in their respective communities.

In view of the existing dependency of the school administrator on school boards and the community at large it is often wise if the initiative toward the institution of an expanded program of intergroup education rests with civic groups in the community itself. In the above mentioned community a "Committee on Intergroup Education" was set up in 1943 at the "instigation of a liberal citizens' group" to combine the diverse activities of many interested groups, and to interpret school interracial policies to the community. Having achieved the approval of the superintendent of schools, it included in its membership not only teachers and the president of the parent-teachers council, but also representatives of such diverse organizations as the Union of Social Agencies, the NAACP, the League of Women Voters, the Council of Churches, and the central Labor Union.[5] Such broadening of the "leadership necessary for the building of a good program in intergroup education" should extend into the school system itself. Committees of teachers and students, may be asked to cooperate in the planning and execution of programs.[6]

PERSONALITY AND ATTITUDES OF THE TEACHER

It is obvious that the success of intergroup education in the schools rests primarily on the personality of the teacher, his attitudes and skills. The average teacher shares the traditional prejudice of his community. While he received more education, is often especially indoctrinated to suppress his own prejudiced attitudes in the classroom, his real sentiments may often, intentionally or unintentionally, reveal themselves in the treatment he gives to children whose economic and ethnic background differs from his own. Most teachers are majority members recruited from the lower middle class and share the basic outlooks of their group. Hence they may prefer the behavior exhibited by children coming from their own group and consider the different behavior patterns of lower class or minority children as undesirable.

If they themselves have not suffered from prejudice and discrimination, they may be unable to understand the reactions of minority children to their experiences, become impatient:

> Feelings derived from situations in which racial or cultural groups meet discrimination or segregation are not by any means the most significant kinds of feeling to many teachers in many schools. The only reason they deserve full and careful explanation is that they are not feelings shared by most middle class Caucasian teachers. Expressed explosively in protest, often with a sense of grievance, they mystify and shock many teachers. Unaware of having offended, teachers retaliate by saying these students are "unreasonable, unfair, hypersensitive."[7]

Moreover, there are elements in the lives of many teachers which tend to lead to the accumulation of repressed hostility so conducive to the development of prejudice, which may easily lead to displaced aggression toward minority children. Particularly in smaller communities teachers enjoy little prestige, earn small salaries, are told by the parents how to live. Excessive insistence on conformity and exemplary moral behavior in teachers may add to their frustration, prevent self-expression. Yet the better adjusted the teacher, the more sensitive will she be to the needs of her children, and the greater will be her potential effectiveness in accomplishing her objectives.

We cannot reasonably expect school systems to pick teachers on the basis of their general psychological adjustment, institute a mental hygiene program, or modify excessive demands concerning the behavior of teachers inside and outside of school. Yet we should, through in-training courses, attempt at least to attack the prejudices of the teachers. Only the teacher who believes what she teaches can be really effective in reducing prejudices among her pupils. Children are influenced not so much by what is said, but by how it is said. More than adults they see through pretensions and react to people's feelings rather than words. They are sensitive to minute gestures, inflexions of the voice of the adult. The teacher of intergroup relations, therefore, must be sincerely convinced of the basic equality of different ethnic groups and not pay mere lip service to the ideals of democracy.

SCHOOL AND COMMUNITY

Equally important as the school setting and its personnel is the relation between school and community. It is difficult to conduct good intergroup relations programs without the support of the community, and almost impossible if there is active opposition. Even provided that a given community is not directly hostile to intergroup education, great difficulties may have to be surmounted in order to achieve active participation. The community has to be aware of the danger of prejudice to democracy and community living. It needs to recognize the potential contribution the school can make to the release of tension and prejudice, and should have at least rudimentary information about the methods of intergroup education. The community needs to be mobilized in the direction of an acceptance of intergroup education. Such mobilization may lead to the gathering of further information on techniques of intergroup education, and finally may lead to community pressure for action by the school. Only when all these conditions are fulfilled can active participation by the community be expected.

A rough analysis of the state of affairs prevailing in five Northern states indicated that only a small percentage of the population is aware of the dangers of prejudices and tensions to the democratic way of life and that an even smaller number recognize the potential contribution of the schools. Pressure for action by the schools was found to exist in not more than six communities in the five states, and only two actively participated in intergroup education at the time of the study.

The agency best equipped to provide the necessary cooperation between school and community is the Parent-Teacher Association. Other agencies which may coordinate their program with school programs are social and athletic organizations, social work agencies, church clubs and the YMCA or YWCA, boy scouts and girl scouts, which enjoy the respect and confidence of parents and children and in which the children spend a considerable amount of their time.

Unfortunately community-school cooperation in the field of intergroup education of organizations such as the PTA is rare. In one of our largest Midwestern cities only one fifth of all schools, twenty in number, had functioning PTA's and only one was active in the field of intergroup relations. Not one of the PTA's contained both Negro and white parents.[8]

Of all the factors tending to limit the effectiveness of intergroup education none is more important than the existence of discrimination and segregation in the school system or the community at large.[9] When we hear that the school which most constructively participated in Negro history week—by stressing the "similarity of all human beings" and "the contributions of all races and cultures to civilization"—was all white, we may wonder how the child reconciles his learning with the fact of segregation. Children are aware that segregation in schools, swimming pools, and dances is not voluntary and against the will of the excluded group.

To the extent that segregated patterns in education counteract the effect of school teaching, intergroup education needs to be synchronized with the abolition of segregation and discrimination in the school system itself. We must aim not only at the discontinuation of segregation in schools and recreational activities connected with them, but also at the integration of minority personnel in the school systems both among teachers and administrators. The effect of a warm, generous, generally liked Negro teacher may be greater than that of a dozen lessons dealing with racial equality. The contributions of different cultural groups can be discussed more fruitfully in a group in which members of different national origins are present than in a more homogeneous group.

Insofar as progress may be blocked by prejudiced parents it is necessary to integrate the school program with an efficient program in adult education eliciting the help of civic organizations wherever possible. Prejudiced parents are in an excellent position to nullify the gains made in school. Here again civic organizations may take the lead.

ASSESSING THE EMOTIONAL NEEDS OF THE CHILD

Provided we have set the stage for successful re-education, how can we best proceed? Re-education, we found, should aim at an improvement of intergroup living, because prejudicial behavior was found to be partially rooted in disturbances of human relations. Our first task consists in taking stock of the emotional needs of the children, the extent to which prejudices prevail in the classroom situation.[10]

One of the most efficient diagnostic techniques here is the sociometric approach,[11,12] which has been found eminently suited for work with school classes.[13] "Social belonging" as the adherents of this technique point out, "is a psychological necessity; the classroom atmosphere has a profound effect on children. All children need the approval of their age mates. They need to feel that they belong and are important to others. Children can be happy and secure in their sense of belonging to an age group, or unhappy and frustrated in their attempts at social participation."[14]

The method is designed to ascertain social relations in the classroom by finding out whom each child prefers as companions, whom he rejects and for what reasons. It tells us which child is most often chosen by others, and with which child nobody wants to associate. In analyzing the children's choices in terms of their racial and ethnic as well as class origin, the type of home they come from, we are able to ascertain the operation of ethnic and class prejudice within the class. Essentially the technique consists in having each child fill out a questionnaire containing questions such as:

1. With whom would you like to sit? (give three choices)
2. With whom would you like to work?
3. Whom would you like in the same club with you?

Together with further queries, like: "Why did you choose?" or "How did you happen to choose the persons named above?"[15] they enable us to find out whether each child is popular or rejected as well as the reasons for acceptance or rejection.

Many techniques are available to get insight into the problems, activities, and attitudes of the students in his class. Diaries, for example, can answer what the children do after school, give information about their routines and social habits, and insight into how they get along with other children or their parents. They indicate to what extent the home presents a warm and permissive as opposed to a cold, impersonal environment. Frictions at home as well as the child's feeling about his parents may be reflected in his relations to other children as well as her outlook toward life.

In addition to studying the children's personal problems, it is also necessary to find out the hidden and open prejudices of the students.[16] Where the teacher is familiar with the tensions existing in his class re-education can be more successful.

STRENGTHENING THE EGO

Having gained some insight, the next step in the process of re-education consists in the establishment of good human relations in the classroom by taking care of the problems of the individual children. A warm, sympathetic teacher can encourage the timid child and protect the child under attack. It is often possible to help the withdrawn isolated child or the child whose aggression is based on feelings of inferiority and rejection, if the traumatic experiences leading to his problems have not been too deep. Many children are in need of contact with others, require to be given and receive affection. To some extent the teacher may be able to help here by giving such children special attention, encouraging them, and discussing their problems with them.[17]

From a practical point of view a more feasible technique is the provision of contact with others through the establishment of small groups as, for example, panels entrusted with preparing material dealing with a special problem for classroom presentation. Cooperation in small groups provides all children with prolonged experiences in social interaction, permits them to accept and discharge responsibility. Rejected children who never before had an occasion to take over leadership roles are now given an opportunity to assert themselves. Through contributing to the success of the group, they tend to be accepted and hence experience closer feelings of belonging, which in turn may make it easier for them to give up some of their prejudices.

Many different activities have to be organized to permit the expression and utilization of the different talents found in the class. The boy who is unable to contribute to a panel discussion may be eminently suited to lead in sports or to give dancing lessons. The girl who had been a wallflower in school affairs may establish closer ties with the other children by taking a dominant role in the small discussion group working on the class assignment. If skillfully handled such panel discussions can be used simultaneously to improve human relations and to attack prejudice:

The first panel reported on suffrage today and in Washington's day. The children in that group had chosen Agnes as chairman, but Gladys turned out to be the leading force. She was a social outcast in this group and had never before taken a real part in school activities. When they discussed limitations on suffrage today, May, also on the panel, denounced Negroes as a group because they did not keep a clean house and because it was "her training" to dislike them. She was "brought up that way." Gladys quickly came to the defense of Negroes. There was a verbal free-for-all led by May on the one hand and Gladys on the other. In fact, I had to stop the lesson for a little instruction on how to discuss with "more light and less heat."

I had never seen children behave this way over an issue other than a very personal one. As soon as we talked over ways of casting "more light," Gladys ran to her desk, hauled out *One Nation,* and showed pictures to the class. She explained the pictures that bore out her argument. One was a picture of ramshackle houses. May seized this opportunity to accuse Negroes of neglect. The girls confronted each other, faces almost touching. Arms akimbo, Gladys asked May, "If you had only five dollars to buy food for your children or a tool to fix the porch, which would you buy?" May admitted she'd buy the food. Gladys then turned to the class and told of circumstances in her family not long ago when their ceiling was falling. She pointed out that only after several people in her family were able to find jobs was there money for household repairs. May was told she'd have to find better reasons for feeling as she did.

The next day the panel continued. By this time I realized that I would have to do something to protect May, for she laid herself wide open to attack and would only draw more rejection upon herself. . . ."[18]

May had been a child rejected by her family and unable to gain acceptance by her schoolmates which she very much desired. Having been rejected, she now rejected others. The intensity of her prejudice as well as her inability to establish social contact was related to her unfortunate home situation. Hence she felt on the defensive in the discussion, a condition which rendered her incapable of learning. She needed acceptance as well as an opportunity to release aggression.

CATHARSIS

Inside and outside school, people who feel themselves attacked will not benefit from education. In 1946 Gordon Allport was called upon to give a series of eight lectures to high members of the Police Department of one of our largest cities. The city had been plagued by outbreaks of violence between juvenile members of different racial and ethnic groups and police officials were to be taught modern methods of handling racial tension.

From the beginning, throughout the course the forty members of the group indulged in an aggressive, hostile, prejudiced discourse, directed sometimes against the teacher but more often against the various minority groups. These, as well as the press, were blamed for the disorders and accused of exaggerating the events necessitating the training course.

Their expressions of hostility partially reflected a reaction to the felt threat to the personal status of the officials: "Why do we need this course?" "Why do they pick on us?" were frequently heard comments. As experts they felt that they knew how to handle the situation and considered it an imposition that an outsider was going to tell them how to act. They tended to construe the very fact of being forced to take the course as a sign of public criticism, as being held responsible rather than those who created the disturbances. They suspected that the college professor would feel superior in a field in which they felt competent. To make things worse, underneath the surface there were hidden feelings of guilt for having been unable to cope efficiently with the problem, which had to be kept repressed in order to safeguard their self-esteem.

It is easy to see how the situation invited hostility toward the instructor as well as the course, which needed expression. We saw why people are in a better position to listen and to accept criticisms after they have let off steam, expressed and defended themselves. Feeling threatened, they needed reassurance and sympathy. The teacher had to reassure them that he could and did understand their just grievances, was on their side, before he could begin to explain that a defensive attitude did not solve the problem with which they were forced to deal.[19]

Similar support has to be given in the classroom situation. The teacher needs to be permissive. He must show the prejudiced child that he understands him and can see how it is difficult for anyone to change opinions which he has accepted as right all his life and which he had been trained to believe.

Whenever prejudice exists in a weakened ego, the building of self-confidence and good interpersonal relations is of major importance. Play therapy with school children, for example, led to a lessening of hostility after a frank expression of aggression had taken place.[20] It is obviously impossible to provide psychotherapeutic treatment to everyone who needs help. More realistic is the institution of an extensive mental hygiene program, which aims at the prevention more than the cure of maladjustment. A better adjusted population will be less prejudiced.

GROUP-ORIENTED EDUCATION

Re-education succeeds best if it is group oriented rather than aiming at the conversion of the individual. We tend to depend upon the opinions of our group, like to feel that we are in accord with group opinion. Particularly the more insecure individual hates to go against the attitudes of his group. A study undertaken during World War II showed that it was easier to change food habits through group discussion and decision than through individual education. The participating housewives were more likely to change when they all had agreed upon the new way of buying and cooking.[21]

When the group as a whole discusses the problems of prejudice without emphasizing the particular bias of the one or the other participant, the individual prejudiced member feels less under attack and finds it easier to accept the democratic message. When the group as a whole decides to give up prejudiced beliefs and to adopt new patterns of behavior the individual is likely to follow because he needs to conform in order to be accepted. Acceptance of the new idea brings with it the positive reward of group approval and is particularly strong if the individual feels that he himself took part in the group discussion and decision. He becomes emotionally identified with the change to which he contributed. For the same reason it is important that the teacher participate in such discussions only as a member of the group rather than an outside authority, as a person who may be consulted but not as an individual who tells others what to say and believe. The final decision, the adoption of new values and attitudes, should come from the group as a result of the work of the group.[22]

It is more difficult to change the opinion of the individual group member without achieving prior group change. The individual who would give up part of his prejudiced beliefs before the others are ready to do likewise would thereby get into conflict with majority opinion, be out of tune with the rest of the group. Particularly for the insecure person, the knowledge of such disagreement with group norms would be difficult to bear.

Much will depend here on the individual's closeness to the group. The more important the group for our well-being, the closer our identification with a group, the more important is it for us to agree with their main attitudes. A study of the students in a liberal New England girls' college coming from conservative homes showed that the adaptation of liberal attitudes took place mainly among girls who felt at home in the new setting. Those who were unable to make a satisfactory social adjustment also failed to give up their conservative attitudes.[23]

FINDING OUT FOR ONESELF

A change in attitudes is made possible through catharsis and the strengthening of the ego, facilitated by group support. The next step in the process of re-education consists in the discovery of the facts, to be followed by the accomplishment of greater empathy for the needs and problems of others. This process of "sensitization," showing us to what extent others are faced with the same problems as we ourselves, can finally be supplemented by the achievement of insight into prejudicial patterns of perceiving and thinking as well as our inner need for prejudice.

People remember best what they themselves discover. This is particularly true where the objective facts contradict previously held beliefs. It is much easier to disbelieve other people, teachers, experts, "who pretend to know better," than to distrust the evidence we unearthed ourselves. Sound re-education encourages the "student" to find things out for himself.

In school one may ask working committees of students to canvass the existing literature to find out more about groups about which widespread prejudices are held in their class or community. The pride of discovery will help them to accept what they have learned.[24]

Not long ago a small New England town experienced an influx of Mexican workers. When the issue was first brought up in the fourth grade of the local school, the children were encouraged to express their opinions freely. Class consensus was that they were "strange," "funny," and "did not belong in Westfield." Asked why they thought so, the children replied that they "could not speak English," "wore mustaches," "needed haircuts," "played guitars," were "brown skinned," "lived in dirty quarters."[25]

By and by the teacher asked them whether these were good enough reasons to look down on them, where they had obtained their information, and why they wore blankets to church or lived in undesirable quarters. The discussion revealed to the children that they were unfamiliar with the reasons for the behavior of the Mexicans. They discovered that many beliefs proved to be hearsay or insufficiently documented. "Slowly their laughing and giggling subsided and they became more thoughtful when they found out how little they really knew." Those who still contended that they could make the derogatory judgments they had advanced were asked further questions. "Are Mexicans the only ones who drink? Do others need haircuts besides the Mexicans? What is funny about playing a guitar? Do all people in Westfield speak English? Why do you speak English?" were among the main questions asked.

As the result of such skillful stimulation the class spontaneously asked for more information and decided to orient the social studies course around Mexico and the Mexicans. The authors report that the children were now much more impressed with the likeness rather than the difference, tended to admire rather than to despise the Mexicans:

Some children were so affected by this study that they planned how they would behave toward the Mexicans in the future. No matter what others did they decided that they would not stare at the Mexicans on the street or go peeking in their windows nor say unkind things about them either to their faces or to others. They did not condone throwing peanuts at the bald heads of Mexicans who happened to be in the theater or laughing at their looks. As one boy so aptly put it, "They can't help what they look like. They are human beings like us. I wouldn't like it if somebody laughed at me."[26]

COMMUNITY SELF-SURVEYS

The same basic principle of *finding out for oneself* forms the rationale of the Community Self-Survey, a novel technique developed to combat discrimination.[27] The community self-survey intends to lead to community action against discrimination upon the basis of the information collected by the members of the community themselves.[28] An intelligent attack on violations of civil rights can be initiated only when the extent and nature of the violations are known to those most in a position to act against discrimination wherever it is found, in housing or education, employment or public welfare. Hence the survey has to be initiated by a group of people who suspect that discrimination exists in their community and who want to see it reduced.

Such a group is usually small although it should include some influential individual citizens or organizations in a position to initiate action. Prejudiced individuals or groups may know about the existence of discrimination but choose to deny it in order not to be accused of sanctioning or condoning undemocratic practices. Others may feel ambivalent about the existence of discrimination and prefer to close their eyes to it in order to avoid conflict. Both groups can often be induced to participate by appealing to their democratic principles or their pride in their community. They may be told that one is interested in finding out how their community compares with others. If they state that their community is better than others or has practically no discrimination, one may explain to them that this fact alone would be worth demonstrating.

No community self-survey can succeed until it has obtained the sponsorship of all major influential groups in the community, people whose opinions and recommendations command respect and weight. In the dozens of communities which have conducted surveys, the sponsoring organizations usually included representatives of the major religious denominations, of management and labor, and the fraternal organizations.[29]

One of the most important features of this technique consists in the method of getting at the facts. Traditionally, communities faced with problems of such magnitude employed a group of outside experts to make a survey of their town or city. The result was often the production of a more or less technical report, unknown to most members of the community and considered as inaccurate or doing injustice to the particular conditions prevailing in the community by those opposed to changing the status quo. In the community self-survey in which the members of the sponsoring committee carry the major responsibility for its execution from its planning stage through its execution to the writing of recommendations for action, there is a considerable amount of personal involvement.* The members take pride in their work, identify themselves with the interpretations of the findings as well as the recommendations. While they may have challenged the findings and conclusions of the outside experts they are unlikely to challenge a report which they worked out in group discussions by themselves.

* Not that the work of the outside expert can be dispensed with. Some help may be needed in the construction of questionnaires and the tabulation of the results as well as the training of the interviewers. But the expert here makes no decisions; he is only available for consultation when and if needed. Moreover, the publication of a manual by the Commission on Community Interrelations which in its supplements includes copies of questionnaires for all conceivable purposes may make even the hiring of an expert unnecessary.[30]

In order to extend the benefits of the educational process to the largest number of people it is of vital importance to recruit a maximum number of community members for the project. Not only the interviewers, who go from house to house or plant to plant to interview a cross section of the population, but also the people who analyze and compute the data should live in the town where the survey is taken.

The interview process itself proves to be an emotionally satisfactory affair for the individual participant and thereby provides fertile ground for learning. The interviewer sees himself as a person engaged in a truly democratic enterprise, the spokesman of important and powerful groups in the community. He is engaged in an activity to help others, a fact which is appreciated by the respondents, who feel grateful for the interest taken in them. Since most people are inclined to feel friendly toward those for whom they do things, if for no other reason than that such altruistic activity enhances their self-esteem, conditions for maximum rapport are favorable.

The average interviewer finds it is interesting to come for the first time in face to face contact with people with whom he heretofore only had sporadic contact. He sees the home life of those people whom he had known before only as co-workers or people riding the same bus, tends to become sensitive to what it means to suffer from the effects of prejudice, to live in substandard housing. He learns to empathize with the Negro white collar girl, who tells him of her struggles to get an office job, the Italian who has difficulty in getting decent living quarters.

SENSITIZING THE CHILD TO THE NEEDS OF OTHERS

It is this process of *sensitizing* the prejudiced individual to the needs of others, the creation of empathy with members of different groups, which should constitute one of the major goals of a dynamic re-education. While community self-surveys provide such opportunities for a fairly limited time, their effectiveness is further restricted by the fact that only the more sympathetic and outgoing community members are likely to volunteer. Again the schools are in the best position to make the prejudiced individual aware of the problems of others. A first step here consists in providing the child with at least a modicum of insight into his own problems and the causes and reasons for his own actions. This is to be followed by a demonstration of the similarity of his own actions and reactions, problems and worries, with those of other children.

To increase the social sensitivity of children and adults alike is no easy task. We have seen how the inner needs of the individual make it difficult for him to identify with the underprivileged and outsiders in our own society, not to speak of people in distant regions or lands:

We can extend sensitivity only slowly and must begin with what is familiar and immediate. Thus no matter how we may wish children to appreciate what it means to be hungry and destitute in some far-off land or age, experimental study seems to give evidence that very few children get accurate concepts from teachings about the effects of starvation, plague and other disasters and major deprivations upon the lives and feelings of people. Social sensitivity begins with identification with the feelings of the child in the next seat or the neighbor in the next block. Extending it gradually so that it crosses social distance is a task that demands careful planning as the child develops new appreciation of himself and of people in his community, his state, his nation and the world.[31]

A first step in this process should consist in bringing feelings out into the open, in making people understand their own as well as the emotional reactions of others. Children as well as adults need to realize that all people feel anger, jealousy, fear in situations which frustrate them. They must be made to realize that only situations which are rewarding to the individual bring forth feelings of friendliness, trust, generosity. Our own actions as well as those of others are reactions to the way we have been treated. The understanding of our own problems is a condition for the understanding of others. Once we realize what kind of things make us angry or aggressive we are in a better position to understand what makes others angry or hostile.[32]

It is necessary to show students how it feels not to be accepted. Even among majority members we can find many individuals who have experienced rejection and are in a position to tell about it. One may, for example, ask the transfer students how they felt when they first came to the new school. Typical reactions recorded in this type of approach include: "You don't know what to expect," "You are afraid others will laugh at you," "It makes you feel not wanted, and you don't want to mix in where you are not wanted."[33]

To create empathy with immigrants one may link the problems of the immigrants more directly with the child's own background and experience by asking them to investigate the background of their own parents:

1. Who came and from what country?
2. Why they came?
3. Where they went?
4. What worries they had?

5. What they found here?
6. What kinds of work they found?
7. What adjustment they had to make?[34]

The last years saw the development of reading lists useful for the discussion of a great variety of human relations, patterns of family life and community patterns, economic differences and differences between generations, adjustment to new places and situations as well as experiences of acceptances and rejection: Novels and stories are classified in terms of the particular aspect of human relations which they tend to emphasize and selected for their value in initiating discussions. Acceptance and rejection is treated in a novel by Gladys Malvern, summarized in the bibliography:

Jonica, taken reluctantly as a bound girl by a wealthy New Amsterdam family, had to live down her father's unfortunate reputation. Despite suspicion and unmerited banishment to a distant household, Jonica struggled back to care for the Vandervoorts when smallpox struck them and thus proved her honesty and devotion. The story shows how an individual can demonstrate his belongingness by helping in times of need.[35]

Each section in the *Reading Ladders for Human Relations*[36] is preceded by a short explanation:

The stories on this ladder illustrate, in general, the three ways of reacting to these experiences of being left out: withdrawing into one's shell, adopting defensive and aggressive behavior, or learning how to interact with a group or individuals so as to become socially acceptable. . . . In general, these stories show not only the loneliness and isolation that an individual feels in being left out, but also the ways he may build those social skills which make him an acceptable and contributing member of groups.[37]

A more dramatic method used to sensitize students to the needs of others and at the same time to learn to understand each other better is the role-playing method or psychodrama.[38] The participating individuals are asked to take over the role of another person, with whom they are required to identify. The prejudiced majority member, requested to take over the position of the excluded minority student, may be in a better position to appreciate the latter's feeling and to understand his reactions than he would be if he had only listened to a discussion of the latter's problems.[39,40]

GAINING INSIGHT INTO FALSE PERCEPTION

A final step in the process of re-education may well consist of teaching the prejudiced individual to gain insight into the effects of prejudiced attitudes on his perception and thinking.[41] Realization of the operation of selection and distortion in perception, stereotyping, and projection can be introduced best by demonstrating these mechanisms in areas where the individual is not emotionally involved. If we are able to create a friendly atmosphere and to make the demonstrations amusing, we will avoid hostility and create an atmosphere conducive to learning. Guilt feelings can be avoided by showing that all people engage in these defensive mechanisms and perceive incorrectly.

Selective perception can easily be demonstrated by asking persons with different motivations to record what they noticed in the same setting. A young man and a young woman, a fashion expert and a college dean may note entirely different things while visiting a college class. Both men and women are likely to spend more attention to the opposite sex and note their faces and figures. The fashion expert may only observe their clothes and the dean the relative amount of attention they give to the lecture.

It would not be difficult to show how anti-Semites and relatively unprejudiced people arrive at different interpretations of the same pictures showing the interaction between Jews and Gentiles. We recall a similar experiment showing a clash between striking steel mill workers and the police. Those observers which favored management's position later recorded having seen a picture in which the police were attacked by the workers. The pro-labor observers noticed the police attacking the strikers.[42] Prior attitudes determined perception.

Even more dramatic is the demonstration of the operations of rumors. Four students may be sent out of the class, and the rest told a story which contradicts popular notions, for example of a woman who acts cool and courageous and a man who behaves in a cowardly and indecisive manner, during an automobile accident. The first student is then recalled and the story is read to him. He in turn tells the story to the second student called in next. In this fashion the story is transmitted from mouth to mouth in front of the class which has occasion to follow the consecutive distortions, omissions, and additions which the story undergoes. In the above example, for instance, the woman may become less daring, the man more and more in command of the situation. In a subsequent discussion the teacher can now explain the contribution of rumors to panics or race riots. A small fire may become a major conflagration, an altercation between a Negro and a white man may become enlarged to a major gang fight by the time the tenth person has heard and transmitted the story.[43]

STEREOTYPING AND PROJECTION

From here one may proceed to the demonstration of stereotyped perceptions and thinking. Again a neutral subject may be chosen to introduce the lesson. All students may be asked to close their eyes and

to think of the word "Roman," as in "Friends, Romans, countrymen . . ." A subsequent check-up following the request to all students to write down what they saw before their inner eyes tends to
indicate that the majority of the students saw a man rather than a
woman and an elderly rather than a young man. Our "Roman"
usually stands rather than sits or lies down and is invariably clothed
in a toga. Further trials using the words "Frenchman," "Italian,"
"businessman," "professor," "Jew,'" "worker" will complete the
series. The follow-up discussion would emphasize the common elements in stereotyped perception and thinking, with its characteristic
overgeneralization and lack of individuality.

To cast doubt upon the validity of most common stereotypes one
may want to familiarize the students with stereotypes others hold
about them. One may first ask them to report what the average American, Frenchman, or Englishman is like. They will be then told what
the average Frenchman or Britisher thinks about Americans as well
as about each other.

The discussion will emphasize the discrepancies which occur when
the same group, such as Frenchmen, are viewed by Americans, Eng-
lishmen, and finally by themselves. Taking up group for group one
may point out how unlikely it is that one group only, and coinci-
dentally one's own, has correct notions concerning all other groups.
Who knows the French best, the French themselves, the Americans,
or the British? How do we explain that foreigners have strange notions concerning Americans, while we know the truth about everyone?

We will finally be able to demonstrate the influence of projection
upon our perception of others. Even a relatively young person can be
made to understand how the angry boy is more likely to view others as
aggressive than the quiet boy, how we see others in terms of our own
needs and expectations. The man who raves about the beauty, gay-
ness, and dancing ability of his fiancee, may interpret all these as
signs of superficiality when she has jilted him. If I am pushing to
get into the crowded trolley car or bus I am only asserting myself
and trying to get to school on time; if someone else is pushing me
he is the aggressive, pushing type.

After this point has been made, it is only one further step to discuss how the same behavior which we call "*aggressive*, forward-look-
ing, getting ahead and advancing oneself" for members of our own
group, becomes "*aggressive*, mercenary, pushing, only interested in
themselves" for members of other groups whom we view as competitors.[44] What looks like loyalty and self-protection to the family

experiencing discrimination, appears as clannishness or unwillingness to mix to the prejudiced outsiders.

Attempts toward a dynamic re-education in the field of human relations are of relatively recent origin. Some have already been tried; others, like the above suggestions of ways to create insight into perceptual processes, are still in the planning stage. There has been as yet no systematic attempt to evaluate the success of various techniques in modifying attitudes and behavior.[45] Change may occur on the verbal level only, may be genuine or apparent, and may extend to the level of behavior. There are indications that given a sufficiently intensive and progressive program, led by a warm and well-adjusted teacher, success may be obtained even in such hostile climates as the South.[46]

But educational programs satisfying all these conditions are few and far between, partially as a result of resistances toward change among those who control or influence the school system, partially as a result of the lack of teachers trained in these new methods. We cannot really know the limitations of the effectiveness of intergroup education until we have tried to put into effect what we already know and test it.

A PROGRAM FOR EDUCATION

Yet it is possible to draw conclusions as to the proper role of formal education in a democracy. Education against prejudice must be considered an integral part of general education for citizenship in a democracy. Prejudice is irreconcilable with American ideals of the rights of the individual and of equal opportunity for all. Not only must we try to erase prejudice through education, but we should attempt to make our children resistant to prejudiced influences and propaganda in the same manner as we teach them to beware of foreign ideologies like communism and fascism.

Formal education must not be content with the mere teaching of facts about minorities. The children must be made aware of the evil consequences of prejudice for themselves and others, made aware of its widespread existence even in their own environment. They must be taught to detect prejudice. Applying modern methods in a variety of school subjects, the students must be taught to discover things for themselves, and to reject hearsay, rumors, and false perceptions. Successful immunization may well have its effects long after they leave school.

Effective teaching must proceed in a democratic setting. There must be no discrimination or segregation to counteract it. All groups must be fairly represented, particularly so among the ranks of teachers and administrators. The class room should be made a laboratory in democratic living, in which students learn how to take the initiative, to work together on cooperative projects.

Not only from the point of view of better intergroup relations, but in order to promote better human relations generally and to obtain a healthier citizenry, the school authorities should attempt to answer the emotional needs of their charges. Where possible, an organized program of mental health should be established. Even in its absence teachers can be trained to become aware of the emotional needs of their students and respond to them by providing opportunities which make them feel wanted and give them a sense of belonging. Through making the class members aware of their own needs and problems, they can be sensitized to the needs of others and learn to identify with them.

Finally, the school should attempt to reach the parents in order to avoid conflict between the teachings of the school and the parents. Through parents who are interested in the education of their children it is perhaps possible to involve and educate an adult group otherwise beyond the age of formal education.

SELECTED READINGS

1. Taba, H., and Elkins, D., *With Focus on Human Relations.* American Council on Education, Washington, D. C., 1950.
2. Heaton, M. M., *Feelings are Facts: An Intergroup Education Pamphlet.* National Conference of Christians and Jews, New York, 1951.
3. Brameld, T., *Minority Problems in the Public Schools.* Harper & Brothers, New York, 1946.
4. Harding, J., "Some Basic Principles of Self-Surveys." *Journal of Social Issues,* 5:2, 1949.
5. Lewin, K., and Grabbe, P., "Conduct, Knowledge and Acceptance of New Values." *Journal of Social Issues,* 1:3, 1945 (technical).

REFERENCES

1. Brameld, T., *Minority Problems in the Public Schools.* Harper & Brothers, New York, 1946, chap. VIII.
2. *Ibid,* p. 240.
3. *Ibid,* p. 239.
4. Cook, L. A., *College Programs in Intergroup Relations.* American Council on Education, Washington, D. C., 1950, vol. 1, p. 351.
5. Brameld, *op. cit.,* p. 12.

6. Bostwick, P., *Brotherhood Week*. National Conference of Christians and Jews, New York, 1951.
7. Heaton, M. M., *Feelings are Facts*. National Conference of Christians and Jews, New York, 1951, p. 25.
8. Brameld, *op. cit.*, p. 29.
9. Cook, L. A., "The Frame of Reference in the College Study." *Journal of Educational Sociology*, 21:31-42, 1947.
10. Taba, H., and Elkins, D., *With Focus on Human Relations*. American Council on Education, Washington, D. C., 1950.
11. Bostwick, *op. cit.*, p. 25.
12. Moreno, J. L., *Who Shall Survive?* Nervous and Mental Diseases Monographs, 1934, Series 58.
13. Jennings, H. Hall, *Sociometry in Group Relations*. American Council on Education, Washington, D. C., 1948.
14. Taba, H., Brady, E. H., Robinson, J. T., and Vickers, W. E., *Diagnosing Human Relations Needs*. American Council on Education, Washington, D. C., 1951.
15. *Ibid*, chap. 5.
16. Trager, H. G., and Radke Yarrow, M., *They Learn What They Live*. Harper & Brothers, New York, 1952.
17. Taba and Elkins, *op. cit.*, p. 36.
18. *Ibid*, p. 41.
19. Allport, G. W., "Catharsis and the Reduction of Prejudice." *Journal of Social Issues*, 3:3-10, 1945.
20. Axline, V. M., "Play Therapy and Race Conflict in Young Children." *Journal of Abnormal and Social Psychology*, 43:300-310, 1948.
21. Lewin, K., *Forces Behind Food Habits and Methods of Change in the Problem of Changing Food Habits*. Bulletin of the National Research Council, No. 108, Washington, D. C., 1943, pp. 35-65.
22. Lewin, K., and Grabbe, P., "Conduct, Knowledge and Acceptance of New Values." *Journal of Social Issues*, 1:53-64, 1945.
23. Newcomb, T., *Personality and Social Change*. Dryden Press, New York, 1943.
24. Brown, S., *They See For Themselves: a Documentary Approach to Intercultural Education in the High School*. Harper & Brothers, New York, 1945.
25. Merril, J. V., and Lesnizk, J. B., "From Prejudice to Straight Thinking in the Fourth Grade," in *Learning World Goodwill*. The National Elementary Principal, 25th Yearbook, 1946, pp. 160-164.
26. *Ibid*, p. 163.
27. Wormser, M. Haas, and Selltiz, C., *How To Conduct a Community Self-Survey of Civil Rights*. Association Press, New York, 1951.
28. Harding, J., "Some Basic Principles of Self-Surveys. *Journal of Social Issues*, 5:21-29, 1949.
29. Wormser, M. Haas, "The Northtown Self-Survey: A Case Study." *Journal of Social Issues*, 5:5-20, 1949.
30. Wormser and Selltiz, *op. cit.*, 5-20.

31. Heaton, *op. cit.,* p. 51.
32. Brown, *op. cit.,* pp. 37 ff.
33. Taba and Elkins, *op. cit.,* p. 155.
34. *Ibid,* pp. 146-152.
35. Malvern, G., *Jonica's Island.* Messner, New York, 1945.
36. Taba, H., *Reading Ladders for Human Relations.* American Council on Education, Washington, D. C., 1947.
37. *Ibid,* p. 49.
38. Moreno, J. L., "Psychodrama and Mental Catharsis." *Sociometry,* 3:209-244, 1940.
39. Shaftel, G., and Shaftel, F. R., "Report on the Use of a Practice Action Level in the Stanford University Project for American ideals." *Sociatry,* 2:243-253, 1948.
40. Lippitt, R., *Training in Community Relations.* Harper & Brothers, New York, 1949, chap. 9.
41. Lewin and Grabbe, *op. cit.,* pp. 57 ff.
42. Proshansky, H., "A Projective Method for the Study of Attitudes." *Journal of Abnormal and Social Psychology,* 38:393-395, 1943.
43. Lee, A. M., and Humphrey, N. D., *Race Riot.* Dryden Press, New York, 1943.
44. Asch, S. E., "Forming Impressions of Personality." *Journal of Abnormal and Social Psychology,* 41:258-290, 1946.
45. Rose, A., *Studies in the Reducation of Prejudice* (ed. 2). American Council on Race Relations, Chicago, 1948.
46. Simpson, F., "Teaching Racial Tolerance in the South," in *Improving Human Relations.* National Council for Social Studies, Bulletin 25, 1949, p. 87.

CHAPTER 14

CHANGING PREJUDICE THROUGH CONTACT

After a long and perilous expedition during the past war, a Southern officer on a submarine chaser was overheard saying, "Half way through the trip I forgot they were black."[1]

Attitudes may change through the mere experience of living together without any attempt at education. Education may often not even be the best way to tackle people's prejudices. Even the young child was found to be impressed with the discrepancies between the teachings of school and the realities of life. It was considered unlikely that he would learn to give up his prejudices if the adoption of new attitudes brought him into conflict with his prejudiced environment.

We compared the limited amount of time during which most individuals are exposed to the teaching of brotherhood inside and outside school, with the constant influence of the exposure to prejudice and prejudicial practices. Granted that good education, combining deeds and words with satisfaction of the emotional needs of the prejudiced pupil, may make a considerable dent in the solid wall of prejudice, such superior education was found to be rare.

There is reason to be sceptical about the likelihood of substantial improvements during the near future. Hence, we are interested in a better technique for the reduction of prejudice, and this is available in the provision of contact between the prejudiced and his victim.

HARMFUL AND BENEFICIAL CONTACTS

Not all types of contact will lead to a reduction of prejudice. Biased individuals claim that their unfavorable attitudes toward minorities are the result of unpleasant experiences. While we have seen that prejudice makes us perceive minorities in an unfavorable light, it is unquestionably true that some experiences reinforce prejudices and others help to erase them. The same naval officer who was favorably impressed with the Negro members of his crew, may have found his prejudice reinforced if forced to ride side by side with Negroes during the crowded rush hour in a New York subway train.

Contact may be harmful where competition along racial or ethnic lines is prevalent, for example, competition for jobs. A Jewish and a Protestant student studying together for an examination in college may be expected to view each other more positively than the same students competing with each other for medical school. One of the worst incidents in the armed forces during World War II was reported from Guam where a group of white Marines fired on a group of Negro sailors and ran them from the main town of the island because of their attention to local Guamian girls.[2] Race riots, we noted, tend to break out where contact is close, involuntary, and provocative, where minority members move into an overcrowded neighborhood hitherto occupied by majority members, or on a hot, sultry day on an overcrowded beach.

A main condition of favorable contact lies in the rewarding character of the contact experience. Rachel DuBois hit upon the idea of bringing together mothers from different ethnic groups in a high tension area for the purpose of celebrating public holidays such as Thanksgiving. Coming from different cultural and religious backgrounds, the participants discussed how the holiday was celebrated in their homeland or the part of America from which they came. From holidays the talk shifted to other aspects of life, child rearing and courtship, the preparation of food.

Such cooperation is emotionally rewarding. Reminiscing about childhood creates a pleasant mood and adds to mutual understanding through the discovery of many similarities and common problems. The fact that everybody is asked to contribute raises their self-esteem. The pride in the uniqueness of one's own culture, which develops as the result of the interest of the other participants, counteracts negative feelings about one's own group often found to be a source of the need for prejudice among minorities. The mothers benefited by learning new songs or cooking recipes useful in pleasing children or husbands.[3]

An attempt to foster understanding between the nations as well as between different racial and ethnic groups is made by the "International Houses" found near the campus of famous universities in New York, Chicago, and Berkeley. Each house provides dormitory space and recreational facilities for several hundred students of all races and from all nations. During an average year they house students from forty to fifty different countries in addition to Americans from all parts of the nation. Beautifully situated and tastefully equipped, the houses provide a rich and varied educational and entertainment program; from discussion groups on world affairs and religion to concerts and dances; from sports to formal Sunday dinners followed by addresses of nationally famous speakers. The students (chosen from the large list of applicants) are selected for their potential contribution to International House living as well as their ability to utilize the experiences of international contact and acquaintance with the problems of different lands in their future careers.

The experience of living in the houses is rewarding and may explain why even prejudiced students from the South or from regions outside the United States prefer to live there. There has been practically no trouble of any serious form in the associations between members of different races and ethnic groups. On the contrary, many students are said to have acquired a more tolerant and understanding attitude toward members of other groups and other races. Unfortunately, the effectiveness of this type of contact is limited by the small number of similar institutions and the fact that the students living in the house represent a selected group.

PREDISPOSITION FOR CHANGE

The importance of the interaction of environmental and personality factors was demonstrated by the effects of contacts between Negroes and white boys from New York who attended an interracial summer camp. The white group as a whole did not change its attitude toward Negroes. Those boys who made a good adjustment to the camp situation tended to acquire a positive attitude toward the Negro boys.

On the other hand, those who did not find the camp experience rewarding and felt frustrated, tended to become more rather than less prejudiced. The children whose prejudices increased were characterized by strong aggressive feelings and the need to defy authority, as well as a generally unfavorable view of society, which were displayed toward the Negroes who furnished a convenient target.[4] The manner in which we experience our environment as well as our inner needs determines at least in part whether contact has a beneficial or detrimental effect.

The influence of changes in environment and psychological adjustment in bringing about changes in attitude was highlighted by an exploratory study of a cross section of the Queens Borough population of New York City. Mail ballots were sent to 2500 residents of the borough asking the recipients whether their feelings toward Jews or Negroes had changed at any time during their life.* A move

* Altogether 460 people replied. After eliminating those whose attitudes had not changed, who did not sign their name, or could not be reached for other reasons, 45 people were selected for intensive interviews. Considering the nature of the sample, the project does not permit conclusions about the population as a whole but only yields tentative suggestions for further study.

toward a more liberal attitude tended to be associated with leaving the parental home, taking one's first job, going to college, or joining the army. Such change coincided with the move from adolescence to adulthood, a period in our life where we tend to free ourselves from the values of our childhood environment and tend to re-evaluate parental teachings.

Changes of residence also were an important factor in the modification of attitudes. Northerners moving South tend to become more prejudiced, Southerners settling in the North less prejudiced towards Negroes. Moving not only brings us into contact with different types of minority members but also with different attitudes. Finally, increased emotional satisfaction, a rise in prestige and status, were frequently found to be associated with improved attitudes toward Jews and Negroes.[5]

Changes in personal satisfaction may be the results of accidents in the person's life history or be inherent in the contact situation. Some contact situations are gratifying and others punishing. Favorable attitudes are most likely to occur when people work together toward the accomplishment of a common goal. Negroes and whites working together in the same union committee, Italians and Irish on the same tenant committee tend to like each other, provided the group accomplishes its objectives. Otherwise it is possible that members of the other group are blamed for the failure. This danger is, of course, minimized where a committee of long standing has undergone a long series of successes as well as failure.[6]

In bringing together members of different racial and ethnic groups it is always preferable to emphasize the common goal rather than the establishment of better relations between the groups. An interracial camp or brotherhood week meeting established explicitly for the purpose of improving human relations often tends to succeed only in making its members self-conscious and to put the more prejudiced participants on the defensive. The members of the minority may feel humiliated by the emphasis on race relations or feel that they must be on their best behavior. Majority members may feel uncomfortable in the thought of being there in order to learn more democratic attitudes and to lose their prejudices, whose existence they may deny.

In a camp experience the emphasis should be on the enjoyment of vacations, in a "mixed" labor management committee on the common task of improving industrial relations. A civic council with representatives from different ethnic groups located in a mixed neighborhood may concentrate its effort primarily on an improvement of recreational and school facilities. Orientation to the common goal is more likely to make us see the members of other groups as individuals with interests common to our own rather than as members of a different group toward which we are prejudiced.

EQUAL STATUS CONTACTS

Of major importance is the choice of the participants in interracial contact. Moderately prejudiced persons having no neurotic need for their prejudice may be more likely to benefit from contact than highly prejudiced individuals.

To the extent that high status and prestige are related to the likelihood that we may develop more tolerant attitudes, the position of the individual within his own group may need to be considered. Where different groups associate, the more secure majority person, who enjoys prestige and status in his own group, is more likely to benefit from contact. Within each group the leader rather than the follower is in a better position to change. He needs less to conform and, being more secure, is less likely to envy members of the other group.

There is substantial agreement that contact between two ethnic groups is most likely to have positive results when they are of equal status, when middle class Negroes mix with middle class whites or upper class Protestants with upper class Jews.[7] People of equal status have a common outlook toward life, similar manners, share the same interests. We have seen that ordinarily a majority of white middle class persons meet only lower class Negroes, who serve to reinforce their stereotyped beliefs that all Negroes are dirty, dumb, and emotional. Experiences along equal status lines tend to run counter to the stereotypes of the prejudiced individual.

Equal status contact is not experienced as either degrading or humiliating by the participating groups, does not constitute a threat to the participants. When an upper class member of the majority is brought into contact with a lower class member of the minority, we may easily activate his class prejudices in addition to his ethnic prejudice. Nor is the lower class member always happy about unequal status contact. While it may perhaps flatter him, it also tends to arouse more or less conscious envy, mobilizes feeling of inferiority and resentment about the imagined or real condescension of the majority member.

While equal status contact is generally the most desirable, there may be exceptions depending upon the nature of the stereotypes held by the majority, as well as the satisfaction derived from the situation. A few years ago a group of forty-six students from Teachers College responded to an invitation to spend two week-ends on a conducted tour through Harlem, which included visits to the theatre, lectures by prominent Negroes, teas and dinners in the homes of Negro writers and artists. The visitors showed a decided increase in friendly attitudes toward the Negroes, which was found to persevere for at least a year.[8] *

The meeting with upper class minority members tended to contradict the usual stereotypes about Negroes as lower class. Whatever envy may have arisen about the better standard of living among the middle class students was overshadowed by the unanticipated behavior of the prominent Negroes and the enjoyment derived from meeting celebrities and being royally and amusingly entertained. Similar results were obtained when residents of Boulder, Colorado, were asked how they felt about the Japanese in their community. Considerable improvement in attitudes occurred after a number of Japanese-American language instructors had resided a few years in the town.[9]

We may not necessarily obtain the same results when prejudiced middle class Protestant students meet with upper class Jews. If they believe Jews to be rich and running the country, contact with well-to-do Jews may reinforce their original stereotypes and lead to feelings of envy and resentment. They may feel that they, rather than the Jews, should have first call on positions of renown and prominence. Much depends on the specific beliefs held by the prejudiced. If they believe all Jews to be bankers they may benefit from visiting the poor Jews on the lower East side. If they think that most Jews are low class communists, noisy and unwilling to assimilate, a visit with conservative, cultured upper class Jews may be beneficial.

The real complexity of the factors influencing the effects of contact is illustrated by the experiences of a Jewish college professor who bought a house in a neighborhood known for its anti-Semitism. He first met with aloofness and slight suspicion, was held to be snobbish. A dent in the neighborly reserve appeared when he attempted to plant flowers in his garden, a skill which the academician did not possess to a marked degree. After a short period the neighbors, whose egos were bolstered by the apparent inability of the professor in areas in which they felt competent, came to his help. Sometime later the professor was in a position to help when one of the neighbor's children got into trouble. Each one had something to contribute and learned to appreciate the other. The neighbors learned that the professor was not as superior as they had thought. They had been looking for manifestations of the type of behavior which would verify their original prejudiced beliefs and it took intimate association over a period of time before close relationships were established.

* Both the experimental and a control group matched for degree of prejudice and socioeconomic characteristics took attitude tests prior to the visit of the experimental group, soon after the visit, and eleven months later.

DEGREE OF INTIMACY

Superficial contact is not sufficient to produce a general change in attitude. A study of college students indicated that anti-Semitism increased with the frequency of personal contact, but tended to decrease when the contact was of a more intimate type presumably designed to give a fuller picture of the person. But even intimate contact is most likely to reduce prejudice, mainly if it counteracts prejudicial stereotypes. Students in a socially prominent Eastern college tended to develop increased prejudice against Italians within the school with whom they became intimately acquainted. The Italians' more "emotional attitude" toward life, the result of yet incomplete assimilation, were presumably considered as undesirable by our "old" Americans whose upbringing permits less expression of "emotionality."[10]

When we find that white salesgirls in department stores working side by side with Negro salesgirls do not develop a more positive attitude toward Negroes than others not subjected to similar experiences, we may again suspect that the contact was perhaps not close enough.[11] The group of white salesgirls who had worked with Negro salesgirls differed from another group not having had that experience only in so far as they were willing to take a new job in which white and colored people were doing the same type of work. No general change in attitude developed.

In most jobs one does not have an opportunity to see the whole personality of one's partner. At work many people more or less tend to play a role and not to present themselves as they really are. There is also the possibility that white workers may perceive the Negroes as competitors.

One may surmise, therefore, that contact related to one's leisure-time activities, sports, and recreation, may be more beneficial. Particularly valuable is the potential benefit of mixed teams in competitive sports. Competition occurs between the teams, whereas members of different racial or religious groups cooperate with each other within each team. In games between the Dodgers and Giants, both players and audience tend to see Jackie Robinson as a Dodger rather than as a Negro.

Of all aspects of life providing an opportunity for contact, none is as all-encompassing as housing. We tend to be more concerned about the persons with whom we live than about the persons with whom we work or worship, sit together in school or in the movie. We spend more time at home, are more ourselves than on almost all other occasions. It is difficult, if not impossible, to avoid meeting one's neighbors. Housing provides one of the few opportunities for interracial contact, intimate and prolonged enough to lead to general changes in attitudes.

The growth of public housing during the last ten years has given an opportunity to study the effect of such interracial housing. A sufficient number of racially mixed housing projects has been built to enable us not only to study the effects of mixed housing on attitudes, but also to give an answer to the proponents of segregation in public housing who state that trouble would result when Negroes and whites live as neighbors and that a policy of nonsegregation is not feasible.

INTEGRATED AND SEGREGATED INTERRACIAL HOUSING

Interracial housing in the United States is of two types. There are segregated housing projects in which Negroes and Whites live in different parts of the project or at least in different houses within the project. An example of the last type is the so-called checker-board system in which "white" and "Negro" houses are arranged in alternating order. In the "integrated interracial" projects, however, Negro and white families live in the same houses, often on the same floors. Assignment of an apartment is made solely on the basis of the date of application. Eligibility is determined by income and priorities (e.g., for veterans) without regard to race and religion.

The existence of segregated and integrated housing projects in the metropolitan area of New York which differed only in regard to the occupancy pattern provided an opportunity of studying the effects of the two major types of interracial housing through interviews of a cross section of the tenants. Deutsch and Collins and their interviewers talked to roughly 100 housewives in each of two segregated and two integrated projects.[12] They found that the inhabitants of both groups of houses came roughly from the same socioeconomic background, included similar proportions of educated and uneducated people, and held similar attitudes toward Negroes prior to their moving into the project. If anything, more housewives who had previously held unfavorable attitudes toward Negroes were found in the integrated projects, hence any differences in attitudes occurring as the result of a few years of living in the project should be attributed to the contact experience.

The two types of housing projects differ in important aspects. In the segregated housing projects the institution of segregation appears to constitute official sanctioning of the practice. In the context of the history of race relations in the United States segregation connotes the idea that Negroes are inferior and should not associate with the superior whites.

In the integrated projects, on the other hand, we find implied an official sanctioning of interracial association on the basis of complete equality. In such projects more opportunities exist to meet members of the other race in hallways or elevators, at the laundromats or the benches in front of the houses.

The results of these differences in occupancy patterns were pronounced. In "Koaltown" and "Sacktown," the integrated projects, white and Negro tenants soon develop close neighborly relations. They visit back and forth, help each other with shopping and taking care of the children. They join together in informal club activities, such as card or ironing clubs, even go to the movies together.

Not only are there fewer opportunities for meeting in the segregated projects, but whatever opportunities exist are not used for getting acquainted: "They stay on their side and we stay on our side. We're in separate parts," explains a housewife from the separated "Bakerville" where a broad street divides the project into the colored and white section.[13]

IMPORTANCE OF SOCIAL NORMS

Close neighborly contact between Negro and white families in the integrated projects is not only the result of the greater opportunity to get acquainted, but is determined also by the *social norms* implicit in integration or segregation as manifested in the administrative policies of the housing authority.

As a result of these differences in policy considerably more white women in the segregated project express ideas such as: "It's best for colored and white not to mix," "We should stay on our side and they should stay on their side." In addition there is more frequent spontaneous mention of social pressure not to mix exerted by other whites in the segregated projects:

"They'd think you're crazy if you had a colored woman visit you in your home. They'd stare at you and there'd be a lot of talk." Another said, "I used to be good friends with a colored woman who worked with me at Westinghouse before I moved here. She lives on the other side of the project but I never have her over to my apartment—it just isn't done. Occasionally I go over and visit her."[14]

Social pressure in the integrated project runs in the opposite direction: "They resent you if you are not friendly. You are liable to find yourself in plenty of trouble around here if you try to be snooty."[15] Bakerville and Frankville are characterized not only by better relations between Negroes and white families, but by a warmer, more cordial and cooperative spirit pervading the project as a whole. There is more visiting between whites, more community sponsored activities. Perhaps the feeling of being different from the prejudiced outside world throws the tenants in the integrated projects closer together. The white women have the same problems. What does one do when the prejudiced mother-in-law drops in for a visit and one does not want to offend the Negro friend next door? How does one reconcile one's behavior inside and outside the project?

Table 9. Neighborly Contacts, Feelings toward Negro People, and Beliefs Concerning Racial Differences, of White Tenants in Integrated and Segregated Public Housing Projects

	Integrated projects		Segregated projects	
	Koaltown (%)	Sacktown (%)	Bakerville (%)	Frankville (%)
Proportion of white women hav- ing neighborly contacts with Negro women in project	39	72	1	4
Attitudes of whites toward Negroes				
Likes them, desires to be friendly	42	60	9	5
Mixed or reserved feelings	30	12	12	27
Avoids them	28	28	79	68
Beliefs concerning Negroes				
Respects Negroes, views them as equal	72	79	43	39
Neutral or ambivalent	17	8	20	26
Believes Negroes are inferior, childish, primitive, etc.	11	13	37	35
Negro families Living in Project	40	70	66	50

Adapted from Deutsch, M. and Evans-Collins, M.[12] *Interracial Housing,* University of Minnesota Press, 1951, tables 2, 11 and 12.

Not only are actual relations between Negro and white families better in the integrated housing projects, there also is a marked change in prejudiced feelings and stereotyped beliefs:

"We get along beautifully. They're really wonderful. When I was sick, Mrs. Jones across the hall noticed it and she came in to help. She used to bring food in and go shopping for me. A lot of white people wouldn't do that for you. . . ." "They're nice to get along with. They treat me fine. They're the same as everybody else."[16]

More people in the integrated project than in the segregated project find nice things to say about the Negroes. The people of Koaltown and Sacktown not only have come to consider Negroes in the project as equals, but tend to change their attitudes toward Negroes as a whole, not withstanding the fact that their projects border on a low class, deteriorated Negro slum.

PROPINQUITY AND MUTUAL INTERDEPENDENCE

The Deutsch and Collins study suggest that contact between equals in a setting where the prevailing social standards emphasized equality of treatment was most likely to reduce prejudice. An important factor was the closeness of contact between white and Negro families living in the same house as well as the large proportion of Negroes in the projects. But projects in which approximately equal numbers of white and Negro families live are fairly rare. Because of the importance of their findings for future planning as well as for our knowledge of the factors reducing prejudice a follow-up study was conducted in projects in which Negroes represented a small minority, a situation typical for the majority of integrated bi-racial housing. Two projects, one integrated and one segregated, located in small New England towns and two other projects in Philadelphia and Pittsburgh were chosen for comparison. In each project about 10 per cent of the tenants were Negroes.[17]

At first glance this study seems to invalidate the earlier study. No differences in prejudicial attitudes were found to exist between the integrated and the segregated projects. Further analysis, however, revealed the essential likeness of the results. The crucial factor turned out to be the relative propinquity of a white family toward a Negro family. Those whites having Negroes as next door neighbors showed the largest shift in the direction of more favorable attitudes. There was a smaller shift among those who lived in the same house but not on the same floor. Some change occurred among those who lived in a house without Negroes but with a Negro family in the adjacent house. The smallest change in the direction of reduced prejudice was found where the next Negro family lived more than one house away.

Perhaps the most intimate type of contact between Negroes and whites can be found in the merchant marine. On ships manned by members of the National Maritime Union a strict anti-segregation policy is enforced. An attitude test comparing NMU members with those of craft unions not having such a policy indicated strong anti-Negro prejudices among only 4 per cent of the former but 71 per cent of the latter. Prejudice was related to the number of times a white seaman had shipped out with Negro sailors. Whereas 54 per cent of those who had sailed on ships without Negro crew members were prejudiced, and those who had been on two journeys with Negroes included 24 per cent with prejudice, those having sailed more than four times with Negroes included only 10 per cent prejudiced sailors.[18]

Equally impressive has been the effect of Negroes and whites going together into battle during the last war. Asked whether they thought it "a good idea or a bad idea to have the same company in a combat outfit include Negro platoons and white platoons," only 18 per cent of those who had never fought with Negroes answered in the affirmative. In contrast, 64 per cent of those who had been in companies with Negroes considered mixing a good idea. Both commissioned and non-commissioned officers completely changed their ideas about Negro troops after they had personal experience with Negroes in combat units. Prior to serving with companies having white and Negro platoons two thirds of the officers had been unfavorably inclined toward the idea and thought it would cause trouble. Having served with mixed companies 77 per cent of the officers developed more favorable attitudes and thought that colored troops performed just as well as white troops (69 per cent of the commissioned officers) if not better (17 per cent).

As in the previous study no marked differences between Northerners and Southerners were found. "The evidence indicates that white and colored soldiers got along together best in those units in which they shared the heaviest combat."[19] Perhaps few contact experiences are as likely to lead to a change in attitudes as those in which the participants are mutually dependent upon each other, and often must cooperate in order to survive.

EFFECTS OF INCONSISTENT SOCIAL NORMS

Do favorable attitudes and behavior patterns persist when the prolonged close association and friendships between colored and white servicemen during the war are terminated? What happens when the soldiers or sailors return to a society in which segregation constitutes the social norm?

I recall one specially poignant experience related to me by a returned veteran from the Pacific. He had many close friends, he thought, among the white boys overseas. And this was true enough when they were sequestered on lonely islands and divorced from the outside world by a limitless stretch of ocean. In the pathetic security of his own naivete the Negro soldier imagined that this newly-discovered cameraderie was something indestructible and enduring. Imagine then the cruel disillusionment on his return home. Mercifully the first glimpse of his native country as seen from the ship's side brought no immediate shock of understanding. It was only with disembarkment that realization came swiftly, surely, unmistakably.

The young Negro soldier had assumed that he and his white "buddies" would go to eat and drink together, to celebrate in song and hilarity his first night's return to glorious America. But it was not thus to be. The white boys disillusioned him with careless remarks whose cruel thrust they could not realize. The parting to them was a casual affair. "Of course you won't go with us now," they said. And he in dumb recognition assented.

So the ship's side was their parting place. They walked down the gang-plank together, but into two different worlds. Yes, he was back home in America and nothing was changed. He took off his uniform to don once again the garb of his inferior role and status.[20]

Uncounted thousands of colored, Italian, and Jewish servicemen must have undergone similar experiences. While the return to a preju-diced atmosphere alone led to changes of the white servicemen toward more prejudiced behavior, deliberate attempts were often made to restore the status quo. After both world wars prejudiced Southerners were worried about the return of the Negro veteran, fearful that he become "uppity" and "no longer know his place." They were deter-mined to see to it that the old patterns of racial suppression were preserved.

Unfortunately no studies on the long-range effects of contacts of white persons separated from the army or navy or moving out of interracial housing projects are available. Such changes in behavior as recorded for the veteran returning from the Pacific theatre of war only indicate that we tend to conform to local patterns of behavior, the norms of our society, sometimes perhaps regardless of more friendly feelings and beliefs derived from contact. Some of these white veterans at least may have changed sufficiently to fight for greater Negro rights in the South.

There is some reason to believe that lasting changes in general attitudes and beliefs toward minorities are more difficult to achieve than changes in behavior. Particularly where social pressure against prejudiced behavior is strong and personal maladjustment outspoken, there may be mere superficial compliance to the demands of the situa-tion rather than changes in underlying attitudes. When the oppor-tunity is favorable, prejudiced attitudes will again be expressed.[21]

It is, however, certain that persons who have had intimate and favorable contact with minority members over a long period of time are more likely to develop a positive attitude toward entering again into such contacts. The person who once worked with Negroes in a factory or fought side by side with them in the army is more likely to work or serve again in an interracial setting. He has seen that his original fears concerning close contact were not substantiated by reality. The Negroes in the housing project did not turn out to be dirty, childish, or aggressive. The colored comrades were as reliable and as good fighters as the next white man.

On the other hand there is the danger that in the long run the effects of favorable contacts which have been terminated may wear off if the person who had developed more favorable attitudes moves back into a highly prejudiced and discriminatory setting. At first he may behave in a discriminatory fashion only because he needs to conform. But to the extent that we tend to make our attitudes and beliefs fit in with our behavior in order to avoid inner conflict a slow deterioration of attitudes in a prejudiced direction may be expected. In a public address Roper reported that persons who were politically liberal and unprejudiced in a liberal college atmosphere reverted to a more prejudiced and conservative attitude, in response to the social climate of their environment, when they became successful bankers or businessmen.

The relative independence of a person's behavior from generalized attitudes toward minority members becomes even more apparent whenever the same individual participates in a number of situations in which different social norms prevail. The passivity with which the individual will accept apparent contradictions in the mores is perhaps rarely as clearly revealed as in the following story related by Minard in his study of race relations in the West Virginia coal fields:

"Do you see that white woman in that jitney?" the man asked me. "She will ride in that back seat crowded in close physical contact with Negro men and never offer an objection. But if she were on the public bus that goes to Belmont and a Negro sat down beside her, she would jump into the aisle and create a scene." The fact of course that the man sat on the edge of the seat and a foot and half away from her would have made no difference.

It is interesting to discover how this contradiction in folkways arose. The driver of the jitney cannot wait until the back seat fills up with white customers. They might not come at all or for a long time, and time is worth money. Both he and his customers are in a hurry, so if Negroes come to ride he simply puts them in with everybody's assent and approval. The white woman therefore suffers no social censure for riding in that manner, and does not object. Group expectations have developed in a different pattern on the public bus, and the white woman accepts them without question in both areas. She plays her customary role in either situation with a surprising amount of emotional indifference, save as she conforms to group expectations.[22]

McDowell County in West Virginia is full of such contradictions. Within the coal mines we find Negro and white miners working together as equals in a spirit of general good will. In some cases Negroes were found to work in a superior status position as motormen on mine lorries or company physicians without any friction whatsoever. But while they ride together on the mine bus in the community itself the white miners again become members of a superior caste. On the interstate bus as well as in the community itself separation is the rule.

Needless to say, the extent to which such "segmentalization" of basic patterns exists, depends somewhat on differences in prejudicial attitudes. A Negro miner explained that "Some men will walk along as fast as they can after they come out of the mine, as if they didn't want to be seen with you . . . other men will tip their hats to your wife when you are out with her or if they have their own wife along with them they will introduce you to her and say, 'This is my buddy.' " About one fifth of the white miners behaved consistently prejudiced and another fifth consistently unprejudiced inside and outside the mine, but the majority adopted different ways of behavior in mine and community. Within the mine they accepted the social norms set forth by the management which assigned workers according to their "efficiency in production," "resourcefulness," and "decisiveness." Outside the mine the Southern system of segregation prevailed.

In the same communities one may observe the combined effect of earlier acquired attitudes, economic factors, and social norms. The majority of the miners were indigenous to the region. There also were a considerable number of poor whites, divided into migrants from the deep South and native white mountaineers. Prejudice against Negroes was intense among the migrants. The myth of Negro inferiority served them as an important compensation for feelings of inadequacy resulting from their depressed status on the bottom of the social ladder. The more class conscious mountain whites on the other hand, not in direct competition with the Negroes, tended to identify and to mix with them.

These opposing forces which influenced the communities toward or away from further integration, constituted an equilibrium which could easily be changed through immigration of a more or less prejudiced population or through economic change. In one community, for example, the influx of relatively unprejudiced Italian immigrants led to a partial breakdown of residential segregation.

SET AND EXPECTATION

A final factor determining the effects of contact is the operation of mental set and expectation. We are likely to change attitudes as the result of contact with minorities not only in proportion to the intimacy and length of time we have spent with Negroes or Jews, but also in terms of our expectations concerning the length of the contact. Participants in an interracial summer camp know that they are soon to return to a prejudiced environment. To a lesser extent this holds true also for soldiers who are in the army for the duration. An entirely different situation exists for members of the regular army or inhabitants of a housing project. They expect to remain in the same situation for a long time and are therefore more likely to attempt a permanent adjustment in terms of behavior as well as attitude than those aware of the temporary nature of the association.

This may explain partly why we find not infrequently that travel fails to be educational. In 1932 the National Education Association[23] sponsored a trip to Japan for a group of California high school pupils whose attitudes were tested before leaving and after returning from the journey. While they had picked up considerable information about Japan, no significant change in attitude toward the Japanese was recorded. To some extent the insufficient and superficial contact over too short a period may be held responsible for the absence of change. Partly, however, such inflexibility may be due to the operation of the wrong set of mind. Being prejudiced they may have seen only the "negative" aspects of Japanese life. The traveller who is convinced of the superiority of everything American can travel through all of Europe and only note and later remember the bad plumbing, the beggars, the dirty and uncomfortable trains, and the lack of orange juice for breakfast.

But let us presume that our traveller is impressed with the beauties of Italy, likes the gaiety and carefree behavior of the Italians. He may still be able to maintain his prejudice against the Italian immigrants living in his home town by failing to connect his experiences at home and abroad. He may fail to realize that the colorful and happy Italians abroad are of the same background as the downtrodden exploited Italian immigrants living under semi-ghettolike conditions in his neighborhood. He may continue to look at the Italians in Italy as exotic—he travels to meet different peoples—the Italians in his home town as unassimilated immigrants, foreigners with bad manners. Education here may facilitate learning by pointing out the assets of the culture and by emphasizing the common origin of Italians here and abroad.

The natives of foreign countries appear different to the soldier at war, the businessman there for trading, the pleasure-seeking tourist. The soldier wants to go home, where there is security and life goes along in the old and familiar way. The businessman distrusts foreigners because of their strange ways of conducting business. But the tourist, who goes there voluntarily, likes them for being different, looks at his visit as a break from a humdrum everyday life. The motives which have led us to establish contact influence what we see.

Our incidental experiences in a new setting also shape our perception. If the hotel accommodations and the weather are good we are more likely to view the natives as pleasant. Similarly, the tenants in an interracial housing project are likely to develop favorable attitudes toward Negroes if the project is run efficiently. Where morale is low and hence bickering and hostility develop, they are likely to be channeled into interracial aggression.

The tenants of the interracial housing project had moved from dilapidated slums into attractive and modern houses surrounded by pleasant lawns. They could obtain such desirable accommodations only at the price of living with members of another race toward whom they were more or less prejudiced. It is doubtful whether they would have moved there if an equally attractive project for whites only had been available. When the hostility toward interracial housing is too great, as perhaps it would be in the deep South, it is doubtful whether interracial housing could function at the present time or whether white tenants would not prefer slum living to a loss of status and general hostility by the community.

Public housing projects house at present only a very small segment of the population. Can contact on an equal status basis be as easily developed in private housing for example? Here the outlook is considerably darker. The influx of colored families into a previously white neighborhood, we noticed, is experienced as a deterioration of the neighborhood and resented by the white tenants. The opposition to race mixture in lower class neighborhoods has its parallel in upper class neighborhoods, where one's social status depends at least partially on living in a restricted suburb where Jews and perhaps Catholics are not wanted. The prestige of colleges and even more, fraternities depends on the extent to which the "right" people are found there perhaps as much as upon their scholastic status.

Yet the situation is not altogether hopeless. Where enlightened private investors build unrestricted houses which compete favorably in desirability with restricted houses, even fairly prejudiced individuals might be attracted. If colleges of high scholastic standards begin to accept Jewish, Catholic, as well as Protestant white students on the basis of merit only, prejudiced majority and minority people might be brought together on an equal status basis. If more business and industrial firms would hire minority people on an equal basis contact could be multiplied. While there is little doubt that favorable contact is one of the best methods to attack prejudice, the problem with which we are faced now is the discovery of ways and means to bring about such contact.

SELECTED READINGS

1. Deutsch, M., and Evans-Collins, M., *Interracial Housing: A Psychological Evaluation of a Social Experiment*. University of Minnesota Press, Minneapolis, Minn., 1951.
2. Minard, R. D., "Race Relations in the Pocahontas Coal Field." *Journal of Social Issues*, 8:1, 1952.
3. Nelson, Lt. D. D., *The Integration of the Negro in the United States Navy*. Farrar, Straus and Young, New York, 1951.
4. "Opinions about Negro Infantry Platoons in White Companies of Seven Divisions." Information and Education Division, U.S. War Department, in *Readings in Social Psychology*, ed. Newcomb, T. M., and Hartley, E. L. Henry Holt, New York, 1947.

REFERENCES

1. MacIver, R. M., *The More Perfect Union*. Macmillan, New York, 1948, p. 234.
2. Nelson, Lt. D. D., *The Integration of the Negro in the United States Navy*. Farrar, Straus and Young, New York, 1951, p. 83.
3. DuBois, R. D., *Neighbors in Action*. Harper & Brothers, New York, 1950.
4. Mussen, P. H., "Some Personality and Social Factors Related to Change in Children's Attitudes toward Negroes." *Journal of Abnormal and Social Psychology*, 45:423-441, 1950.
5. Watson, J., "Some Social and Psychological Situations Related to Change in Attitude." *Human Relations*, 3:15-56, 1950.
6. Watson, G., *Action for Unity*. Harper & Brothers, New York, 1947, p. 60.
7. Allport, G. W., and Kramer, B. M., "Some Roots of Prejudice." *Journal of Psychology*, 22:22-25, 1946.
8. Smith, T., *An Experiment in Modifying Attitudes toward the Negro*. Teachers College, Columbia University, New York, 1943.
9. Irish, D. P., "Reactions of Caucasian Residents to Japanese-American Neighbors." *Journal of Social Issues*, 8:10-17, 1952.
10. Saenger, G., and Flowerman, S., "Stereotypes and Prejudicial Attitudes." *Human Relations*, to be published.
11. Harding, J., and Hogrefe, R., "Attitudes of White Department Store Employees toward Negro Co-Workers." *Journal of Social Issues*, 8:18-28, 1952.
12. Deutsch, M., and Evans-Collins, M., *Interracial Housing: A Psychological Evaluation of a Social Experiment*. University of Minnesota Press, Minneapolis, Minn., 1951.
13. *Ibid*, p. 53.
14. *Ibid*, p. 66.

15. *Ibid*, p. 67.
16. *Ibid*, p. 79.
17. Wilner, D. M., Walkley, R. P., and Cook, S. W., "Residential Proximity and Intergroup Relations in Public Housing Projects." *Journal of Social Issues,* 8:45-69, 1952.
18. Brophy, I. N., "The Luxury of Anti-Negro Prejudice." *Public Opinion Quarterly,* 9:456-466, 1945.
19. Mannheimer, D., *Opinions about Negro Infantry Platoons in White Companies of Seven Divisions.* Information and Education Division, U.S. War Department, 1945, Report No. B-157.
20. Minard, R. D., Unpublished Study.
21. Cook, S. W., *Contact and Intergroup Attitudes: Some Theoretical Considerations.* Research Center for Human Relations, New York University, New York, 1952, mimeographed.
22. Minard, *op. cit.,* p. 39.
23. *Character Education.* Tenth Yearbook, National Education Association, Dept. of Superintendence, Washington, 1932, Study No. 65, p. 145.

CHAPTER 15

FIGHTING DISCRIMINATION AND SEGREGATION

George Carter, American Negro, is probably less concerned with the prejudiced attitudes of his white fellow citizens than with their refusal to give him a decent job and a decent place to live in. He demands the same opportunities as his white neighbors, limited only by his own personal abilities and endeavors.

The fight against discrimination and segregation is in many respects more important than the fight against prejudiced feelings and beliefs. Minorities do not suffer as much from what others think about them as from their actions. A person's beliefs and feelings may be considered a private matter. Discrimination and segregation, however, are matters of public concern, because they affect the right of the individual to equality and freedom of opportunity.

Moreover, any reduction of the overt manifestations of prejudice is likely to lead to a reduction of prejudiced beliefs and feelings. In abolishing discrimination and segregation we make it possible for majority and minority members to meet each other as equals. By abolishing discrimination, we succeed in raising the standard of living of underprivileged minorities and in making them less resemble the stereotype of the dirty uneducated and unambitious outsider. We manage to reduce minority hostility toward the majority and its manifestations, ranging from abject submission to defiant aggression— neither of them conducive to mutual respect and harmonious living.

MOTIVATIONS FOR INTEGRATION

Unless compelling motives force them to do so, most members of society prefer the familiar status quo to change in an unknown and perhaps dangerous direction. Particularly the more prejudiced individuals are unlikely to give up traditional patterns of discrimination, and tend to resist social innovation in the field of race and ethnic relations.

How then, can progress be initiated? Advances in the fight against

232

discrimination and segregation may originate with relatively unprejudiced persons in a position of power, who can dictate the behavior of the more prejudiced whom they can influence. Pressure can be exerted by organized minority groups aided by civic organizations which cross racial and ethnic cleavages like the National Council of Christians and Jews, as well as committees within the Catholic and Protestant churches. Mere moral considerations by themselves are less likely to bring about change, although the increased educational efforts which have characterized the last decade should not be entirely discarded.

Advances are facilitated when it becomes advantageous for the prejudiced person to give up discriminatory patterns of behavior in the interest of more important gains. The decline of immigration from Europe which provided a cheap labor supply for the lower skill levels has been instrumental in the growing acceptance of Negro labor in industry.[1] The greatest progress was made during World War II when the "shortage of manpower forced industry to look to Negroes as a source of factory labor."[2] Economic considerations have occasionally even been able to effect the abolition of segregatory patterns:

Mendota, California, maintained segregated schools for whites and Mexicans for over thirty years, when a new superintendent, who had had successful experience with mixed schools in Madera, also in California, tried to merge Mendota's separate schools. His opportunity came when it was found necessary to build fences around the schools in order to protect them against the acts of vandalism. He pointed out to members of the school board that two fences would measure about 3,175 feet and cost over $10,000 while one fence to enclose one consolidated school would measure only 2,075 feet and cost half the price. Besides, the cost of maintenance would go down, duplication of staffs could be avoided, and better education given to all children. In spite of pressure by townspeople the unification took place, enrollment increased.[3]

Material advantages explain partially why more or less prejudiced white tenants move into an interracial housing project. Not only are the accommodations in modern housing projects vastly superior to the slum areas from which the occupants came, but there often are no other equally adequate shelters available.[4]

RESISTANCES TO INTEGRATION

While the armed forces can decree the abolition of discrimination and segregation in the services, the contemplation of such a step usually raises considerable fear and anxiety as to the consequences, such as a potential decline in morale, unrest, or inefficiency.[5] Similarly in industry, although management has usually enough power to abolish discriminatory practices it may not proceed if it fears that such a step would interfere with production. In other situations those interested in the abolition of prejudiced practices may have no control over the people who would be most immediately affected by such innovation. The store owner who decided for the first time to hire Jewish or Negro sales personnel, can influence the other salesgirls but not his customers.

While even an enlightened management may thus hesitate it is easy to envisage the reluctance of many representatives of management who themselves share common prejudices. Fearful of the consequences of hiring Negroes they tend to see a racial issue in any difficulty in which Negroes are involved:

In a typical case of this kind the management frantically called the representative of an agency that tries to settle such matters to say they were having race trouble and would have to establish separate locker rooms. The investigator found that the plant had grown tremendously during the war, without any increase in locker-room facilities. For two years employees had been complaining of crowding in the locker room and of having to share their lockers with workers on other shifts. When Negroes were hired, the matter came to a head; the white employees demanded separate locker rooms. This case was settled by immediately building new but not segregated locker rooms well placed about the plant.[6]

It is only too easy to understand that managers will avoid hiring Negroes. They dislike being burdened with new problems particularly since any trouble which ensues may be held against them by other members of management. They tend to view an intended innovation not in terms of actual happenings in other plants—with which they are largely unfamiliar—but in terms of their own biased notions concerning the "nature" of the new group about to be hired, and the "difficulties resulting from race mixture."

The apprehensiveness about entering a new and untried path is further reinforced by the fear of going against local customs. While these undoubtedly influence the ease of integration, Southall expresses the conviction that these patterns are not as important as generally believed. Actually we find even in the South firms where Negroes and whites work together unsegregated. An evaluation of personnel policies of the different units of the International Harvester Company located in various parts of the nation was unable to detect any correlation between community patterns and progress in Negro-white integration. Some plants in the South and border states were found to be more advanced than units in Northern cities where no legal segregation existed.[7]

We have already seen why workers in industry resist the coming of all new groups, immigrants or women, Negroes or Mexicans. They are viewed as a threat to the job security of the established groups. New workers also represent a threat to the worker's status and prestige: "The kind of people hired for a given job determines to some extent the job's prestige. If women are hired for a job that only men have done, the men may take the hiring of women not as proof that women are rising in status, but as proof that the job's status is threatened." The job becomes known as "women's work," a derogatory term.[8]

The difficulties anticipated in the path of the abolition of discrimination are not necessarily realized. Of the dire predictions concerning the consequences of hiring women in heavy industry during the war, none came to pass. What actually happens will depend upon external conditions, the amount of prejudice of those opposing the cessation of discriminatory practices, and the extent to which their behavior can be controlled by those responsible for the innovation. Such control reaches a maximum in the armed forces, is of considerable strength in business and industry as well as public housing, and achieves a minimum in social situations, recreation, the behavior of customers in stores. What happens will depend largely upon the actual procedures used to abolish discrimination with a minimum of friction.

In discussing these methods three different periods may be distinguished:

1. *The Period of Preparation*: During this period announcement of the intended change may be made to the public. Plans can be prepared how to introduce and integrate a minority group into a new setting.

2. *The Period of Innovation*: During this period a particular type of discrimination is abolished. The innovation is news to all concerned, conflicts may arise and adjustments will be made.

3. *The Period of Accommodation*: During this period integration is completed. The innovation is no longer news, no longer discussed. Conflicts have been resolved and adjustment achieved.

ASKING PUBLIC CONSENT

Various practices have been used during the initial period of preparation. Some have thought to avoid later trouble by attempting to ascertain public sentiment concerning intended changes as, for example, the hiring of Negro bus drivers where they had not previously been employed. They attempt to gain public consent for their policy. Others simply announce the intended change in policy without asking for public approval. A third group, finally, goes ahead without any prior announcement and presents the public with a *fait accompli*.

On the surface it appears tempting to insure the success of the intended action by gaining public consent, sounding out how people in general feel about one's plan to introduce minority members in new settings. But we know that prejudiced individuals can be found almost everywhere. Even under the best circumstances we shall never achieve results which indicate that everybody approves of the plan. Depending upon the situation there may be 5, 10, or 50 per cent of those we asked who will disapprove of the project.

Regardless of how low the figures are, the manager of the store or factory planning to hire female workers or Negro sales persons will be alarmed because he may believe that most of the people who express negative sentiments will also react negatively when confronted with the members of the new group. Even the loss of 5 per cent of all customers may appear too high a price to the manager of the store who intends to hire Negro salesgirls. Confronted with the results of a public opinion poll which states that 5 per cent of the customers would not buy in a store hiring Negro sales personnel, he will actually believe that the customers will act as they said.

In using opinion polls to predict future behavior we assume of course, that the questions asked of the public were unbiased, which can by no means be always taken for granted. The Washington Transit Company contemplating the wisdom of introducing Negro bus and street car conductors asked a cross section of the public:

1. Will present operators walk out when Negro operators are employed?
2. Will present operators resort to acts of violence if Negro operators are employed?[9]

The suggestive influence of these questions is obvious. But even where we succeed in asking fair questions, prejudiced individuals anticipate the consequences of minority advancement not in terms of the reality of the situation, but in terms of their stereotyped version of future reality, their prejudiced image of the Negro or Jew. When asked whether Jews should be permitted in a heretofore restricted community they envisage the invasion of a horde of noisy, aggressive individuals rather than the arrival of a highly diversified group with quiet and noisy, retiring and aggressive individuals, just as in their own group. We can, therefore, be practically certain that the anticipated behavior predicted from the replies to opinion polls will be at odds with the behavior which actually will occur once the initial step has been taken.

The most obvious disadvantage of asking for prior public consent before going ahead is the almost certain mobilization and crystallization of hostile sentiment against the innovation. The more vociferous, aggressive prejudiced person has time to make himself heard and to express his opposition in no uncertain terms. He will threaten action against the proposed measure sometimes quite out of proportion with what he is able and willing to do.

The fact that the sponsors of the proposed action ask for his opinion indicates to him as to everyone else that they are in doubt as to the advisability of the innovation. Given advance notice of the intended action he has time to get together with other like-minded individuals and to organize for protest or violence:

In Detroit, the efforts of the Federal Housing Agency to find a suitable site for Negro housing led officials to sound out various communities about their attitudes. What happened as a result was a solid congealing of the haters in each community prior to any official action. When it became imperative to select a site despite opposition everywhere, near riots took place. Would it not have been better for the FHA to have announced decisively that Negroes are about to be housed in a site already selected?[10]

Announcing a proposed interracial housing project lends itself to some of the same dangers as asking for public consent. The difference is that the mere announcement without asking for public opinion indicates a feeling of strength. The authority here appears determined, has made up its mind.

While it might perhaps be better to proceed without prior announcement, such procedure is often inapplicable. Negroes will have to be informed of the interracial character of the housing project in order to secure their applications. Where minority members are to be introduced in a complex setting such as a large industrial concern or business where resistances may be expected, it is often indispensable to prepare the ground for the intended innovation beforehand, to educate management and the supervisory personnel, and sometimes the rank and file as well.

THE "FAIT-ACCOMPLI" APPROACH

Wherever possible, it is usually best to go ahead without public announcement and discussion, to confront the public with a *fait accompli*. In this manner the change may be introduced without getting much attention, and thus avoid the crystallization of hostile sentiment.

A study illustrating the effectiveness of this method analyzed the reactions of customers in New York department stores to the hiring of Negro sales personnel, was able to demonstrate that the existence of prejudiced feelings does not necessarily lead to discriminatory action.[11] Partly because of the New York state law against discrimination, nine of the fifteen major metropolitan department stores had begun to hire Negro salesgirls by 1947. If prejudice was going to determine the reaction of their customers, it was reasonable to assume that the more bigoted person would refrain from dealing with Negro clerks. He might even change to stores employing only white clerks. To test this hypothesis, trained interviewers were stationed near sales counters where white and Negro girls sold side by side. This made it possible to distinguish customers who dealt with Negro clerks from those dealing with neighboring white girls. All customers thus observed were later interviewed to discover their attitudes toward the Negro personnel. The fact that they were not being told that they had previously been observed made it possible to compare their attitudes with their behavior.

Many customers did not hesitate to voice their prejudice. One out of five New Yorkers interviewed expressed disapproval of the employment of Negro clerks. Some of these stated that they would not buy in stores which hired them. Another 20 per cent gave limited approval. Negro salesgirls were all right, but they would not like to see them selling in departments handling food or clothing. At first glance the fears of management seem justified and it is easy to imagine what would have happened if these figures had been known to representatives of management before they began hiring the colored girls.

Actually there was no relationship between what people said and what they did. There were as many prejudiced customers among those dealing with Negroes as there were among those dealing with white clerks. In both groups 38 per cent either disapproved of Negro clerks or wanted them excluded from certain departments of the stores. Not only did we fail to find any relationship between prejudiced attitudes and discriminatory behavior, we even observed some women buying from Negro clerks who told our interviewers half an hour later that they would not buy from Negroes under any circumstances.

To appear certain of the results another group of New Yorkers was interviewed in streets and parks. Considering the relatively small number of Negro clerks then employed it was reasonable to assume that most of these had never encountered Negro clerks on their shopping trips. If prejudiced customers would refrain from buying in stores with Negro clerks, more prejudiced New Yorkers should have been found in the street sample. Actually, the proportion of prejudiced persons was slightly smaller than that found among customers observed in stores with Negro clerks. The conclusion is inevitable that department store customers from all walks of life and ranging from the most tolerant to the most prejudiced, do not act out their prejudices.

Table 10. Attitudes toward Negro Sales Personnel among Department Store Customers Dealing with White or Negro Salesgirls

| "What would you think if all New York department stores hired Negro sales personnel?" | Observed with: | | Random street sample (%) |
	Negro clerk (%)	White clerk (%)	
Approve	64	64	75
No opinion	16	15	11
Disapprove	20	21	14
Number of cases	61	53	142

Saenger, G., and Gilbert, E., "Customer Reactions to the Integration of Negro Sales Personnel." *International Journal of Opinion and Attitude Research*, 4:61, 1950.

The story of the New York department store customers constitutes no isolated event. Contrary to dire predictions and in spite of considerable prejudice no major disturbances occurred when the New York City and Cleveland transit systems hired Negro bus drivers without prior announcement.[12] The Southern part of New Jersey abolished segregation in the elementary school system involving thousands of students, parents, and teachers, without any trouble.

INNER CONFLICTS AND SUPPRESSION OF PREJUDICE

What explains this glaring discrepancy between prejudiced people's attitudes and opinions, and their actions? Our department store customers are able to answer this question. Asked how the public would feel about the hiring of Negro clerks, a New York mail carrier replied:

About half of the public probably wouldn't like it because they aren't accustomed to it, but like anything else you have to get used to it. I wouldn't mind myself because if I want to buy something and that department store has it I don't care who sells it to me. I want the article and especially in department stores, the article sells itself.[13]

The biased person is faced with a conflict between his desire to buy and his prejudice. How the conflict resolves itself depends at least in part on the relative strengths of his desire to give in to his prejudice and his desire to shop where he finds it most comfortable and convenient.

Such conflict did not exist when the customer was asked to express his opinion. He did not stand to lose time and money merely by expressing his prejudicial attitudes. Not being asked before he bought he is not committed to act in accordance with his beliefs in order to appear consistent to himself and others.

As has been shown earlier there is in our culture an ambivalent attitude toward prejudice, a conflict between yielding to one's prejudice or following one's basic democratic impulses. On the one hand, we believe in the American creed of equal opportunity for all, "giving the other fellow a chance." On the other hand, we found deeply ingrained prejudices, the desire to occupy a privileged position in the struggle for existence:

"After all, this is a free country. Everybody is entitled to make a living; if a Negro is better qualified for a job than I am, I don't see why he shouldn't get it." Shortly afterwards, however, our customer's prejudices gained the upper hand and she continued: "Yes, they have to make a living the same as anybody else. The store could always put them into the basement or somewhere. I don't think the majority of them are intelligent enough to do a good job. I wouldn't object if they were there, but I would rather not have them there."[14]

The inner conflict between prejudice on the one hand, and the desire to live up to our democratic ideals on the other, explains in part why in many situations prejudice is not expressed in action. In a conflict situation either of two conflicting desires may win out. The individual can act in accordance with his prejudices or in accordance with his democratic beliefs.

The actual outcome of such conflicts depends not only upon the relative strength of the conflicting desires, but also upon the social pressures exerted upon the prejudiced and the situation in which the conflict occurs. The desire to conform with prevailing public opinion is foremost in his mind. Though he would like to express his prejudices in action, the prejudiced individual yields to local custom:

"To be frank with you, I'd say that if I went in and there were two people there, one colored and one white, I think I would undoubtedly prefer to deal with the white person." But only a few minutes later the same person, a middle aged auditor, adds, "Occasionally, I go into the —————— restaurant and *it's taken for granted there* so you can't object. I will say that in the stores I have been in that have Negro sales people, they appear to treat the customers as nicely as a white person would, perhaps better. I guess it is largely a matter of habit with me since I don't have much occasion for contact with them."[15] [Our italics.]

The need to conform, which we found strong particularly among the more prejudiced people, also determines action. The decisive factor is not even the actual division of public opinion, which the customer could not know, but rather his impression of what others think. The very fact that Negroes are found in these stores seemed to indicate to him that the public approved of their presence:

"They wouldn't be there if people would object. We have to respect public opinion whether we like it or not. I don't know why people feel like this about it, but I guess I'm not the man to change things."[16]

The insecure, conformist customer is unlikely to defend his prejudices and complain to management, a step which takes time as well as courage. It would be a different matter if he would know that he was not alone in his feelings about the hiring of Negro personnel, for example in regions where prejudiced people know that public opinion is on their side, as in the South. But even there progress has been registered; there are by now a few department stores in the deep south which have Negro clerks.

Advances are often tolerated by prejudiced individuals through a reinterpretation of the situation which makes it possible for them to accept the innovation without seemingly to give in. Prejudiced customers tended to rationalize their acceptance of Negro salesgirls by stating that "salesgirls are basically servants," and "Negroes make good servants." When we also find that not fewer than 20 per cent of those who bought from a Negro clerk and 33 per cent of those standing next to her had even been unaware that there were Negro sales people in the store, we are in a better position to understand why there had been no resistance to their presence. The customer is so intent on the buying process itself that he often remains unaware of the skin color of the salesgirls provided she is courteous and helpful and he likes what he bought. Public announcement of the change would only have heightened such awareness.

The integration of Negroes in industry may not always proceed with as little trouble as the public acceptance of Negro salesgirls and bus drivers. Here prejudiced people know each other, have a greater chance to discuss the issue, which affects a larger part of their life. Where trouble may reasonably be anticipated it may be possible to take appropriate steps to prevent it as much as possible and to plan in advance how to counteract any resistance which may develop in spite of careful planning.

PREPARATION OF INTEGRATION

In modern industry the handling of human relations is usually the task of the industrial relations department. While it may be preferable if the initiative for the advancement of minorities rests with top management, progress can be made also when the former takes the first step. A preliminary task confronting the industrial relations staff is the appraisal of the actual situation in the plant before the introduction of women or the upgrading of Negroes. It is necessary to study first the extent of discrimination existing in the plant, the types of jobs held by minority members, if any, compared to their skills and education. Next it may prove advantageous to study the attitudes of the representatives of management, the supervisory personnel, and union leadership—in short, of all people who are instrumental in implementing the new policy. The success of the new policy will depend upon obtaining their cooperation, which may require not only a certain amount of education and reassurance of apprehensive members of the managerial hierarchy, but in some cases also the teaching of ways and means of handling trouble. The industrial relations officer "must make certain that key personnel within his own company understand the policy, accept it, and are willing to apply it."[17]

Important here is the indoctrination of the lower supervisory personnel, who often constitute the main obstacle to successful integration. A study of the experiences of thirty-three firms located in various parts of New York State and ranging in size from 100 to 30,000 workers indicated that:

. . . despite a clear cut, definite declaration of policy by top executives to employ Negroes, and an acceptance of this fact by the rank and file employees, a barrier sometimes difficult to surmount has been hesitancy and even hostility of supervisors. . . . Many of the supervisors are long-term employees . . . firmly steeped in their prejudices, and others simply do not believe that the company is sincere in its declaration that it wishes to follow democratic hiring practices.[18]

While it is more difficult to deal with resistances of the supervisors than with obstruction by the rank and file, it is necessary to win over the foremen. In many firms they can accept or reject the applicant hired by the personnel office and are responsible for the training and work assignment of the newly hired minority member. Industrial relations personnel in large concerns should be trained to lead discussions on the new policy in such manner as to give full freedom of expression and to answer all questions which may be asked by supervisors or office managers:

A Japanese American girl was employed as a telephone operator by one of the large paper companies. Before she reported to work, the chief operator voiced her objections to the vice-president of industrial relations. In view of the company's no-discrimination policy, she did not say—what was undoubtedly true—that she was prejudiced against Americans of

Japanese descent for this, that, or the other reason and did not want to work with the girl; instead she rationalized her objections on the grounds of interest in the company. "Is it wise to have a Japanese girl in the telephone department?" she asked. "Won't her strange accent interfere with company business?"

He refrained from pointing out that the new operator did not have a "strange accent," that, in fact, she had been chosen especially because of the quality of her voice, and excellent pronunciation of English. Such a response might have antagonized the chief operator, and the industrial relations officer was intelligent enough to recognize the need of helping her to save face. He did so by asking her to come back to see him if any problems developed when the girl started work. The operator did not repeat her visit.[19]

Opinions are divided concerning the necessity to announce the new policy to the rank and file members of the work force beforehand. Reports of successful integration without prior and with prior announcement can be found.[20, 21] It may be that prior announcement is better where resistance is expected. Discussion with the rank and file workers again permits the crystallization and accumulation of hostile sentiments. Yet many firms have considered it advantageous to announce and occasionally discuss the new policy with their workers in departments known to be hostile to the integration of Negroes, so that the employees are prepared and, if necessary, can receive some education.

The personnel officer called a meeting of the department and told them that a qualified Negro had applied for a job opening and that he wanted them to frankly express their feelings. One man said: "You know me, I'm prejudiced, I was born and raised in Kentucky." Others expressed similar sentiments, in generalities. Quietly and concisely, the personnel director gave a rational answer to every objection. When one employee said belligerently, "They smell," he answered, "We wouldn't hire any employee, white or Negro, who smelled." Another announced, "They are lazy," and the personnel officer countered with "The company is not interested in spending money on any employee who cannot give us a day's work for a day's pay." In reply to the positive statement that "They all have venereal diseases," he stated "Every one here is given a medical examination." He punctured the objection that "They don't know their place" with "We expect all our employees to cooperate with their co-workers. Any over-aggressive employee—whether white or Negro—becomes a disruptive force in the office and will not be tolerated."[22]

Such objections are by no means rare but reflect general prejudiced conceptions of the workers. Even though they may not be the real reason for resistances—the same worker who objects sharing washrooms or eating with a Negro accepts him as a janitor or waiter—it pays to answer them.[23]

Minority groups generally know where they are not wanted and hence fail to apply for jobs unless the new policy has been publicized to the community. Information about the change in policy must be communicated to employment agencies, vocational counsellors in schools, minority publications, and civic agencies. In seeking qualified minority personnel nondiscriminatory employment agencies like the YMCA, state employment agencies, and settlement houses may be contacted to advantage. Skilled Negro personnel is often referred by the local branches of the Urban League, and Jewish workers through the Federation Employment Service. To facilitate the hiring of suitable Negro personnel it might be a good idea to use Negroes in personnel departments.[24]

Where skilled minority personnel is not available, training facilities have to be opened for them. In high discrimination areas vocational counsellors advising Negro youth are faced with the dilemma of either considering only the client's interests and ability, or taking into account the restrictions of opportunities existing in the community. They often choose the latter alternative, thereby accepting the status quo. In the same vein parents and neighbors often discourage minority children, especially Negroes, from continuing school beyond the grammar or junior high school level. In spite of the manpower shortage in the early stages of the last war, Negroes were often excluded from vocational training for semi-skilled and skilled defense jobs with the active connivance of prejudiced individuals inside and outside the government.[25]

FIRM STAND OF AUTHORITY

Even more than in the preparatory period a firm stand in support of the new policy is perhaps the single most important factor determining its success after it has been put into effect. Those in authority must make it known that they identify themselves with the new plan and that any revolt against it will be regarded as a revolt against the leadership.

Archbishop Ritter of St. Louis succeeded in having a reluctant community accept Negroes in parochial schools by refusing to yield to protests and threatening excommunication to objectors. Within a short time the revolt was effectively stopped and Negroes integrated without friction.[26] When management in industry takes the position that it will under no circumstances change its policy or be affected by threats, and that those who want to leave rather than work with Negroes or women may do so, it is rarely necessary to actually dismiss people. When the International Harvester Company began to hire Negro women for general office work, not a single one of the six hundred employees left in spite of previous protests and only one had to be threatened with dismissal.[27]

Even in the rare cases where walkouts occurred during World War II a firm policy tended to quell the disturbance in short order. In the case of the Hudson Motor Company, white workers went on strike the day Negro workers were added to their shifts. When management, backed by unions and the government, refused to withdraw the Negroes, the white workers returned within hours after the main agitators had been dismissed.[28]

On the other hand, where the leadership is vacillating and appears to be fearful of the consequences of the new policy, objections against it will abound and revolt is likely. Housing officials agree that it is not enough to hire a staff, from executive director down to the janitors, that identifies wholeheartedly with interracial, integrated housing. While it may be opportune to wait with the announcement of its policy until applications are received in order to avoid the possibility of opposition, once the policy is announced "it should be definite and unswerving."[29] "Eligibility for housing on the grounds of race should not be a matter of debate," tenants must not be given the alternative of choosing an apartment close or far from Negro families.

The handling of people who refuse to abide to a nondiscrimination policy by the National Maritime Union may be considered as a good example of enforcement strategy:

NMU LEADERSHIP TRAINING SCHOOL

WHAT TO DO WHEN A SEAMAN REFUSES TO SAIL WITH A NEGRO BROTHER

(This approach is not one that can be automatically applied to all cases of discrimination. However, it will be effective in the majority of cases.)

1. The first step is to call a meeting of the entire crew, except those that are needed for the safe navigation of the ship.
2. At this meeting you state the problem that some brothers refuse to accept the Negro brother. Then you ask the brothers who object to the Negro to stand up. Have each brother who objects to the Negro brother state his reasons.
3. His arguments are to be answered point by point. His arguments are invariably fallacious and easy to expose.
4. In the event that these men refuse to accept logic, or to discuss it with a view of settling it, then invoke the Constitution of the NMU. Ask those men if they believe in the NMU Constitution. They will invariably say yes. Ask them if they believe in all of the Constitution; not in parts of it. They will again say yes. Then, ask them if they

believe in the clause that states that there will be no discrimination. If they say no, then obviously they do not believe in all of the Constitution. If they say yes then what the hell are we arguing about?

5. If that is not successful, then tell the brothers that they are not obligated to sail with a Negro, so they can get off the ship. And, in order to save a lot of inconvenience, they can leave their union books because their books will be no good to them.[30]

A milder and less authoritarian technique using social pressure can be used in institutions like the International Houses harboring members of all nations and races. A girl who refuses to dance with a member of another nationality or race because of his origin, may simply find herself without anybody to dance with. The need to avoid conflict with a strong authority, to protect one's job, to be accepted and to belong, furnishes the motive power inducing compliance with the antidiscrimination policy.

SELECTION OF MINORITY MEMBERS

Resistance to the integration of a new group can further be minimized by a careful selection of the first members of the group to be admitted. When male students in graduate schools objected to the registration of female students as flirtatious, illogical, incapable of sustained intellectual effort, care had to be taken to see to it that the first female students were women of exceptional ability, industry, and seriousness of purpose.

The first members of a minority in a specific branch of business or industry should be chosen to contradict existing stereotypes and ought not only to be well trained but also outstanding for their personality and of pleasant appearance. Their behavior will be carefully scrutinized by the older workers who consider their performance as proof for the success or failure of the program. If they do well, resistance to future minority group employees will decline; if they fail this is considered evidence that the group is incapable of adjusting to the new surrounding.

Yet they may still be considered as exceptions. One prejudiced department store customer with rare insight mentioned his pleasant experiences with Negro employees in restaurants and stores but continues "Of course, one unpleasant experience would turn me against all of them."

There is always the problem that the first and most desirable members of the minority, who serve as good will ambassadors, may be considered exceptions. Therefore, as soon as the old employees have accepted the new members, more average members of the minority should be hired. A well-known chain of inexpensive restaurants in

New York introduced Negro waitresses by hiring first girls of more than average beauty. When time had passed and the customers had become accustomed to the Negro waitresses, the firm changed gradually and almost imperceptibly to more average looking girls.

ADMISSION TO INFORMAL ORGANIZATION

After minority members have been hired, steps have to be taken to insure their acceptance by their fellow workers. To facilitate acceptance, steps should be taken to prevent feelings of a loss of prestige and status among those working in departments into which women or Negroes are introduced. We noted earlier that if these groups enter a particular shop in a factory, the work in the shop becomes reclassified in the mind of the workers as "cheap work," "Negro" or "women's work." It is, therefore, a good idea to introduce the minority into *all* shops of the factory at the same time. This method prevents the rise of a differentiation into better "male" or "white shops" as opposed to inferior "mixed shops."

The same danger occurred in regard to the hiring of Negro sales personnel. Had only some stores hired Negroes, these stores would in the eyes of the prejudiced customers henceforth have become inferior stores with "cheap" help. It was important that all stores hired Negro personnel. Actually, this procedure was not followed; instead a different equally beneficial situation arose. It so happened that some of New York's most famous Fifth Avenue stores were among the first to hire colored sales help, stores which by no stretch of the imagination could be considered as cheap or inferior.

It is important to integrate Negroes simultaneously not only in all departments on a horizontal level but also on all skill levels. If Negroes are hired only as skilled manual workers but not as office secretaries the danger arises that the white workers may say: "They aren't good enough for the boss but we have to be satisfied with them." It is advantageous if the boss gives an example by hiring not only Negro white collar secretaries but also, if possible, Negro officers.

To succeed in industry the new worker should be admitted to the informal organization usually found among all those who work in a particular shop. Whether the work is done by mutually interdependent teams working together on the same machine, exchanging tools and materials, or whether each worker is on his own, all workers depend more or less on the cooperation of their fellow workers.

The informal organization regulates to a considerable extent the output. It decides what is to be considered a good day's work. It may help those who are slow, curb those who produce more, lest they ruin the job for the diligent but slower workers.[31] The new worker will find it hard if not impossible to adjust unless he is accepted by the older members. Particularly where team work is required, it has sometimes been impossible for management to break the resistance of older workers:

> In a certain plant, Negroes were first hired in a department that, though dirty and smelly and without prestige, has a very stable working force. The men in it, mostly elderly Poles, work in groups of three that produce as units and are paid so as to make team work the key to a good income. It was thought that these men would not have much prejudice and that the isolation of the department would allow the hiring of Negroes without much comment. Of several Negro men hired, none stayed more than a few days. The management was disturbed, for it thought that the Negroes were confirming the common opinion that Negroes are unreliable. Interviews with these men brought out a consistent and simple story. The workers in the department had practiced every obvious and subtle art to let the newcomers know that they were not wanted and would never learn (i.e., be taught) the work.[32]

Such occurrences are not necessarily indicative of prejudice against the specific group to be hired. They indicate mainly that the workers believe that their particular type of job should be reserved for their own group.[33]

The evidence collected by Hughes suggests that Negroes are often not admitted into existing teams and cliques of white workers in industry. In one such situation described by the author, admission to the central clique is denied to the Negro workers in spite of the fact that otherwise the ten colored women working together with twenty-eight white women in the same room are "accorded tolerance and a measure of friendliness." In the two years they had worked together prior to the study, Negro and white workers met each other with good will on the job and carried on conversations while working, but such friendliness did not extend beyond the work situation. The two groups did not eat together in the plant cafeteria, nor did their conversation touch important personal problems as was customary among the roughly one half of the white girls who were clique members.

Considering the importance, for one's own protection, of belonging to a clique, why did the Negro members fail to form a group of their own? Fear of forming a rival group which may be resented by the dominant central clique, which set the tone, might have been one reason. But contributing to the lack of such informal organization among the excluded Negro girls was the greater anxiety concerning their jobs, in part caused by the attitude of management as represented by the foremen:

"You are on trial. I doubt whether you can make it, but if you do I will give you credit. Most people of your kind can't make it. I shall be astonished if you do. If you do, you will certainly be an exception. You've got to show me."[34]

Such attitudes are likely to invite individualistic competitive behavior, the feeling that everyone has to look out for himself. The fact that the Negro girls are not being rewarded by clique membership if they accept group discipline further discourages the assumption of a more cooperative behavior. Far from realizing the causes of Negro behavior the white girls tended to blame it on Negro personality, a potential source of friction. As one white girl put it to the interviewer:

"Some colored girls . . . don't care what the next person does. They're that way about everything. If one of them makes a hundred and ten [a very high production], the rest of them don't care. Now when a white girl makes that much, we make her slow down because we know how hard it is for some of them to make the average."

"Why do you think the Negro girls don't try to pull their rates down?"

"Well, they're just like that about everything. They don't even try to help each other."

"What do you mean?"

"They don't get into a group. They just mingle with everybody. I don't think the colored girls have any little groups like we have. . . ."[35]

The lack of integration into the informal group found by investigators like Gardner and Hughes does not mean that the job cannot be done. As Hughes himself states, it only means those interested in integration must not neglect the importance of the informal organization.

Several methods facilitate the integration of minority personnel in the work situation. An insurance firm and a public utility company both located in New York City followed the practice of having the supervisor personally introduce the new employee to those with whom she was assigned to work. In addition he took her to lunch and presented her in the cafeteria to as many people as possible. This method, while it indicates to the worker that management is definitely interested in making the minority employee feel at home, has to be used in an informal and casual way to avoid embarrassment, a feeling of forced cordiality and paternalism.

Management can help also through brief orientation talks to the new workers, in which they emphasize that the new employee will be treated like everybody else and in which he is familiarized with the policies of the company. One organization made it a point to reassure particularly those workers who either had not previously worked in a mixed group or had been subjected to unpleasant experiences which had left an attitude of fear and resentment. They were told that they could discuss their personal problems with the personnel office whenever they desired.[36]

Union officers can be of even greater help. In one Buffalo department, for example, management simply informed the union when members of its alteration department refused to work with the new employees. When the business agent let it be known in no uncertain terms that objections would not be tolerated, the older employees acquiesced, and a few years later the Negro member had advanced to the position of union steward.[37]

Union stewards, who are in charge of grievances of the workers, are usually in an excellent position to help in the integration of the new workers into the informal organization. Unfortunately, in many cases, where the union leadership itself is progressive, the stewards may be prejudiced. This is not astonishing considering that they are recruited from the rank and file. Moreover, being dependent upon the membership for re-election, sometimes even unprejudiced shop stewards may not dare to go against the opinions of their membership. A remedy lies in an educational program for the stewards conducted either by the union or by outside agencies. The New York State Commission against Discrimination, for example, conducted work shops for union stewards using sociodramatic presentations of situations with which the participants may be confronted. The stewards discussed such questions as how to deal with a member of the minority group, who has a "chip on his shoulder," or how to act when a new worker is about to quit because of the opposition of his fellow workers.[38]

Integration on the social level can be furthered through company- or union-sponsored social activities. In the thirty-three firms studied in New York, Negroes participated in such activities as baseball, bowling, softball, picnics, plays, and company dances, with only two minor incidents. Management and unions can do their share by endorsing or sponsoring only those programs that bring workers from different ethnic groups together rather than to separate them.[39]

The success of integration finally depends on the adequate training of the leadership. It is not enough for majority leadership to take the appropriate steps. Ideally, majority leadership should be taught to understand the problems of minorities. It should understand that minorities will see through mere lip service to democracy. When management or union committees on discrimination fail to include minority members there is reason to doubt not only their sincerity, but also their efficiency. The ways of life of the factory, the importance of cooperative democratic practices must be taught to minority as well as majority members, a task for which the leadership of both groups must take responsibility.

DISADVANTAGES OF GRADUALISM

In spite of the progress made in recent years, more remains to be done. Practitioners as well as theoreticians have often been concerned with the optimum pace of progress. We noted earlier William's statement that too rapid advances may create uncontrollable "nativistic" reactions. It has been stated that prevailing social customs limit the speed of progress.

This does not necessarily mean that progress in any particular setting, industry, housing, the armed forces, has to progress step by step. Gardner claims that it is easier to hire Negroes simultaneously on all skill levels in a factory where none had previously been employed than to upgrade them in rank in plants where they had previously been employed only at relatively low levels. The latter procedure is more difficult because it violates established traditional patterns.[40] A gradual progress leads to a freezing of discriminatory lines at each new, though advanced, level.

In practice, partly due to the fears of those responsible for social innovations, progress is often introduced in steps. Department stores first hired Negroes as cashiers and wrappers, a few years later as salesgirls, and again later began to integrate them into office work. At the time when Negro girls were first hired as salesgirls, many customers were found to be opposed. The same questionnaire indicated that at this time hardly any objected to their employment as wrappers and cashiers. They had been doing these jobs for some time, and everyone was accustomed to seeing them working in these capacities for a number of years. But one may be almost certain that objections would have been more frequent at the time when Negroes were first employed on these lower skill levels, had the customers been asked.

A timid manager seeing the results of the poll may perhaps have taken Negro salesgirls only in those departments against which no objections were made. We recall that one out of every five white customers interviewed stated that Negro salesgirls in general were all right except perhaps for those departments where they had to handle intimate things such as food or clothing. Paranthetically we may note that the same women who wanted Negro girls excluded from these departments as "unclean" said that "Negroes were all right as cooks or maids." They may employ Negro maids but consider them as exceptions.

Hence they need to see Negro girls working in specific places in order to have them accepted there. We did not find a single customer who, after seeing Negro clerks in the food department, wanted them excluded from that section. Many, however, said they did not want Negroes to handle clothes. On the other hand, those who had observed Negro women selling lingerie and other intimate garments, were among those who wanted Negroes excluded from the food departments. It is not too much to expect that had any customers seen Negroes in both departments they may not have objected to their working in either.

It seems as easy if not often easier to introduce minority members at several levels than on any one new level. People learn by favorable contact experience. If we move one step at a time, we only have to undergo the same process of adjustment the next time we are ready to move ahead.

ACCOMMODATION AND PACE OF PROGRESS

Since gradual progression is often the method used, it may still be important to know how long it takes after a social innovation has been instituted for accommodation to set in so that the next step can be taken. Had the stores begun to hire Negro salesgirls before the customers and employees had become completely accustomed to see and accept them on the lower skill levels, there may have been a possibility not only of resistance against colored salesgirls but also a retroactive resistance to their being hired on the lower level.

A few years ago baseball fans throughout the nation discussed the hiring of Jackie Robinson by the Dodgers. Now Negroes are found in practically all major baseball clubs and are no longer subject to controversies. Southerners argue about the admission of qualified Negroes to graduate schools. Perhaps, in a few years they may be taken for granted on the higher levels of the universities and the fight may rage about the "advisability" of permitting Negroes on the college level in Southern schools. While no data are available one may venture the guess that the period of accommodation may last anywhere from half a year to two or three years, after which period the issue is dead and new advances may be introduced more safely.

Actually it appears doubtful whether progress often proceeds at the maximum speed which the step-by-step method allows. The slow pace of progress is dependent not only upon the willingness and ability of the general public to accept innovations. It is often caused by a leadership which is sometimes not only prejudiced, but also has vested interest in the continuation of discriminatory practices. At other times the leadership is afraid to go ahead at too fast a pace.

The same people who exert pressure for the use of the gradual method rather than the simultaneous integration on all levels may at any one time when a new step is contemplated, prevent progress by declaring that the time is not yet ripe. They may even try to arouse public opinion against the intended innovation. Moreover, the gradualistic approach also runs into the danger of not making maximum use of otherwise favorable conditions such as prosperity and full employment. If one waits until mass unemployment and depression occurs the chance for speedy progress may be over.

Persons favoring the gradualistic approach often claim also that any one step paves the way for subsequent progress. They believe that experiences with Negroes of a favorable sort in one situation will make it more likely that they will be accepted in another situation. But research demonstrated that with the exception of such long-lasting, intimate experiences as exist in housing, there is little transfer of learning. In the field of employment, favorable work experiences with unskilled Negro laborers do not necessarily make it easier for them to be accepted on the skilled level. The same irrational arguments will be advanced, the same emotional resistance to their progress will be aroused.

We have discussed the general advisability of achieving complete integration rather than proceeding in piecemeal fashion in any particular field of human relations such as employment in a given industry, housing, the armed forces. It is another question whether the simultaneous attack on discrimination in prejudiced regions of the country would not lead to uncontrollable popular resistance and thwart progress altogether. Here one may indeed advocate concentration on those areas of life in which resistances may be expected to be smallest, and where control from above is greatest, such as army or industry.

A twofold approach may be recommended. There should be broader education of the population as a whole in regions like the Southern United States, spearheaded perhaps by labor unions, educational institutions, a liberal press. Progress in the South owes considerable impetus to the Southern liberal who is more apt to be heard than the disliked Northern reformer. We noted that most people do not want to be taught the "errors" of their ways by outsiders.

In general, however, to the extent that those in authority set the norms, and even though not always prejudiced themselves, may be timid and reluctant to institute progress by themselves, it will be often necessary to prod the leadership into action. Progress can be made in rather short time provided the right techniques are used. Wherever the leaders do not voluntarily take the initiative—which is more desirable—legal means of abolishing discrimination appear in place.

SELECTED READINGS

1. Southall, S. E., *Industry's Unfinished Business*. Harper & Brothers, New York, 1950.
2. Saenger, G., and Gilbert, E., "Customer Reactions to the Integration of Negro Sales Personnel." *International Journal of Opinion and Attitude Research*, 4:1, 1950.
3. Weaver, R. C., *Negro Labor, a National Problem*. Harcourt Brace, New York, 1946.
4. Hughes, E. C., "The Knitting of Racial Groups in Industry." *American Sociological Review*, 11:5, 1946.

REFERENCES

1. Southall, S. E., *Industry's Unfinished Business*. Harper & Brothers, New York, 1950, p. 61.
2. Feldman, H., The Technique of Introducing Negroes into the Plant. *Personnel*, 19:461-466, 1942.
3. Johnson, D., "They Fenced Tolerance In." *Survey Graphic*, 1947, 36, 398-399.
4. Watson, G., *Action for Unity*. Harper & Brothers, New York, 1947, p. 107.
5. Kennworthy, E. W., "The Case Against Army Segregation." *Annals of the American Academy of Political and Social Science*, 275:27-32, 1951.
6. Hughes, E. C., "Race Relations in Industry," in *Industry and Society*, ed. Whyte, W. F. McGraw-Hill, New York, 1946, p. 119.
7. Southall, *op. cit.*, p. 63.
8. Hughes, *op. cit.*, p. 120.
9. Watson, *op. cit.*, p. 71.
10. *Ibid.*, p. 72.
11. Saenger, G., and Gilbert, E., "Customer Reactions to the Integration of Negro Sales Personnel." *International Journal of Opinion and Attitude Research*, 4:57-76, 1950.
12. Watson, *op. cit.*, p. 71.
13. Saenger and Gilbert, *op. cit.*, p. 65.
14. *Ibid*, p. 67.
15. *Ibid*, p. 65.
16. *Ibid*, p. 67.
17. Southall, *op. cit.*, p. 147.
18. Seidenberg, J., *Negroes in the Work Group*. New York State School of Industrial and Labor Relations, Cornell University, Research Bulletin No. 6, 1950.
19. Southall, *op. cit.*, p. 78 f.
20. Seidenberg, *op. cit.*, pp. 8-11.

21. Southall, *op. cit.*, pp. 147-154.
22. *Ibid,* p. 90.
23. Gardner, B. B., *Human Relations in Industry.* Irwin, Chicago, 1945, p. 259.
24. Seidenberg, *op. cit.*, p. 24.
25. Weaver, R. C., *Negro Labor, a National Problem.* Harcourt, Brace, New York, 1946, chap. 4.
26. Granger, L. B., "A New Problem for Negroes: Integration," in *Race Prejudice and Discrimination,* ed. Rose, A. Knopf, New York, 1951, pp. 580 ff.
27. Southall, *op. cit.*, p. 152.
28. Weaver, *op. cit.*, pp. 72 ff.
29. Deutsch, M., and Collins, M. E. *Interracial Housing.* University of Minnesota Press, Minneapolis, Minn., 1951, pp. 20 ff.
30. Watson, *op. cit.*, pp. 119 ff.
31. Hughes, E. C., "The Knitting of Racial Groups in Industry." *American Sociological Review,* 11:512-519, 1946.
32. Hughes, E. C., "Industry and Society," *op. cit.*, p. 113.
33. Collins, O., "Ethnic Behavior in Industry." *American Journal of Sociology,* 51:293-298, 1946.
34. Hughes, "The Knitting of Racial Groups in Industry." *Op. cit.*, p. 518.
35. Hughes, *ibid,* p. 518.
36. Seidenberg, *op. cit.*, pp. 14-15.
37. *Ibid,* p. 25.
38. *Democracy at Work.* Troy Council of the New York State Commission against Discrimination, mimeographed report. 1952.
39. Southall, *op. cit.*, pp. 158 ff.
40. Gardner, *op. cit.*, p. 261.

CHAPTER 16

THE LEGAL APPROACH

Laws can be used to sanction or prohibit discrimination. We distinguished earlier between official and private discrimination. The fight against discrimination is concerned, therefore, with the abolition of discriminatory laws and governmental practices on the one hand, the elimination of private discriminatory practices on the other hand.

ABOLITION OF DISCRIMINATORY STATUTES

Under the provisions of the fourteenth amendment legal discrimination is unconstitutional; there can be no laws which discriminate against any one group. The poll tax was not considered unconstitutional because it applied equally to all members of the population. In 1896 the Supreme Court, in the case of "Plessy *vs.* Ferguson," declared that separate but equal facilities for Negroes did not discriminate. This decision opened the door to a host of state legislation prescribing segregation in education, recreation, transportation, etc.

Between 1868 and 1937 the large majority of court decisions tended to restrict the civil rights of minorities. They made it impossible for all but a few Southern Negroes to vote in the essential primaries, and through upholding restrictive covenants, interfered with the freedom of minorities to live where they wanted. The chance of obtaining a fair trial was lessened by the court's failure to declare that all-white juries sitting in cases involving Negro defendants were unconstitutional.[1]

In more recent years the Court has tended to strengthen civil rights. Until the settlement of the "Norris *vs.* Alabama" case in 1935 "it was necessary in order to prove discrimination to present direct evidence that the exclusion (of Negro jurors) was on racial grounds alone. In the Norris case however, the Court held that discrimination could be inferred from the contrived absence of Negroes from the lists of jurors and from juries."[2]

The opinions given in support of earlier Supreme Court decisions tending to preserve the caste system rather than to promote greater equality are irreconcilable with modern scientific theories. In a prejudiced society one cannot expect all white juries to act impartially in a case involving a Negro defendant. With hardly any exception, social scientists today consider segregation a basic form of discrimination. In "regulating the multitude of daily contacts between races, segregation has become the primary symbol of Negro inferiority."[3]

One might argue that the exclusion of one segment of the population against its consent by itself constitutes discrimination. More important is the contention that segregation would interfere psychologically and materially with the welfare of the excluded group even where equality is approached. The Negro knows that he is excluded because he is "considered inferior," thought not to be worthy of the company of the "superior" white, and hence kept apart. Segregation was found to contribute to the rise of feelings of inferiority and disturbed feelings of belonging among members of the excluded group.

From a legal point of view it would be desirable to distinguish between the relative contribution of segregation and prejudice or discrimination to such detrimental effects. This is difficult because segregation and discrimination inevitably go together. Yet we can say that enforced segregation tends to reinforce and lead to prejudiced behavior, lends official sanction to discrimination, which could be rejected easier if it were only a mere individual manifestation of a prejudiced mind.

In practice, separate but equal facilities are rare. Segregation almost always led to large differences in the quality of facilities offered to Negroes and whites. Because of the long history of inferior Negro schools, for example, a greater number of qualified teachers are available in white institutions, particularly in those regions of the country where segregation prevails. In spite of great improvements in recent years, the South as a whole still spends less money per capita on the education of Negro than on white children. The situation has been somewhat ameliorated also by grants to Negro schools from the privately endowed Rosenwald Fund.

Even if we could equalize Negro and white schools, going to segregated institutions prevents the Negro graduate student from establishing valuable associations needed for his later business or professional life. It is even doubtful whether segregation could theoretically coexist with complete material equality. Why should real estate operators in a competitive capitalistic democracy offer the same quality houses to segregated Negroes at a price equal to that paid by whites, since minority members have no opportunity to leave segregated districts and look for better housing elsewhere?

In view of the earlier Supreme Court decision, court suits in behalf of Negroes have been fought on the ground that equal facilities were not provided. As a result of these suits an improvement of the facilities open to Negroes has been gained, but segregation was not challenged. Partly because it was felt that the advance of scientific thinking concerning the detrimental effects of segregation has made such action possible, the National Association for the Advancement of Colored People has now begun to challenge the institution of segregation itself. At the time of this writing the Supreme Court has agreed to pass judgment on the question of segregation in Southern elementary schools.

There is precedent to indicate that the Supreme Court has occasionally arrived at new interpretations based on new scientific evidence. While it ruled twenty years ago that movies do not make opinion and hence do not come under the protection of the Bill of Rights guaranteeing freedom of the press, it reversed its stand in 1952, influenced perhaps by the fact that a great number of studies demonstrated that films are a major factor in the shaping of public opinion. If the Supreme Court has been reluctant so far to consider the constitutionality of segregation, changes in scientific opinions not withstanding, fear of the consequences of such action has been considered a factor:

Behind the Supreme Court's insistence on a factual showing of inequality in educational segregation cases may be a reluctance to remove too abruptly the basic props of the Southern social system. In part this reluctance may stem from fear that sudden change would have harsh effects on Negro children presently in school. Forcing them into a hostile mixed school atmosphere might, during the transition period, produce more unfortunate psychological consequences than segregation. However, since this may also occur when segregation is abolished piecemeal, some immediate harm to Negro children seems inevitable if the long-run goal of a healthy educational environment for both Negroes and whites is to be achieved. A more decisive factor in the Court's "go slow" policy may be its fear of precipitating widespread social unrest and possible violence. This fear could easily arise from repeated warnings of southern leaders that no interference with the established Southern racial structure will be tolerated.[4]

Since there appears to be some reason to believe that the Court is often "reluctant to cause social revolution by fiat,"[5] it has become important to demonstrate to the judges that segregation would not lead to any major social upheaval. We noted that over one thousand Negroes have in recent years been peacefully integrated into Southern graduate schools without major social ostracism. The state legislatures of Illinois, Indiana, and New Jersey have abolished elementary school segregation without trouble. In the face of continuous threats of violence by some Southern leaders, white primaries, all white juries, and segregated interstate travel have been partially abandoned through court procedures.[6] Integration in the traditionally segregated Navy has been accomplished within a period of five years through executive order.[7]

FEDERAL AND STATE LAWS AGAINST DISCRIMINATION

While progress had thus been registered in the abolition of discriminatory laws, advances in laws against discrimination by private individuals have also been made.

A distinction must be made here between the protection of the fundamental civil rights embodied in the federal and state constitutions —such as the constitutional right to vote or the right of equality before the law—and the passage of specific laws or regulations explicitly forbidding specified types of private discrimination—for example, discriminatory employment practices. To administer the latter type of law special federal, state, or municipal committees or commissions have been set up for the purpose of receiving and judging complaints by individuals or of conducting their own investigations. The prototype of this kind of organization was the federal Fair Employment Practice Committee (F.E.P.C.) set up by executive order in 1941 to insure adequate representation of minority manpower in war industries.

The F.E.P.C. owed its existence to wartime exigencies, the shortage of manpower during the war, and a favorably disposed administration. With the end of the president's wartime emergency powers in 1946 it went out of existence. Attempts to establish a permanent F.E.P.C. through congressional action since have failed. But after the end of the war a number of states, beginning with New York, have set up their own F.E.P.C.'s. They are in many respects superior to the original federal committee which had no enforcement power and insufficient personnel.

In 1951 commissions modeled after the New York law existed in New Jersey, Massachusetts, Connecticut, Rhode Island, Washington, Oregon, and New Mexico. The New York State Law originally applied only to discrimination in employment and forbade discrimination in hiring, firing, wages, working conditions, and promotion as well as discrimination by labor unions or employment agencies:

Unlawful Employment Practices

It shall be an unlawful employment practice:

1. For an employer, because of the race, creed, color or national origin of any individual, to refuse to hire or employ or to bar or to discharge

from employment such individual or to discriminate against such individual in compensation or in terms, conditions or privileges of employment.

2. For a labor organization, because of the race, creed, color or national origin of any individual, to exclude or to expel from its membership such individual or to discriminate in any way against any of its members or against any employer or any individual employed by an employer.

3. For any employer or employment agency to print or circulate or cause to be printed or circulated any statement, advertisement or publication, or to use any form of application for employment or to make any inquiry in connection with prospective employment, which expresses, directly or indirectly, any limitations, specification or discrimination as to race, creed, color or national origin, or any intent to make any such limitation, specification or discrimination, unless based upon a bona fide occupational qualification.

4. For any employer, labor organization or employment agency to discharge, expel or otherwise discriminate against any person because he has opposed any practices forbidden under this article or because he has filed a complaint, testified or assisted in any proceeding under this article.

5. For any person, whether an employer or an employee or not, to aid, abet, incite, compel or coerce the doing of any of the acts forbidden under this article, or attempt to do so.

NEW YORK STATE *Law Against Discrimination*
Chapter 118, enacted March 12, 1945.

In 1952 the New York State Commission also became entrusted with the administration of a law which forbids discrimination in places of public accommodation such as hotels, restaurants, swimming pools, and resorts, a law which has existed for some time in New Jersey. Fair educational practice laws exist in two states. Six states have forbidden discrimination in housing built with the assistance of the state.[8] But with the exception of New Mexico, state laws are found only in the more liberal regions of the country having large foreign populations, where political resistance to the enactment of such measures was relatively small and considerable public support for the enactment of such measures could be found.

CAN LAWS COUNTERACT SOCIAL MORES?

The lack of federal legislation as well as the fact that only a few states have been able to pass laws against discrimination may be attributed in large measure to the effective opposition of prejudiced people in power. Arguments against such legislation by prejudiced persons as well as by misguided friends of minority rights are often based on the belief that discrimination cannot be curbed by legislation, that laws cannot change people's feelings.

The belief that laws cannot affect discrimination is related to the assumption that laws generally are an expression of the ideology and the prevailing mores of a society. They follow rather than precede social change, and cannot by themselves change the folkways of a society. The sociologist Sumner declared that "stateways [laws] cannot change folkways" and that legislation is as futile as preaching in changing basic social patterns.[9]

Sumner's theory has been effectively challenged by Myrdal who emphasized the constant changes and conflicts that have been typical of our modern Western world, and in which laws have often played a role.[10] Evidence that norms superimposed by authority have been able to change dominant patterns of feeling and acting has been furnished by the study of integrated interracial housing, mentioned earlier:

> We are, in effect, rejecting the notion that has characterized much of sociological thinking in the field of racial relations: the notion, originating with William S. Sumner, that "stateways cannot change folkways." The evidence of our study is that official policy, executed without equivocation, can result in large changes in beliefs and feelings despite initial resistance to the policy.[11]

But although few social scientists still adhere to the old theory, the popular notion that widespread prejudices prevent laws against discrimination from becoming effective is still widely held. In 1948 not fewer than four out of every ten persons questioned in a nationwide poll believed that "people can't be forced to change deep rooted prejudices by passing laws."[12]

In earlier decisions the Supreme Court argued akin to Sumner's theory, that laws could not control attitudes. In the case of Plessy *vs.* Ferguson dealing with racial segregation on common carriers, the Court not only argued that the law could not control social prejudice but also spoke of a "racial instinct" beyond the power of the law. The absurdity of this reasoning has been expressed by MacIver:

> Racial attitudes are made eternal as racial instincts, although these attitudes are often changing. Then the inference is drawn that law is powerless to control them. Why should this inference apply only to laws that reject discrimination and not to laws that enforce it? If the one kind is vain why not the other kind? Even if law has no power over prejudice why should it have none over discrimination, which is not an attitude but an action? Laws often check behavior to which the attitudes of people prompt them.[13]

Because of the often heard objections to the passage of laws against discrimination that they are unable to influence feelings, it cannot be sufficiently stressed that it is the object of all law to regulate actions rather than to control feelings. The prejudiced New Yorker is less likely to bar a Negro from his restaurant if it may cause him to lose his license. Lynchings and other acts of violence against Negroes may be reduced by making certain that the culprits will be apprehended and tried before an impartial court. No laws would be required if the strength of the mores alone would prevent people from acting against social norms. Laws are effective to the extent that they act as deterrents, and therefore, effective to the extent that they are enforced. If clearly stated and enforced they tend in the long run to become part of the norms.

The correlation between the enforcement of traffic rules and the number of violations is generally known. But one may argue that public opinion is by and large in favor of traffic rules. It views them as necessary for the common good. The question has been raised whether laws can be passed and effectively enforced when they run counter to the feelings and beliefs of a substantial segment of the population, as was the case with prohibition laws. Opponents of laws against discrimination, particularly in the Southern part of the country, claim that it could not be enforced and would meet with widespread resistance by an aroused public opinion insisting on the maintenance of the status quo.

While the ultimate test of this contention would be the enactment of such laws, there are reasons to doubt the accuracy of this prediction. We had occasion to note that the average American is in a dilemma concerning the justice of discriminatory practices. Many persons in the North as well as in the South are firmly convinced of the need to strengthen democratic practices at home. While it is probable that Southerners are more opposed to granting social equality to Negroes than Americans in other parts of the country, we also noted that they are more willing to grant economic than social equality. Much will depend upon the type of legislation proposed at a given time. Although it is perhaps foolhardy to proceed too fast against solid opposition, there is some evidence that even in the South substantial portions of the population are no longer opposed to legislation against some forms of discrimination. A survey of factory workers in 1948 showed that 48 per cent of Southern workers approved a federal fair employment practice law.[14]

Much discrimination is rooted not in prejudice but the desire to conform to prevailing social standards.[15] In order not to find themselves at odds with prevailing public opinion, many Southern workers express prejudiced opinions in public but privately feel differently. A prominent labor leader conducted during the last war an opinion poll in a Southern shipyard to ascertain workers' opinions toward the integration of Negroes, in which most workers expressed themselves against their admission. Dissatisfied with the results, this labor official repeated the poll, using secret ballots. This time a majority of the workers came out in favor of hiring the Negroes. It is possible that the opponents of laws tend to overrate the proportion of prejudiced people and the actual opposition to laws. In general people tend to believe that the feelings of others parallel their own thinking.

The argument that the abolition of discriminatory practices by law would lead to complete chaos, would necessitate a sudden and complete change in the social fabric, is equally fallacious. Experiences with the administration of existing laws against discrimination indicate the occurrence of a gradual and slow change. It is unlikely that laws can be passed which go too far ahead of changing public opinion:

> . . . our legislative bodies are so slow to move, so resistant to new ideas, so packed with representatives of rural areas that legislation really in advance of popular understanding and support will not be enacted. The civic agency which seeks a legislative reform need not be deterred, therefore, by a fear that it is acting precipitately. It will not succeed until the legislators who possess more sensitive instruments for listening to the public pulse believe the times are ripe.[16]

CIVIL RIGHTS LEGISLATION

In terms of the prevailing state of public opinion as well as the potential resistance expected to the enactment of federal and state laws for the protection of minority rights, progress may be expected to be slow. Advances are impeded as the result of the entrenched political power of those interested in the status quo. The effective blocking of all civil rights legislation in the United States Senate through the filibuster is too well known to deserve further discussion.

What is less well known is the fact that filibustering could be effectively stopped through the application of the cloture rule, which has, however, been impossible through the active cooperation of a majority of Republican and Southern Democrats. Equally important is the institution of seniority rule which gives the South an inordinately great influence, far out of proportion to its actual population. Senators from the one-party South tend to remain in office longer than legislators from other parts of the country and hence are able to control many important committees.[17]

To a certain extent the remedy to this situation can be found in the South itself. The control of the South by a reactionary leadership is tied to the institution of white primaries, the poll tax, and the low state of political education, which has effectively disfranchised approximately 80 per cent of its voters. But as the result of recent Supreme Court decisions, large inroads into the system of white primaries have been made, and the proportion of Negroes who vote for the first time has been steadily increasing. The poll tax has lost much of its efficiency because of the relative prosperity during the last decade, in the South as well as the rest of the nation. It has now been abandoned by a majority of Southern states.

Even discriminatory educational requirements have been unable to prevent an increase in the Negro vote.[18] Although reactionary elements sometimes manage to hold on to power through a prejudiced electoral system giving the backward rural regions a disproportionately large influence and discriminating against the city vote, even in the state of Georgia the emergent liberal forces have recently managed to defeat Talmadge running on a white supremacy platform. The steady increase in the power of Southern liberals must not be underrated.

Sound strategy of minority groups throughout the nation, if they can be effectively organized, can exert considerable pressure.[19] Minority groups, if united and organized, can throw their bargaining power to the side which does most to advance their liberation, provided they do not advocate revolutionary and extreme programs which neither party could dare to support.[20]

For the foreseeable future the need for federal legislation is obvious, if we consider the small likelihood that the Southern and border states will enact legislation to protect minorities. Minority groups can use their bargaining power to see to it that state F.E.P.C.'s are established wherever possible, and existing legislations strengthened.

By the end of 1951 legislation existed in states or cities which held 32.5 per cent of the nation's population, including over one sixth of the colored, one half of the Catholic, and three fourths of the Jewish population. While these figures are somewhat deceiving in so far as not all laws are equally well written, considerable progress has been made.[21] Apart from their effect in improving the minority situation a successfully administered law tends to alleviate the apprehensions expressed prior to its passage by many people. It opens the path for more advanced legislation in the same state and imitations of the law in other states.

Prior to the passage of the New York Law, fears had been expressed that the law would drive business out of the state and would interfere with normal business routine. It was expected to result in large-scale resistances by employees and customers, and mass complaints by cranks and disgruntled failures. None of these fears was realized.[22] Three years after the passage of the law a poll of a cross section of the population of New York City showed that disapproval of the law was smallest among business men (5 per cent disapproved, 4 per cent were undecided, and 91 per cent approved of the law) as compared to professional, white collar, and manual workers (disapproval rates, 16, 14, and 12 per cent respectively). The law succeeded, therefore, in winning over those most immediately affected by its provision.[23]

The small number of complaints also contradicts the fear that disgruntled individuals would use the law to air their grievances. Parenthetically one may note that research has indicated that the proportion of individuals who tend to rationalize their failure by claiming discrimination, small as it is, is probably still smaller than the proportion of minority members who tend to deny experiences of discrimination in order to protect their self-esteem.[24]

EMPHASIS ON PERSUASION AND CONCILIATION

Much can be learned by analyzing the administration of the state laws. The success of the New York State Law, which may serve as an example, can be attributed to its stress on conference, persuasion, and conciliation rather than on punishment and coercion. The process of a complaint has been outlined by the New York Commission in its 1951 report:

Any person claiming to be aggrieved by an unlawful employment practice may file with the Commission a verified complaint.

The chairman of the Commission designates one of the commissioners to make a prompt investigation.

If the investigating commissioner determines there is probable cause to credit the complaint, he endeavors to eliminate the unlawful practice by conference and conciliation.

If conference and conciliation fails, a public hearing is held before three members of the Commission.

If the respondent is then found to have engaged in an unlawful discriminatory practice, the Commission issues a cease and desist order.

All cases are reviewed approximately six months after settlement in order to assess the extent and effectiveness of compliance with conciliatory agreement.

In practice, during its five years of operation in which approximately two thousand complaints were received, only three public hearings were necessary, and only one case led to court action. In all other cases where discrimination was discovered to exist in the company, employment agency, or labor union, conciliation was successfully concluded. The success of this approach is due probably to the fear of the unfavorable publicity ensuing from a public hearing (conferences are held in secret and not publicized), as well as the commission's power to apply sanctions if conciliation should fail.

The main effect of the conciliation procedure lies not so much in the satisfaction of the individual complainant but in the resulting change of the discriminatory employment pattern. Although only 28 per cent of all complaints were found to be verified, the ensuing investigations disclosed discriminatory policies in 61 per cent of all companies investigated during the life of the Commission.[25] The conciliation agreements reached, stipulated as a minimum more than the immediate elimination of all discriminatory practices and a general commitment that the respondent will obey the letter and spirit of the law in the future. It also required the hanging of Commission posters where employees and job applicants can see them, as well as the right to periodic investigations of the firm.

Provisions for redress to the complainant were often made and steps taken to sensitize and educate the personnel in the successful integration of minorities.[26] Help was given also to advise the companies in securing minority labor by presenting them with a list of employment agencies which had a nondiscriminatory policy or were specifically designed to serve minority groups, such as the Archdiocesan Vocational Service or the Urban League.

In addition to complaints the Commission also initiated 647 investigations of its own and disclosed discriminatory practices in 76 per cent of all such cases. Finally, specific attention was given to employment agencies of which more than 1000 were examined during the life of the Commission. The Commission analyzed 3557 application forms for the presence of unlawful questions which would have made it possible to identify the race, creed or national origin of the applicant. The most common type of unlawful employment practice found by the commission here was the refusal to refer applicants when the agencies knew or suspected that a customer does not favor employees from a specific racial or ethnic group. The commissioners remark that:

> Experience has shown that employment agencies are frequently wrong in their judgment of whom an employer will or will not accept in terms of race, creed, color or national origin. Since the enactment of the Law against Discrimination, many employers have changed their employment policies. Employment agencies are not always cognizant of these changes. More important, an employer may have a stereotyped concept of a Negro, Italian, or Jewish person, but may be willing to hire a particular Negro, Italian, or Jewish person on the theory that he is "different."[27]

The efficacy of laws against discrimination can by no means be expressed only in terms of the number of complaints brought before the Commission. Depending upon the size of the firm, each successfully adjusted complaint opens the door of opportunity for a great many minority members:

The Telephone Company, which previously employed no Negroes on its switchboards, now employs colored girls on all its switchboards, throughout the state. The same is true of the Metropolitan Life Insurance Company, where Negroes now work side by side with whites at many skills from which Negroes were formerly excluded.[28]

It is particularly the Commission's emphasis on review which increases the chance of a permanent change in employment policy. In a case against an insurance company, the Commission found a dearth of Jewish employees. A review of this case showed that the conciliation agreement concluded with the Commission was being carefully observed and that a number of Jewish clerical workers from many nationality groups were on the roster of the organization. One large banking company which had had no Negroes on its clerical staff, upon review was found to have 72 Negro clerks among its 2200 employees.[29]

Not the least important factor in the work of the New York State Commission consists of its educational work carried out by a full time staff in cooperation with specially created community councils in the twelve largest counties of the state. The councils, consisting of prominent citizens representing various interests in the community, help in interpreting the Commission's work to the community through schools, civic groups, and meetings with employers and labor groups. Together with the field representatives of the Commission, they are active in the areas of vocational guidance and hold conferences with employer and labor groups to popularize and interpret the law, thus insuring voluntary compliance.

The education division of the Commission has cooperated with various school boards in order to make the students aware of their future rights of fair employment and to see to it that vocational guidance stressed ability and interest as the only criteria for occupational choice. This division is also charged with the task of making the law known to all concerned. In 1951, for example, it held 2150 showings of a specially prepared film explaining fair employment practices, which was seen by an audience of 225,000 persons. Publicity was provided further by posters, through radio and television, and by addresses by the members of the Commission.

SHORTCOMINGS OF EXISTING LAWS

Laws against discrimination can be put on the statute books to appease minority groups and then prevented from functioning adequately by providing no appropriations or insufficient ones, as was the case in New Mexico. Perhaps the only state having a fully adequate staff and sufficient appropriations is New York. It is possible to staff an agency with political appointees chosen for their conservative attitude and timidity. Insufficiently trained investigators who fail to see discrimination where it exists, or, perhaps somewhat less likely, see discrimination where none exists would also do harm. The remedy to this danger may lie in cooperation with experienced civic agencies working in this field, as well as the appointment of an experienced staff drawn from civil service lists.

Table 11. Budget, Staff, and Case Load of State Agencies against Discrimination

	N.Y.	N.J.	Mass.	Conn.	Wash.	R.I.	Oregon
Effective date	1945	1945	1946	1947	1949	1949	1947
1950 budget in thousands	357	65	59	58	25	40	15
Full time staff	63	12	9	14	2	4	2
Total cases docketed since inception	2448	974	751	177	64	?	21
Discrimination found	54%	52%	65%	60%	25%	?	29%
Not found	46%	48%	35%	40%	75%	?	71%

Adopted from Berger, M., "Fair Employment Practices Legislation." *Annals of the American Academy of Political and Social Science,* 275:38, 1951.

In analyzing the work of the Commissions we noted the relatively small number of complaints. In New York the average annual number of complaints lies in the neighborhood of 450 cases. It is unlikely that the small number of complaints can be explained solely by the small staff of the Commissions. New York, with its relatively large Commission, received only somewhat more than one complaint per day in a state whose minority membership numbers several millions.

One might suspect that the small number of complaints may, at least in part, result from ignorance of the law. In 1948, three years after the passage of the law, only 8 per cent of the New York City population was sufficiently familiar with the law to be able, if necessary, to make use of its provisions. What makes it worse, the proportion of people familiar with the law was smallest among those most likely to experience discrimination, the more uneducated members of the minority groups. While it might be expected that the massive educational effort of the New York State Commission has led to a wider knowledge of the law since the completion of the aforementioned study, it is easy to imagine what would happen in states where smaller budgets for the dissemination of the present inadequate publicity are provided.

EFFECTIVENESS OF LAWS

Knowledge of the law alone does not lead to complaints. Only those who have faith in the administration of the law are likely to utilize it. In 1948 only 16 per cent of New York City's Jewish and 26 per cent of its Negro population believed that the law would be efficient in curbing discrimination. To some extent such attitude reflects apathy and resignation based on previous experience. One third of the population of the city believed that nothing could be done against discrimination and that all the talk about it would only make things worse. Many people expressed the opinion that employers would be able to circumvent the law. Perhaps one of the best ways to circumvent such defeatist attitudes would be wider publicity of the positive results accomplished thus far.

It will take time for the law to prove itself and to be recognized as efficient by the population. Yet the New York State Commission in its 1952 report to the Senate Subcommittee on Labor and Labor Management Relations was able to report that it has already been able to "affect" positively the "morale of the so-called 'minority group': Observing the day-to-day improvement in employment practices, they have been encouraged to train and qualify for more responsible positions, regardless of past patterns of employment."[30]

Minority group members tend to apply for jobs in those occupational fields in which they believe that they have their best chance. If Jews believe that they are more likely to get jobs in retail stores than in banks they will apply at these stores. Many firms believed to practice discrimination are not singled out for complaint simply because Negroes, Jews, or Italians do not seek employment in them. Finally, we suspect that the average minority member is too much afraid to appeal to the authorities even if he knows that he is entitled to such complaint and familiar with the provisions of the law. Officers of the law are formidable persons from whom one may prefer to stay away. He may not be sufficiently motivated or educated to realize that such complaint helps not only him but other members of his group. He wants a job and not a "law suit."

These shortcomings of the legislative procedure could perhaps be avoided by making provisions for the channelization of complaints through trusted minority organizations, whose officers are personally known to the victim of discrimination. State commissions could be run more efficiently by relying to a larger extent on charges brought in by their own investigators after careful surveys.[31] If we consider that in New York City no less than three out of every ten Negroes and Jews stated that they had encountered job discrimination, in spite of their tendency to apply where they believed they would be accepted, the number of complaints to the State Commission appears pitifully small.

In spite of all shortcomings the state commissions have been able to reduce discrimination. A study by the National Community Relations Advisory Council indicated that discriminatory advertisement and employment agency practices in 1945-1946 were much greater in 11 cities outside New York not covered by local F.E.P.C.'s. While in New York 7 per cent of all applicants reported that they had been refused jobs because of religion, the corresponding figure in other cities was 15 per cent. Similarly, employment opportunities for Negroes in New York were better than in states not covered by law.[32] A more recent report by the National Urban League[33] concerning the integration of Negroes into skilled defense jobs in the nation's larger cities showed that progress, though highly unsatisfactory in most of the nation, was much better in Buffalo and New York City.

Needless to say, existing laws may be circumvented or not enforced even where adequate machinery exists. In New York State, for example, discriminatory advertising was forbidden by law in 1943. Since that time resort places advertising in the New York newspapers simply substituted the phrase "near churches" for the outlawed phrase "restricted clientele." While New York State possesses a law which forbids discrimination in higher education it has been singularly ineffective. There have been only three complaints made to the enforcing agency. A study made by the American Jewish Congress in New York revealed that, out of 72 college graduates whose ability was demonstrated by the fact that they had won state medical school scholarships, 86 per cent of the Protestants, 59 per cent of the Catholics, and 46 per cent of the Jews were admitted to medical schools in New York State.[34] The report claims that the "aura of respectability surrounding the large private universities makes public officials, civil organizations and rejected applicants hesitant to challenge openly their clandestine practices."

From a technical point of view it is hardly ever difficult to demonstrate the existence of discrimination. It is suspicious if in 1951 Cornell Medical School according to the same source, accepted only two out of thirty Jewish applicants. The New York State Commission has been ingenious in tracking down various evasive attempts of employment agencies to circumvent the law. Conspicuous among these attempts is the use of confidential code numbers for applicants or specification of the region from which applicants are not wanted.

In the Detroit riots of 1943 in which several dozen Negroes and whites were killed and several hundred injured, the police not only failed to act in time but also failed to break up mobs before they had gathered sufficient strength to become menacing. The police not only failed to protect the Negroes from violence, but actually sided against them. In many instances the police stood by without interfering "when the white mob ran amok pulling Negroes from automobiles and streetcars."[41] The riots came under control only after federal troops intervened.

In contrast to the Detroit riots which extended over several days the immediate and decisive action of city officials in the case of the Harlem riots may serve as a model of effective riot control. "Within two hours of the outbreak of violence many white and Negro CIO officials were touring the streets of Harlem urging its residents to remain peaceful and return to their homes."

Mayor F. H. LaGuardia immediately (1) took control of the situation, (2) utilized as many Negro policemen, military police, and air raid wardens as he could make available, (3) quarantined the areas of disorder and sizable adjoining areas, (4) concentrated sufficient police power in every dangerous block to halt looting, rioting, and other hoodlumism without further ado . . .[42]

In addition to quarantining the riot area in order to prevent reinforcement from other areas to add to the fight, to call the state militia or regular army, it is of importance to keep high school children in school. Juveniles were found to be the major contributors in the Detroit riots. Finally, intelligent handling of reports to the public via the mass media of communication is required in order to avoid adding fuel to the flames. Instead of inciting reports of the fighting it may be wise to minimize the actual severity of the disturbance and to broadcast appeals by popular leaders of the two conflicting groups.[43]

It is far better to prevent the outbreak of race riots than to wait with ameliorative measures until trouble has started. We may distinguish here long-range measures designed to reduce underlying interracial and ethnic hostility and short-term measures designed to prevent the outbreak of hostilities.

Measures have to be taken to combat delinquency by meeting the needs of young people in the conflict areas, such as the creation of wholesome recreational facilities. As a result of a survey sponsored by the Mayor's Committee on Unity of the City of New York, a number of such recreational centers were established in underprivileged areas of Upper Manhattan and staffed by specially trained group leaders from the College of the City of New York. These centers were arranged on a mixed basis bringing together the different warring factions, whites and Negroes, Jews and Irish. Because of the danger that prejudiced parents would not allow their children to attend these centers, their establishment had to be coordinated with an adult education program. Finally, in order to direct the aggressive needs of the gang leaders into constructive channels, they were organized into a new organization for the improvement of the neighborhood, entitled "Washington Heights Youth, Inc."[44]

On the adult level, the establishment of favorable contact helps to forestall riots. In Detroit "people who had become neighbors in mixed Negro and white neighborhoods did not riot against each other. The students of Wayne University—white and black—went to their classes in peace throughout Bloody Monday. And there were no disorders between the whites and black workers in the war plants."[45] Contacts must be provided particularly for those elements most likely to participate in riots, the uneducated, lonely individuals, those who frequent the beer halls and poolrooms. In addition to the provision of bi-racial experiences, a sound educational program through radio stations, churches, and labor unions may be helpful.

Important is the early detection of rising tension. The Detroit riots had been predicted months before by the experts. In addition to polls, the setting up of "reportorial machine" assuring frequent and frank reports from selected social workers, ministers, policemen, bartenders, judges, and others in a position to have immediate and candid contacts with the neighborhood may be advantageous.[46] Such procedures make it possible to pinpoint the major trouble spots and to take immediate action, which should be under the supervision of bi-racial committees, one representing the citizenry (churches, unions, patriotic societies, parent teachers associations, women's clubs, etc.), and the other the various branches of the city or state government.[47] Particular attention may be given here to the training of those likely to be called upon to handle race and ethnic tension. Classes may be established for policemen, ministers, teachers, and social workers.

But most important is the removal of the deeper underlying causes of tension, segregation, and discriminatory treatment of minorities, the prevention of overcrowding in housing and transportation, job insecurity. Political and legal measures alone may otherwise not suffice to prevent the building of tension between groups.

SELECTED READINGS

1. Berger, M., *Equality by Statute.* Columbia University Press, New York, 1952.
2. "Grade School Segregation: the Latest Attack on Racial Discrimination." *Yale Law Review*, 61:730, 1952.
3. Shannon, J. B., "Political Obstacles to Civil Rights Legislation." *Annals of the American Academy of Political and Social Science*, 275:53-60, 1951.
4. Lubell, S., *The Future of American Politics.* Harper & Brothers, New York, 1951, chaps. 5 and 6.
5. Lee, A. M., and Humphrey, N. D., *Race Riot.* Dryden Press, New York, 1943.

REFERENCES

1. Berger, M., *Equality by Statute.* Columbia University Press, New York, 1952, chap. 2.
2. *Ibid*, p. 80.
3. "Grade School Segregation: The Latest Attack on Racial Discrimination." *Yale Law Review,* 61:730, 1952.
4. *Ibid*, pp. 738 ff.
5. *Ibid*, p. 739.
6. *Ibid*, p. 741.
7. Nelson, Lt. D. D., *The Integration of the Negro in the United States Navy.* Farrar, Straus and Young, New York, 1951.
8. Maslow, W., "Prejudice, Discrimination, and the Law." *Annals of the American Academy of Political and Social Science,* 275:9-17, 1951.
9. Sumner, W. G., *Folkways.* Ginn and Co., Boston, Mass., 1911, p. 95.
10. Myrdal, G., *An American Dilemma.* Harper & Brothers, New York, 1944, pp. 1032 ff.
11. Deutsch, M., and Evans-Collins, M., *Interracial Housing.* University of Minnesota Press, Minneapolis, Minn., 1951, p. 127.
12. Maslow, *op. cit.*, p. 10.
13. MacIver, R. M., *The More Perfect Union.* Macmillan, New York, 1948, p. 171.
14. *Factory*, pp. 103-106, 1949.
15. Chein, I., "Some Considerations in Combatting Intergroup Prejudice." *Journal of Educational Sociology,* pp. 412-419, March, 1946.
16. Maslow, *op. cit.*, p. 17.
17. Shannon, J. B., "Political Obstacles to Civil Rights Legislation." *Annals of the American Academy of Political and Social Science,* 275:53-60, 1951.
18. MacIver, *op. cit.*, pp. 178 ff.

19. *Ibid*, p. 181.
20. Lubell, S., *The Future of American Politics*. Harper & Brothers, New York, 1951, chaps. V and VI.
21. *Civil Rights in the United States in 1951*. American Jewish Congress and National Association for the Advancement of Colored People, 1952, p. 41.
22. Statement of the New York State Commission against Discrimination before the United States Subcommittee on Labor and Labor Management Relations, April 16, 1952.
23. Saenger, G., and Gordon, N. S., "The Influence of Discrimination on Minority Group Members in its Relation to Attempts to Combat Discrimination." *Journal of Social Psychology*, 31:106, 1950.
24. *Ibid*, pp. 115 ff.
25. New York State Commission against Discrimination, Annual Report, 1951.
26. Edwards, E. W., *et al.*, "Patterns of Conciliation under the New York State Law against Discrimination." *New York Law Journal*, April 6-12, 1951.
27. *Ibid*, p. 6.
28. *Ibid*, p. 4.
29. New York State Commission, Annual Report, 1951.
30. Statement of the New York State Commission, 1952, *op. cit.*, pp. 10 ff.
31. MacIver, *op. cit.*, p. 163.
32. Rackow, F., *Combatting Discrimination in Employment*. New York State School of Industrial and Labor Relations, Cornell University, Research Bulletin 5, pp. 30-34.
33. Urban League Report of Feb. 5, 1952.
34. Civil Rights in the United States in 1951, *op. cit.*, p. 57.
35. New York State Commission against Discrimination, *op. cit.*, p. 40.
36. Civil Rights in the United States in 1951, *op. cit.*, p. 40.
37. New York State Commission against Discrimination, press release, 1952.
38. Civil Rights in the United States in 1951, *op. cit.*, pp. 22 ff.
39. *Ibid*, p. 23.
40. Lee, A. M., and Humphrey, N. D., *Race Riot*. Dryden Press, New York, 1943, p. 73.
41. *Ibid*, p. 77.
42. *Ibid*, p. 100.
43. *Ibid*, p. 137.
44. Saenger, G., and Shulman, H. M., Some Factors Determining Intercultural Behavior and Attitudes of Members of Different Ethnic Groups in Mixed Neighborhoods, The *Journal of Psychology*, 25: 365-380, 1948.
45. Lee and Humphrey, *op. cit.*, p. 130.
46. *Ibid*, p. 126.
47. *Ibid*, p. 122.

PART IV. IN CONCLUSION

CHAPTER 17

THE WAYS AHEAD

To advance the attack on prejudice requires the cooperation of the government as well as the individual citizen, business and labor, churches, schools, and numerous other social agencies.

Attention should be given to the removal of the underlying causes of prejudice and discrimination. Intergroup education has to be extended and improved. We must continue to work towards the removal of discriminatory barriers by legal means as well as through volunteer efforts.

LESSENING ECONOMIC AND SOCIAL CONFLICT

Prejudice and discrimination are related to poverty and economic insecurity. If government and industry work together to preserve full employment and to establish economic security, it will help to remove an underlying cause of prejudice. Price controls in times of inflation, unemployment insurance and work relief during times of depression are needed. Better still is the prevention of future unemployment through planning that involves credit controls, stimulation of trade, and government spending for public works programs.

It is equally important to increase the chances of advancement for everyone regardless of class or caste, religion or race. Improvements in educational opportunities, vocational guidance that steers young people into careers for which they are best fitted, are measures which will advance the cause of intergroup relations no less than of the national welfare.

The leadership for such action can come from political parties as well as civic organizations, from education as well as from industry. Members of organizations interested in intergroup relations will support such programs once they are made to understand the dependence of their own welfare on the broader welfare.

Attention has to be given to racially or ethnically mixed high-tension areas. Friction is related to low income, inadequate housing,

279

insufficient social services. We can combat tension and prevent the occurrence of race riots by raising the standard of living of backward communities. Public housing can be provided by the city or private organizations.

Delinquency can be ameliorated through the establishment of social service and mental hygiene programs in mixed schools. Adequately supervised playgrounds and settlements in such areas can be provided by the community or religious organizations. Interracial settlements such as Union Settlement House in New York—used by Negro, Puerto-Rican, Italian, and Irish children—may serve as a model. Group leaders are students from the local colleges who thus supplement their academic training in the social sciences.

Where shifts in population lead to tension the government can take a hand. The problem created by the rapid influx of Puerto Ricans into New York City required the cooperation of the federal government and the city authorities. Through a program of economic aid and development in Puerto Rico, the federal government aims at lessening the urge for emigration from this island. New York City sees to it that the newcomers are not economically exploited and are paid decent wages. In this endeavor they have received the cooperation of the International Ladies Garment Workers Union and enlightened manufacturers in the dress business, in which large numbers of Puerto Ricans are employed.

Public employment services can steer foreign immigrants into areas which have a labor shortage. Privately financed social agencies such as the National Refugee Service have been active in providing advice to the newcomers. It initiated a resettlement and retraining program for newcomers whose employment chances could be improved by training them for jobs in which they would not come into competition with native labor.

MINORITY ADJUSTMENT

Immigrants can be helped to become assimilated through courses familiarizing them with the language and customs of their new country. These have been provided by schools, colleges, and the adult education movement. Church group and civic organizations have invited displaced persons to special gatherings. Libraries can be provided with special personnel to plan educational programs for the education of newcomers' children. In the South, the Rosenwald Fund supplemented inadequate funds for Negro education.

Immigrant clubs facilitate the process of assimilation. They give the newcomers a needed feeling of belonging and at the same time prepare the ground for integration into the local scene. Organizations interested in working with minority group members will find these agencies the best possible source to contact them.

Prejudices often block attempts to admit newcomers to the organizations of the older population, such as parent-teacher's associations, unions, and churches. The initiative can be taken here best by the leaders of the majority organizations or prominent members. Since there is often fear that the admission of newcomers would destroy the harmony and intimacy of the organization, one may well proceed gradually. The children of displaced persons can be invited to some functions especially arranged for them. Once the ice is broken, the membership itself may ask them to join as permanent members.

Exposure to prejudice leads to a lowering of the minority's self-esteem. Their adjustment can be promoted by strengthening identification with their native group through raising pride in their own background and culture. Such identification differs from the development of "racial pride," which implies the rise of a feeling of superiority of one's group as a defensive reaction to prejudice and suppression. Rabbis, priests, Sunday school teachers, and minority group leaders addressing their own organizations should aim at the development of a sound self-esteem and combat the tendency to look down on other groups. Talking about the heroes and accomplishments of their own national or religious groups, they can stress parallel deeds of other groups and indicate how the great men of different groups cooperated and learned from each other.

FIGHTING AUTHORITARIANISM

Intergroup relations can be improved also by attacking the psychological causes of prejudice. Attention must be given to the social causes of maladjustment as well as to the creation of healthier personalities through proper childhood upbringing and mental health programs.

The present uncertainty of the world situation furnishes fertile ground for the development of prejudice. A growing emphasis on conformity has been found related to growing intolerance toward difference, as witnessed by the increased attacks on academic freedom. Thwarting self-expression is in itself a source of frustration leading to aggressive tendencies. These tendencies are reinforced by the growth of fear and anxiety resulting from the communist threat and the danger of another war.

The presence of the external threat should be used to emphasize the need for internal unity based on cooperation among diverse groups rather than on blind conformity. We must fight the tendency to brand all opinions which deviate from our own as communist or fascist.

In some cases even the preoccupation with the fight for minority rights is impaired by the fear that such activities may be branded as communistic.

The fight for freedom of expression and freedom of association has to emphasize that these principles characterize democratic societies as opposed to totalitarianism from the left or right. How limitations of these freedoms may curb scientific enquiry has been pointed out by the American Association of University Professors. School classes where students are encouraged to challenge and discuss the teacher's opinion, to find facts for themselves, produce better informed students, who are creative and independent in their thinking.

It is the job of our educational institutions and our newspapers, of radio and television, associations of management and unions, to point out the dangers of authoritarianisms and to fight it wherever necessary.

BRINGING UP A HEALTHIER GENERATION

Totalitarian trends in the individual may result from a rigidly disciplined childhood upbringing that is lacking in warmth. The manner in which parents bring up their children depends on their own development and character structure as well as upon their opinions upon methods of child training. Mental health programs leading to a better adjustment of the parents will enable them to act more affectionately and permissively toward their children. Erroneous methods of child rearing often result, not from parental inability to give love or from neurotic instability, but solely from lack of knowledge.

Love and affection are not enough to build a strong ego able to withstand the inevitable frustrations of life. The child needs to acquire a high degree of frustration tolerance, which will enable him to contain hostility rather than to release it toward those weaker than himself. He has to learn to control his behavior from within, to govern his actions by relying upon the values and taboos taken over from his parents and his society rather than to rely mainly upon external approval or condemnation. He must learn early to accept responsibility.

These goals can be achieved through consistency of discipline, which makes the world appear orderly and manageable. The child must be made to understand why he is punished, and punishment must be related to the severity of the transgression. Above all, it must not be accompanied by a withdrawal of love. Love is needed to compensate for the sacrifices accompanying the process of socialization, the curbing of asocial and destructive tendencies. While self-expression, even the release of some hostility is necessary for a sound development, it is important to curb harmful modes of self-expression endangering the child or his associates, and leading to feelings of guilt and anxiety. Children need to learn the limits within which they can move.

To acquire a sense of responsibility, children must be allowed to make their own decisions as early as possible. The parents may act as advisors and point to the consequences of different behavior, but should leave the choice of the alternatives to the child. Through trial and error, by being forced to accept the consequences of their choice, children acquire a feeling of strength and self-confidence. Finally, children need recognition of their own accomplishments rather than praise for things not of their own doing, such as prettiness, possessions, or status.

Modern methods of child rearing are now taught in many communities through lectures, films, television programs, and group discussions. The initiative for such programs may rest with the community itself, social agencies, the schools, parent-teacher associations, and civic clubs. Materials can be obtained from the Child Study Association, the federal government, group leaders provided through universities, or school psychological centers.

PSYCHOLOGICAL ADJUSTMENT AND CHANGING VALUES

The attempt to create more prejudice-resistant individuals cannot be fully effective until a new and psychologically healthier generation has grown up. We must concern ourselves also with the more immediate solutions of some of the psychological difficulties which make adults prone to prejudice.

The development of spontaneity, of the individual's capacity for self-expression, needs encouragement. Each person has talents which can be constructively utilized in his leisure time activities. We can develop the lonely individual's ability to make friends, see to it that he attains a feeling of belonging. The most violently prejudiced are people who are isolated, frightened, lacking emotional satisfactions.

Programs aiming at reducing these needs can range from the development of recreational centers for adults through adult education to group and individual psychotherapy. Emphasis on human relations in business will be as helpful as the development of community organization that provides for the needs of the lonely and arranges for their participation in the social life of the community. Marriage clinics and psychiatric services attached to hospitals and welfare agencies may be mentioned here. There is, at present, a lack of trained personnel to take care of these needs. More psychiatrists, social workers, group leaders, and teachers with psychological insight are needed. An encouraging trend is the growing number of clergymen taking courses in counseling and mental hygiene to better serve their parishes.

Our society is characterized by the conflict between business values with their emphasis on getting ahead, and religious values of cooperation and neighborliness. Where self-esteem is based on material success, failure to get ahead deflates the ego. Even those who succeed feel insecure because they can never be certain of the future.

We can diminish the psychological need for prejudice by making the individual's self-esteem more dependent upon the realization of inner values than upon external success and recognition. Constructive attempts to stress noncompetitive values can be made through college courses in family relations, art appreciation, and the psychology of adjustment. Adult education can teach the individual how to enjoy nature and art. Teachers can counteract the trend to accumulate knowledge solely to gain status, to impress others with empty facts and cultivate instead the enjoyment of reading for its own sake. Television and radio can help by putting more emphasis on educational programs. Religion can counteract the stress on crude materialism by emphasizing the values of piety, goodness, and love.

IMPROVING EDUCATION

In the past, education against prejudice centered around the attempt to change beliefs rather than changing the prejudiced individual's personality. Instead of the ineffective attempt to teach children that there are no innate differences we must get them to understand the causes of the existing differences, to learn how prejudice distorts the perception of others, to realize how prejudice is caused by the needs of the prejudiced, and how it hurts the prejudiced as well as his victim.

If we give more attention to an understanding of the ways how prejudice arises and how it colors the way we see others, we do not mean to neglect attempts to erase wrong stereotypes. Stereotypes reinforce hostile feelings. College graduates looking for jobs may fear Jews more if they believe the latter to be more intelligent and aggressive than other Americans.

Classroom demonstrations of rumors help to accomplish this objective. Students may also be asked to write from memory descriptions of pictures or movies, and to compare their reports for discrepancies. They may want to compare stereotypes others hold about Americans or foreigners with their own opinions concerning their countrymen or foreigners. Study guides for this approach are available through the Anti-Defamation League of B'nai B'rith.

Social studies classes can discuss how prejudiced people expect to gain from discrimination, can be taught how discrimination is not only undemocratic but operates against the interests of the prejudiced individual. Students can discuss how prejudice in the classroom or at work interferes with the achievement of their own goals. Role playing, visits to minority gatherings, readings and subsequent discussions of novels dealing with minority problems, will supplement this program and make the children more sensitive to the problems of members of different ethnic groups.

A few schools already have satisfactory programs using these techniques, others do not have any education in intergroup relations. The impetus for the institution of such programs can come from minority organizations as well as national agencies devoted to the task of improving intergroup relations such as the National Conference of Christians and Jews. Teacher organizations and parent-teacher associations can get the stone rolling, as can prominent clergymen or lay leaders. But the leaders must learn first. It is important to introduce adequate intergroup relation programs in teacher-training institutions, religious seminaries, boy scout leader-training institutes.

Parents themselves are often prejudiced and indoctrinate their children in ways tending to counteract the beneficial effects of intergroup education. Prejudices of both parents and children can be reinforced or neutralized by exposure to prejudice and antiprejudice propaganda.

To reach prejudiced adults is more difficult than to reach the children. The educational message has to be woven into materials in which they are interested for their own sake—movies and television programs, union newspapers or discussion groups, dealing with love and adventure, "self-improvement," or international relations.

On the preventive side, we have succeeded to a considerable extent in erasing intentional prejudicial slanting from the mass media of communication. Some newspapers, however, still use race labeling in reporting crimes even in the North.

Much remains to be accomplished in erasing the less deliberate reinforcement of prejudice. Stereotyping of minority characters in short stories and on television and radio still continues. Minority characters should be shown more often as average human beings rather than as the exotic or funny individuals as which they are usually portrayed. Movie, television, and short story writers should be persuaded to give up the practice of giving all heroes Anglo-Saxon names, and movie and television stars to forego anglicizing their names. The Actor's Guild, Newspaper Guild, movie directors, and newspaper editors may initiate such a move if made aware of the undesirable effects of prevailing practices.

Thought needs to be devoted also to the problem of neutralizing the effects of disparaging remarks overheard in ordinary conversations affecting children and adults alike. The technique of training adults to answer prejudiced remarks developed by the American Jewish Congress' Commission on Community Interrelations furnishes a useful beginning but needs further implementation. Parents should be alerted to counteract prejudiced remarks which their children overhear outside the home.

Our most crucial task is the creation of equal status contacts under favorable conditions in as many different areas of life as possible. Contact under favorable conditions implies a minimum of competition and a maximum of possibilities for cooperation. It implies the development of close, intimate relations, involving different activities and bringing to light different aspects of personality.

Such associations, which constitute the most efficient method of education, exist in public and private housing, schools and colleges, churches and sports. Because housing provides the widest variety of human experiences, the creation of more integrated, interracial housing projects should be the first concern of civic organizations working in the field of intergroup relations.

Since money for public housing is provided by the federal or local authorities they can demand nondiscriminatory practices. Private citizens and civic organizations can protest against the so-called "gentleman's agreements" used to keep out Jews and other minorities from residential neighborhoods after "restrictive covenants" were outlawed by the courts. In a fashionable suburb of New York, one courageous civic leader and his friends broke the ice by seeing to it that houses were sold to Jews, bringing opposition into the open, and by introducing the first Jewish family to his friends and neighbors at a party in his home.

The fight against segregation in churches and parochial schools has been conducted successfully by leaders of the Catholic and Protestant churches. We recall the successful fight against school segregation in the parish schools of the St. Louis diocese. In the colleges, recent years have seen a frontal attack on exclusionary tendencies within the fraternities. It proved helpful when fraternity chapters in prestige institutions like Amherst opened the way.

MOVING TOWARD INTEGRATION

From the minority point of view, the abolition of discriminatory practices in employment is most important. What can we do to prepare acceptance of the minorities?

We know that the insecure and conformist-minded, prejudiced person is afraid to act against authority or public opinion. Social and legal sanctions against discriminating individuals are, therefore, likely to succeed. Workers in a factory are unlikely to protest against the admission of a minority member if they are informed that the boss not only personally initiated the new personnel policy, but wholeheartedly believes in it and considers any protest as an attack on himself.

The insecure person is unlikely to oppose minority integration unless he feels that others share his opposition. Confronted with a *fait accompli* he tends to take the integration of minority group members as a sign of public acceptance of this measure. Responsible officials should refrain from announcing planned changes in policy. We warn especially against the tendency to ask employees of business organizations how they feel about intended changes, individually or through opinion polls. Questioning only indicates to them that the issue is still undecided. It is interpreted as meaning that those in authority have doubt about the wisdom of abolishing discriminatory practices. Prejudiced people must not be given time to organize for maintenance of the status-quo.

Educational preparation of planned innovations may be useful in regions where prejudiced individuals know that the majority of the population opposes integration. This could include reports concerning successful abolition of discrimination elsewhere. We may do well to mention the increased trend to the abolition of discriminatory tendencies in the region and throughout the nation.

FACILITATING MINORITY INTEGRATION

What techniques can be used to facilitate the process of integration following the abolition of discriminatory practices? The first members of the minority to be hired in a factory or office should be especially skillful, pleasant, and well-adjusted. When their introduction is no longer news, however, principles of selection should be the same for majority and minority.

In large organizations, it is best to introduce new members into all branches of the organization and on all levels of rank simultaneously. If Negroes are hired only in some shops of a factory but not in others, we only succeed in creating "superior" shops free from "contamination" with "undesirable" minority members, as opposed to "inferior" mixed shops. The work in the latter shops becomes classified as Negro or women's work. Industrial leaders should be told that trial units established to find out whether integration works, or for demonstration purposes, are unlikely to work. Attempts to hire new members only on the lower levels may similarly fail. When the boss has a Negro assistant, his workers are less likely to revolt against fellow Negro workers.

Similarly, if only a few colleges alter their admission policies, they tend to lose social standing and to become minority institutions. The simultaneous removal of the quota system will lead to an equal distribution of minority members.

Minority members should preferably be hired only after good grievance machinery and good labor-management relations have been worked out, otherwise aggression resulting from bad practices may be canalized against the new members. Minority members need to be admitted to the informal organizations. Where teamwork exists they should not work with other minority members but be teamed off with majority workers.

Officials in management—particularly the foremen—who carry out the new policies need training. They must never be defensive and discuss complaints by explaining the selection of employees in terms of individual attributes and skills. There is a need for special training institutes for foremen and personnel officers. Lectures on intergroup relations should be included in business college courses on management and labor relations, and more articles on this topic in journals read by executives and engineers.

How can one induce prejudiced persons to work in a racially mixed factory, or join an interdenominational club or fraternity? Workers in a factory are not in a position to say with whom they want to work and will therefore follow a firm stand by management and union. When people have a choice it may be advantageous to offer special inducements. Where interracial housing offers better and less expensive quarters than found in the segregated white slums many people will prefer to live in the integrated projects. Interdenominational college organizations having a more interested membership and more varied program may successfully compete with restricted fraternities.

MOTIVATING THE LEADERS

Even unprejudiced leaders of industry and business, college presidents and housing officials are often afraid to abolish discriminatory practices because they fear negative consequences. The hiring of Negro personnel or the establishment of racially mixed houses appears hazardous. We can facilitate action by acquainting the leaders with the results of successful integration elsewhere.

At the end of the Second World War, the city of San Francisco found itself with the largest Chinese and Japanese settlement on the West Coast. There had been a tenfold increase in its Negro population. In the face of this potentially explosive situation the community, under the leadership of its most prominent industrialists, merchants, public officials, and heads of social agencies, engaged in a concerted attack on discrimination under the formula that discrimination is bad for business and equality is profitable.

The appeal to an enlightened self-interest is a most powerful motivating factor. Labor leaders have learned and taught their unions that the acceptance of minorities in their ranks prevents their use as strikebreakers or as competitors willing to accept lower wages. Army officers have taken note that successful desegregation in the armed forces has increased Negro morale and efficiency, and did not lead to the expected tensions. Appeal to democratic ideals will sometimes help, particularly where public recognition from influential majority and minority leaders is forthcoming.

STRENGTHENING LEGISLATION

Legislation has been one of the strongest incentives in persuading management and union to accept minority group members. It gives official sanction to integration, raises minority morale, and gives them a weapon to fight for their rights.

More emphasis should, therefore, be put on the fight for the abolition of the remaining laws against segregation. We should attempt to bring pressures to obtain the passage of new laws designed to bar discrimination in employment, housing, education, transportation, welfare, and recreation.

Legislation protecting civil rights would best be vested in the federal government since it is unlikely that the more prejudiced states will voluntarily institute effective legislation. Despite assertions to the contrary, federal legislation on these matters cannot be considered a violation of state's rights, for what is involved is the common welfare, not simply the welfare of people in a given state. Prejudice and discrimination are contagious, and a focus of infection in one state not merely endangers that state but the whole country. It does so in many ways. Prejudiced people may migrate to different states and encourage discriminatory practices. The uneducated, untrained refugees from discrimination will depress wages wherever they go.

The prospects for federal legislation in the near future are dim, but by no means hopeless. Chances are brighter to obtain legislation in states not yet covered by laws, and to extend the areas covered by laws in states and municipalities which already have commissions against discrimination. We need legislation to prohibit discriminatory practices in tax-exempt colleges and housing projects as well as restaurants and other places of public assembly. Attention should be given also to discriminatory practices in professional societies enjoying a monopoly in their field. Some of these measures have already been successfully instituted in New York.

We may want to find out whether existing state and city commissions have sufficient budgets, a competent staff, and adequate enforcement powers. Where these exist, the individual citizen may want to join the work of community councils cooperating with the commissions.

State commissions should be allowed to institute their own investigations rather than to wait for complaints. Civic organizations representing minority groups should be permitted to act as complainants. They also need to teach minority group members to make fuller use of the existing legislative machinery than heretofore.

The task of getting more and improved legislation can be facilitated by publicizing the beneficial results of existing legislation. We may desire to publicize the extent to which laws have helped to reduce discrimination, raised minority morale and aspirations, and led to a decrease in tension and conflict.

Pressure toward the passage of new laws can best be exerted by a coordinated effort of different minority group organizations working together with the more liberal forces in the majority group. But working committees embracing members of all groups should concentrate on all issues concerning the common welfare, work for better housing and better schools as well as for laws against discrimination.

The individual can help not only by joining or giving money to organizations which fight for the passage of more and better legislation such as the National Association for the Advancement of the Colored People or the American Jewish Congress. He can campaign for such legislation and influence civic organizations in which he is a member to come out for its support. Federal legislation requires the election of senators willing to come out against the filibuster. The citizen can help also by addressing letters in support of legislation against discrimination to his individual congressman or assemblyman, particularly when such bills are before the House. To accomplish this objective he may write for literature to commissions in states which have legislation and discuss it with friends and neighbors.

It is often argued that education should precede legislation but the mobilization of public opinion in the direction of legislation is in itself a major medium for such education. A legislative program instituted as a consequence of community action is worth more than a program instituted by enlightened legislators.

THE INDIVIDUAL AND HIS COMMUNITY

Organization for civic progress as well as toward the passage of laws must have the support of the local citizenry. Laws cannot be enforced properly unless they enjoy community support.

Many areas of intergroup relations are not—and whole areas of intergroup relations cannot be—covered by laws, as for example, social relations. Many states do not yet have laws against discrimination. Here community action is the only remedy.

Community action starts with the individual. The individual citizen can set an example for others by being the first to invite the new neighbor to his home. He can answer prejudiced remarks at parties, or may recommend novels dealing with minority problems to his friends.

As a prelude to action he needs to inform himself about the state of intergroup relations in his community. Has the school initiated an educational program dealing with intergroup relations? His children will be able to tell him. When the issue of tensions comes up in parent teachers meetings, he may be able to make suggestions for action. School administrators often hesitate to introduce intergroup education unless they feel that such a program is wanted.

To make education effective we need to eliminate as far as possible the conflict facing many children between the permissive atmosphere of the classroom and the restrictions of the community. To eliminate these conflicts, Northern communities may attempt to remove discriminatory practices such as discriminatory school zoning or segregated swimming pools. They can increase possibilities for majority-minority contact by attempting to introduce minority members into the schools, elect them as city officials, welcome them into civic organizations and fraternal orders.

In all these endeavors the individual citizen can be most effective by working through the organizations to which he belongs. A first step would consist in bringing existing problems to the attention of the membership. Where discriminatory school zoning has led to segregation and conflict between white and Negro gangs on the borders he can explain to his fellow members in the Elks, the Legion, or the PTA, how conflict arises from discriminatory practices. Few people enjoy exclusion. He can suggest that juvenile delinquency among minority children results from lack of adequate playgrounds and settlement houses. He may explain how untidiness and neglect is related to lack of adequate sanitary facilities in minority housing, may point to the lack of welfare organizations and hospital space available to minority members.

Even more effective than individual efforts is the community self-survey, in which the community under the leadership of its major civic organizations studies itself. This technique is adaptable for use in smaller units, a factory, college, school, and has been used by social agencies.

The spread of information often leads to action. Organization for action, however, often does not take place until everyone is aware that there is serious trouble. It is easier to prevent racial incidents than to attempt to restore good-will after hostilities have broken out. Once the community is trained for action, it can meet new problems more effectively. We do not set up a fire department or Red Cross unit after disaster has struck.

While the average citizen can prepare the ground, action can be initiated most easily by enlightened and generally respected community leaders. Clergymen, judges, and officials of social agencies may want to take the lead. More difficult is the eventual involvement of leaders of the more prejudiced organizations. They will not be attracted by emphasis on the improvement of ethnic relations but may often go along with an attack on problems in which their organizations have an interest.

Once the demand for action has led to the initiation of a program designed to improve the community, it is important to involve minority organizations. They know what problems exist in their neighborhoods. Moreover, programs aimed at civic improvement can succeed best when they involve all segments of the population.

Community action finally needs to be supplemented by adult education. Parents need to be educated if the intergroup education program of the school is not to be nullified. To assure attendance even of prejudiced parents emphasis should again be given to topics of general interest, for example, childhood training. After good-will is established and mutual suspicion reduced by the work on common problems, discussions of intergroup relations may emerge by themselves.

In working on common problems, the group discussion method is more successful than lectures. People can express their anxieties and perplexities and hear about those of others. Whatever actions result, they will have to come from the deliberations of the group in order to insure greater identification with adopted plans.

Group discussions and group decisions for action will help to remove the anxieties of the unprejudiced who are afraid to move ahead for fear of community censure. The attempt to improve intergroup relations must be seen as part and parcel of the general fight for social progress and democracy, for the common welfare.

The fight against prejudice in the community and the whole nation is assured as long as there are people interested in the advancement of democracy. It is no accident that all authoritarian systems of government, fascism and communism alike, earlier or later not only suppress people because their thoughts and values differ from their own, but also because of their nationality, color, or religion. Much progress has been made in erasing discrimination and reducing segregation, less in combating prejudiced attitudes and bringing about closer social relations. While there is no room for complacency, the fact that great advances have been made in the fight against prejudice and discrimination must be viewed in the light of our knowledge that in the field of human relations, more than in other fields, progress tends to beget progress.

INDEX

Note: With the exception of "Selected Readings," page numbers after the names of authors relate to the page number in the text in which the author is quoted or otherwise referred to, and not to the references at the end of each chapter.

Date Due

FEB 4 '55			
FEB 2 2 '55			
MAR 2 1956			
MAR 1 6 1956			
MAY 1 1 1962			
MAY 2 4 1963			
OCT 3 0 '64			
DEC 1 1 '64			
MAY 2 6 '66			
OCT 6 '67			
OCT 2 0 '67			
NOV 1 0 '67			
SEP 20 '68			
OCT 4 '68			
DEC 2 0 '68			
MAY 12 '73			
MAY 02 '79			